In Collaboration with British Literary Biography

Jane McVeigh

In Collaboration with British Literary Biography

Haunting Conversations

Jane McVeigh
Roehampton University
London, UK

ISBN 978-3-319-58382-2   ISBN 978-3-319-58383-9   (eBook)
DOI 10.1007/978-3-319-58383-9

Library of Congress Control Number: 2017944102

Cover illustration: EyeEm/Alamy Stock Photo

Printed on acid-free paper

This Palgrave Macmillan imprint is published by Springer Nature
The registered company is Springer International Publishing AG
The registered company address is: Gewerbestrasse 11, 6330 Cham, Switzerland

To

my mother and father

Acknowledgements

This book has been many years in the making and I am indebted to Zachary Leader for his advice and guidance during a long period of learning and relearning in its initial stages. Conversations with biographers in the early years of this project contributed to my thinking and I am grateful for the support of David Ellis, Andrew Lycett, Ray Monk, Adam Sisman, Martin Stannard and Geoffrey Wall, all of whom met with me. Other conversations with Laura Peters, Jane Kingsley-Smith and Cathy Wells-Cole have guided me on my way.

The conversations I have had with Clare Brant, Richard Holmes, Michael Holroyd, Kathryn Hughes, Hermione Lee and Claire Tomalin are published in this book. I am hugely grateful for their interest in this project.

My mother, family and dear friends have listened to me talking about this book for many years and have supported me throughout. Brian is my rock and ultimate guide in this and everything.

CONTENTS

CHAPTER 1

We Tell Stories About Ourselves and Others

This is a story about one person's reading and what she has learnt about how the lives of other people, particularly authors, have been written in British biographies over the last fifty years. It is less interested in what happened in the lives of the people described in these biographies, and more concerned with how their biographical stories have been told. As a reader, I am not looking at what might be better or worse in these different stories but at what different types of story they tell and the different versions of people's lives they re-create.[1]

In common with other readers, I take the view that how a biography has been written becomes part of the story of that life, or group of lives. We all tell stories about our own lives and those of others, but the story may have a slightly different focus or emphasis depending on who is telling it, whom they are speaking to, when the events discussed in the story took place, and how the story is told. This reading aims to have a conversation with British biographers, through actual interviews in some cases, to make their voices heard, to set them talking—a concept important to Romantic biographer Richard Holmes in his biography of Samuel Coleridge—in a reading of both writing about biography and biographies themselves.[2] American historian and biographer John Milton Cooper suggests that "biographers engage in conversations with their subjects" (2004, 90), as they listen, question and talk back to them "by examining their actions, motives, and thoughts" (90). American biographer Phyllis Cole similarly suggests that

© The Author(s) 2017
J. McVeigh, *In Collaboration with British Literary Biography,*
DOI 10.1007/978-3-319-58383-9_1

> Biographers are collectors of manuscripts and fragments of information, but they necessarily write in dialogue with previous biographers, with colleagues and critiques, and finally with the subjects themselves. (2004, 219)

Biography may be understood as a work of collaboration and a conversation between a biographical subject or subjects, and each biographer. Michael Holroyd describes biographers as "messengers" (2003, 19) creating a link between the past and the present, and Romantic biographer Richard Holmes sees the biographer as a kind of ferryman "perhaps even a kind of Charon, crossing back and forth between the Past and Present, over the dark river of Oblivion" (1993, 228). In this context, the collaboration becomes an opportunity to understand the present of the biographer in the context of the past of his or her subject. As a reader, I understand biography as an ongoing collaboration, not only between biographers and their subjects, but between biographers and their readers, like myself, reading people's lives.[3] This book is one reader's conversation with the biographies she has read and the lives they describe, as well as actual conversations that took place in 2016 with some biographers.

This is a reading of British biographies, by Michael Holroyd, Richard Holmes, Hermione Lee and Claire Tomalin in particular, since the late 1960s. It is concerned, on the whole, with biographies of literary subjects, but its main focus is the literary nature of biographies themselves. Michael Benton suggests that in the late twentieth century biography could be described as "The Cinderella of Literary Studies" (2015a, 1), but then "Cinders … was magically transformed, decked out in new clothes by Michael Holroyd, Richard Holmes, Claire Tomalin, Hermione Lee, Peter Ackroyd et al." (1). Other biographers based in Britain, such as Jonathan Bate, Claire Harman, Rachel Holmes, Kathryn Hughes, Alexander Masters, Ray Monk, Andrew Motion, Adam Sisman, Martin Stannard, Jenny Uglow and Frances Wilson, to name but a few, have also transformed the genre and aspects of their writing are also discussed.[4]

My conversation as a reader with biographies and other writing by Michael Holroyd, Richard Holmes, Hermione Lee and Claire Tomalin started some years ago, and in each rereading I have found something that I had not seen before, informed of course by other reading and conversations. Each chapter on their work was completed before I met with them in 2016, or had an exchange over email in the case of Richard Holmes. The topics we discussed were in part designed to find out if there were any echoes between my reading and writing about their work and their own approaches. These topics emerged from earlier reading, in which questions about the nature and authenticity of biography were debated. A meeting with Kathryn Hughes about her approach to biography, and particularly her reviews, set me off on a new path. I am only at the beginning of my reading of reviews and thinking about how reviewers, as readers, influence the reception of each biography and the genre as a whole. A conversation with Clare Brant when this book was close to completion helped to place my reading of biography within the context of recent developments in the field of life-writing.

Hermione Lee is keen to reiterate that biography is not definitive, and she quotes American biographer Richard Ellmann's perspective that all biography comes to be seen more as "historical moments in the interpretations of ... great writers' lives than as definitive monuments" (2009, 90). This book is concerned with a particular moment in the work of some late twentieth century British biographers, albeit with the caveat, which is emphasised in the next chapter, that it is not possible to describe a neat linear history of biography, or indeed of any life-writing. The close reading undertaken considers some of the experimental, performative features in the work of these biographers. The biographers discussed in this book are British, or based in Britain; when a biographer or a critic of a different nationality is mentioned this is made clear.

Biography "is a form of narrative, not just a presentation of facts" (Lee 2009, 5).[5] This reading of biography endorses Lee's perspective that the "possibilities of representation of the self are infinitely various" (4), that "there is no such thing as an entirely objective treatment" (12) given that "there is likely to be some shared experience between the writer and the subject" (12), and that there "is no such thing as a life lived in isolation" (13). Some of the biographers discussed here reserve the right to speculate when hard evidence is not available, recognise that autobiographical evidence may be unreliable and challenge the form and style of traditional realism. The style and tone of a biography may tell us as much about someone's life, or a group of lives, as the explicit statements made in the narrative. This reading aims to illustrate that much of recent British biography, including the work of the biographers discussed in this book, has challenged conventional biographical forms and embraces the dialogic and provisional nature of nonfiction writing.

Biography is relevant to a range of disciplines including history, science, philosophy, visual arts, the humanities and social sciences. All forms of narrative, whether written, visual or spoken, may be fiction or non-fiction, or deliberately blur the distinction between the two. There are many examples of biographies that are hybrid fictional and nonfictional forms, as discussed in Chap. 3. This book is primarily concerned with biographies that are nonfiction narratives. They may not have all the facts to hand about someone's life, and may explore the gaps and silences within it, but they are nevertheless based on extensive research and on the available facts. Some biographies may speculate when evidence is missing and use some of the verifiable evidence in such a way that some critics might consider misleading or inappropriate and as a strategy more commonly associated with fiction. This relates to concerns about the ethics of nonfiction storytelling.[6] This book considers aspects of narrative in nonfiction biography, including the use of figurative language, temporality, tone and naming. It discusses some of the main differences between scholarly and popular biography but is primarily concerned with the unique features of biography that can be understood as popular re-creative nonfiction read by both academic and general readers.

Some may ask why we need different biographies about the same biographical subjects. Andrew Motion's view, in his biography *Keats* (1997), is that "There is good reason to believe that the lives of all important writers need to be reconsidered at regular intervals, no matter how familiar they might be. While the wind of history blows, their stories revolve and alter, offering new attractions and sometimes new difficulties to each successive generation" (1997, xxv). We learn more about people from the past as our understanding of the period in which they lived, and how it connects with our own lives in the present, changes. To some extent, biographies transform the lives of individuals, or groups of people, into cultural artefacts that embody a particular social and historical moment, and reinforce particular values, beliefs and ways of living. In the case of some lives, myths are created, or re-created, and this will influence how these lives are read by their readers. The way that the story of a life is told will change depending on when it is written, and each biography gives a different version of a life, or lives. We do not have the full, embodied, detailed version of someone's life on the pages of a biography, in part because all of the facts about them may not be available to the biographer, or would be impossible to encompass within one narrative.[7] As Lee makes clear:

Biographies are full of verifiable facts, but they are also full of things that aren't there: absences, gaps, missing evidence, knowledge or information that has been passed from person to person, losing credibility or shifting shape on the way. Biographies, like lives, are made up of contested objects … What does biography do with the facts that can't be fixed, the things that go missing, the body parts that have turned into legends and myths? (2005, 6)

She suggests that what biographers try to do is to make "a coherent narrative out of missing documents … a whole figure out of body parts" (8) and in doing so they have to "sort out the myths from the facts" (8). It is inevitable, Lee writes, that "the biographer can't do everything. Biography has to omit and to choose. In the process, some things go missing" (27). Moreover, Lee agrees with Virginia Woolf that, as Woolf comments in *Orlando* (1928), "a biography is considered complete if it merely accounts for six or seven selves, whereas a person may well have as many thousand" (1994, 235).[8] We may read several biographies about the same person because we are interested in how their experiences help us to understand the present day. We also know that people can be read in different ways and each biography offers us a new perspective that we might not have thought about before. Some critics say that biographies do our reading for us, and to some extent that is true. Reading is one way that many people find out about the world. Each biography gives us information and one reading of a life. My reading may be different whatever the biographer might say.

The multifaceted version of a life or lives is influenced by a biographer's approach to the nature of self-fashioning.[9] The story that we read in biography is based not only on the life fashioned by the biographer but also on the biographical subject's own attempts to create a version of his or her life based on a rewriting of their professional and personal lives within the historical period in which they lived. We all perform different versions of ourselves depending on where we are, who we are with and the identity that we hope to portray. The biographers discussed here often interrogate how the lives of others are refashioned not only by biographers and their subjects, but by later generations of readers, performers, theatre directors, film makers and the public. Jonathan Bate suggests that "the Genius of Shakespeare is not a factual hypothesis, but a truth-function of the difference it makes to the lives of those who maintain it" (1997, 325). We may not have all the facts available about

Shakespeare's life, or fully understand his genius, but we do know how other people have maintained a version of his legacy—in performances, in reading his work and in stories about his life—and we know the huge influence that his writing has had on the lives of others. The impact that someone has on the world is formed in part by the use that others, including biographers, make of his or her life and work. To some extent, each biography becomes a contemporary makeover, although it may, of course, not be a version with which some readers, critics or a subject's family, friends or peers are happy.[10] They, in turn, make up their own reading of someone's work and life.

We can consider comparative biography from a number of perspectives, including reading individual biographies, or different biographies about the same subject, by the same biographer, or written in the same historical period by different biographers. Each biography tells its own story, and different biographies about the same person will give us different versions of this person's life. A biography about more than one main subject, a group or relationship biography, may explore how and to what extent each character's story resonates with those of others, or may be representative of wider social, cultural and political issues and historical periods. All biographies are narrated by the biographer seeking his or her own version of the story they want to tell about their subject, but questions may be asked about the authenticity of his or her view. This book is not concerned with specific views about the authenticity of any particular biography, and clearly some may tell stories about a life that are biased towards a particular point of view, or use evidence in such a way that a particular myth about a life is promoted. These are important issues, which impact on the status of any specific biography depending on how it is read.

In 1980, Bernard Crick warns that "the biographer is fooling himself by an affable pretence of being able to enter into another person's mind" (1980, 29). Biography may explore what someone was like by describing what they did, how they behaved and may possibly have had on their mind at any given moment, whilst acknowledging that access to the inner life is impossible. Crick argues that examining the journey that a writer and his or her day-to-day life take together in detail and looking at "what they did together and how they reacted to what happened along the way" (29) will tell us more than focusing on their unconscious. The biographies discussed in this book accept to varying degrees the limitation highlighted by Crick. They are concerned to find out what someone was like and to explore key aspects of his or her personality, but they rarely claim to be able to know what someone was actually thinking or feeling, although they may suggest what might have been on someone's mind, or that particular actions and autobiographical evidence, such as letters, can give an idea about their experience at a given moment. They look for patterns, traces in the journey that Crick suggests, offering a point of view with which the reader may or may not agree.

American Paul John Eakin proposes that "narrative is not merely something we tell, listen to, read, or invent; it is an essential part of our sense of who we are" (2008, ix), and he takes this further, suggesting that "what we are could be said to be a story of some kind" (ix). Popular British literary biographies are also stories.[11] Eakin opens the first chapter of one of his books with the sentence, "We tell stories about ourselves every day" (1), and goes on to say that when we talk about ourselves "we perform a work of self-construction" (2). I would suggest that we tell stories about ourselves and others every day, and that when we talk about them and ourselves we re-create a version of a life or lives. This book is concerned with the versions that some biographers have re-created in collaboration and in conversation with their subjects and readers.

Other aspects of a biographer's approach are concerned with the style and form of the narrative. The close reading discussed in this book aims to identify rhetorical and experimental features of some exceptionally well written late twentieth and early twenty-first century biographies. Our attention may be drawn to the use of chronology, because even in a seemingly chronological biography of someone's life, where the story starts at birth and ends with death, the biographer may use literary techniques such as anticipating the future or recalling the past to influence the rhythm and pace of their story. The biographer may insert pauses if they want to explore a particular theme or point of view, and this influences the tone and pace of the narrative. Each biography may deliver a coherent narrative, but a closer reading may reveal that, for example, some aspects of a life have been explored more than others. The biographer may be interested in themes that have been forgotten or underrepresented in previous narratives. They may also provide evidence of tensions or schisms within a subject's personality, or in his or her relationships, and describe the many different selves that may form part of the make-up of someone's character. Coherent narratives can portray fragmented, complex and messy lives. A close reading of a biography may also consider: how or whether the biographer uses irony or metaphors; how they develop myths or instead seek to demythologise their subject; how they deal with autobiographical material such as letters; and how they use anecdotes or key moments in someone's life. A biography about more than one life may serve to decentre the life of a famous canonical figure, and any single life or group biography may look at the extent to which any individual life is dependent on those of others.

Michael Holroyd wishes that "people didn't make such a hard-and-fast distinction between fiction and nonfiction: 'I prefer creative and re-creative writing. You can't make anything up, but you have to try and recreate it.'" (Wroe 2008, 13). This belief in re-creative writing is central to his approach to biographical narrative:

> Biographies create, or re-create, a world that the reader may enter, where his or her imagination may be stimulated, and some of the emotions, thoughts and laughter experienced in reading—as well as the information—may remain with the reader after the book is finished. (1988, 103)

Holroyd does not think that "the novel and biography are rivals so much as catalysts. They are two branches of our past and present literature which are better described as creative and re-creative writing than fiction and non-fiction" (2014, 231). This makes biography more than a historical record. It becomes a response to the past and one that challenges the traditional laws of genre. This book is a comparative reading of biography that offers one attempt to describe what re-creative writing can mean. In doing so, it is interested in how lives are fashioned by ourselves and others as we each make up aspects of what happens to us in what we say and do. We create a makeover of our identity that we hope is authentic, although others may disagree. In reading and writing about the lives of other people, sometimes as they connect with our own, we ask questions about the identity of ourselves and others and create a form of countersignature, one that is faithful to the facts but creates something that is unique, of its moment, and open to more rewriting and reimagining. Furthermore, in writing about another person, or people, biographers offer a form of remembrance that prolongs or re-ignites a person's impact on the world. In our reading and writing about other people, we maintain their memory and keep them talking.

Finally, some readers of fiction and nonfiction, and biographers themselves, write about their experience of reading and writing about people's lives as a type of haunting.[12] This book is haunted by the re-creative writing of biographers, and they in turn—Richard Holmes and Hermione Lee in particular—are haunted by the lives of their subjects. So, this is also a study of haunting, in which we haunt the lives of others to help us come to a better understanding of our own. This reader of biography is interested in the authorial identity of both the biographer and his or her subject, or subjects, that such a haunting re-creates.

Before moving on to the work of specific biographers, Chap. 2 offers a short overview of biography since the early twentieth century and touches on the impact of literary estates on biographers. A conversation with Clare Brant covers recent developments in life-writing. Chap. 3 discusses some recent examples of experimental biography and considers the conversation that reviewers, particularly Kathryn Hughes, have with biography. Chap. 4 focuses on the haunting nature of biographical narrative in the work of Hermione Lee and Richard Holmes. In Chap. 5, on the work of Hermione Lee, the nature of self-fashioning and biographical makeovers are discussed. The haunting by R. Holmes of British biography and Romantic biographer Richard Holmes's approach to biography as a form of epic narrative is explored in Chap. 6. A reading of Claire Tomalin's biographies in Chap. 7 considers the mediated nature of her portrayals; how she approaches autobiographical evidence; her use of anecdotes and chronology; the use she makes of speculation; and how her work reflects the growth of feminist biography. Finally, Chap. 8 covers Michael Holroyd's fiction and nonfiction narratives, and the nature of both his creative and re-creative writing. The last four chapters end with a conversation between this reader and the biographer whose work has been discussed. They explore how we tell stories about ourselves and others and re-create different versions of life in our writing, reading and actual conversations.

NOTES

1. Romantic biographer Richard Holmes suggests that comparative biography "is based on the premise that every biography is one particular interpretation of a life, and that many different interpretations or reassessments are always possible" (2016, 58).
2. Richard Holmes's biography of Samuel Coleridge aims "to set Coleridge *talking*" (2005, xvi).
3. Some biographies are based on conversations with their subjects and Boswell's life of Samuel Johnson is the seminal example.
4. For another discussion and a different approach to the work of these biographers, see Backscheider, Paula, *Reflections on Biography* (1999).

5. See introductions to literary biography: Benton, Michael, *Literary Biography: An Introduction* (2009) and Hermione Lee, *Biography: A Very Short Introduction* (2009).
6. Michael Benton suggests that the principles of literary biography are "a concern for ethics, a sense of empathy and the exercise of imagination" (2015b, 31), and he sees storytelling as central to a poetics of biography.
7. As Michael Benton proposes, "the picture of the subject that every biography develops is a symbolic image, a figure standing in for the original" (2015b, 61.3). This is a biographical portrayal, a version, of a life or lives.
8. See "Virginia Woolf's Nose" in Hermione Lee, *Body Parts* (2005), 44.
9. In a study about scientific biographies, French academics David Aubin and Charlotte Bigg argue that our sense of self is rooted in place, time and society: "What emerges from ideas of self-fashioning is a dynamic process perpetually recommenced in relation to others, and especially to socio-cultural representations of self made available by individuals' society and body" (2007, 65). This is a dynamic process of self-fashioning as the self "constantly re-creates itself while it seeks to re-create its environment" (66). It is this process of fashioning that some of the chapters in this book explore in the work of particular biographers.
10. Graham Holderness, in an essay about biographies of Shakespeare, reflects aspects of contemporary thinking about the genre and believes that,

> biography must tamper with this realm of the personal, with the hidden life of the subject, and with the efforts of those who try to own and define that life … Biography pursues the elusive personality of the subject, and the biographer needs to have the skills of a novelist, rather than those of a diplomat. Biography should be emotionally involved, not dispassionate; self-reflexive, not neutral; experimental and innovative, not realist and documentary. In addition a biography should be metabiographical, explicitly telling the story of the biographer's engagement with the subject. (2009, 133)

11. Eakin also proposes that "our narrative self-fashioning, oriented as much to the present and future as to the past, may even possess an evolutionary, adaptive value, helping to anchor our shifting identities in time" (xi). This book argues that biographical narrative similarly explores the self-fashioning by a biographical subject and the fashioning in a biography by his or her biographer.
12. Also, see Stoneman, Patsy. "Sex, Crimes and Secrets: Invention and Imbroglio in Recent Brontë Biographical Fiction", *Brontë Studies* 39.4 (2014): 341–352; Wright, Donald, "Reflections on Donald Creighton and the Appeal of Biography", *Journal of Historical Biography* 1 (2007): 15–27.

REFERENCES

Aubin, David, and Charlotte Bigg. 2007. Neither Genius nor Context Incarnate: Norman Lockyer, Jules Janssen and the Astrophysical Self. In *The History and Poetics of Scientific Biography*, ed. Thomas Soderqvist, 51–70. Aldershot, Hampshire: Ashgate.

Backscheider, Paula R. 1999. *Reflections on Biography*. New York: Oxford University Press.

Bate, Jonathan. 1997. *The Genius of Shakespeare*. London: Macmillan.

Benton, Michael. 2015a. First published in 2009. *Literary Biography: An Introduction*. Chichester, West Sussex: Wiley Blackwell.

———. 2015b. *Towards a Poetics of Literary Biography*. Basingstoke: Palgrave Macmillan.

Cole, Phyllis. 2004. Conversation that Makes the Soul. In *Lives Out of Letters: Essays on American Literary Biography and Documentation, in Honor of Robert N. Hudspeth*, ed. Robert Habich, 205–224. Madison: Fairleigh Dickinson University.

Cooper, John Milton. 2004. Conception, Conversation and Comparison: My Experiences as a Biographer. In *Writing Biography: Historians and Their Craft*, ed. Lloyd E. Ambrosius, 79–102. London: University of Nebraska Press.

Crick, Bernard. 1980. *George Orwell: A Life*. Harmondsworth, Middlesex: Penquin.

Eakin, Paul John. 2008. *Living Autobiographically: How We Create Identity in Narrative*. London: Cornell University Press.

Holderness, Graham. 2009. Author! Author!: Shakespeare and Biography. *Shakespeare* 5.1: 122–133.

Holmes, Richard. 1993. *Dr Johnson & Mr Savage*. London: Hodder and Stoughton.

———. 2005. First published in 1989. *Coleridge: Early Visions*. London: Harper Perennial.

———. 2016. *This Long Pursuit: Reflections of a Romantic Biographer*. London: William Collins.

Holroyd, Michael. 1988. How I Fell into Biography. In *The Troubled Face of Biography*, ed. Eric Homberger and John Charmley, 94–103. Basingstoke, Hampshire: Macmillan.

———. 2003. First published in 2002. *Works on Paper: The Craft of Biography and Autobiography*. London: Abacus.

———. 2014. *A Dog's Life*. London: MacLehose Press.

Lee, Hermione. 2005. *Body Parts: Essays on Life-writing*. London: Chatto & Windus.

———. 2009. *Biography: A Very Short Introduction*. New York: Oxford University Press.

Motion, Andrew. 1997. *Keats*. London: Faber and Faber.

Woolf, Virginia. 1994. First published in 1928. *Orlando*. London: Flamingo.

Wroe, Nicholas. 2008. Life in Writing: Interview with Michael Holroyd. *Guardian Saturday Review*, September 13, 12–13.

CHAPTER 2

A Habit of Stories

A brief history of theories and writing about biography since the early twentieth century in this chapter considers how some academics, critics and biographers, Hermione Lee in particular, understand its development—although, as Lee has noted, it can be misleading to try and understand ways in which biography has altered as a tidy, linear progression.[1] On the one hand, some common trends emerge across the centuries as the genre evolves. On the other, the complexity in form, style, structure and medium for biography has changed and biographers have built on and challenged the work of their predecessors. This chapter also touches on the ways in which literary estates have questioned the authenticity of some biographies, and ends with a conversation with Clare Brant, Director of the Centre for Life-Writing Research at King's College, London, on some recent developments across life-writing.[2]

Lee suggests that western biography has its origins in "educational stories of remarkable men" (2009, 22), such as the *Epic of Gilgamesh*, the life of the Assyrian king who ruled in about 2600 BC, and classical stories of public men "judged by their peers and posterity for their behaviour" (22):

> The main events of classical lives are battles, conquests, victories in government and argument, dominance over the populace, the imparting of wisdom, influential deeds and sayings. (22)

© The Author(s) 2017
J. McVeigh, *In Collaboration with British Literary Biography*,
DOI 10.1007/978-3-319-58383-9_2

Plutarch's *Lives of the Noble Greeks and Romans*, also known as *Plutarch's Lives*, is significant because it aims to reveal character as well as glorious exploits. American biographer Nigel Hamilton quotes from Plutarch, who is interested as much in the character of his subjects as in their public lives: "the most brilliant exploits often tell us nothing of the virtues and vices of the men who performed them" (2007, 26). Plutarch argues that "a chance remark or a joke may reveal far more of a man's character than the mere feat of winning battles in which thousands fall" (26). This dual focus can be seen in Roman life-writing, and it persists today:

> the age-old tug of war between idealization and critical interpretation still characterized the biographical enterprise. Some Romans wanted to laud and worship ancestors and past figures ... Others found that this idealization could not square with their curiosity to know more about the psychology and real life experiences of an unidealized individual, the better to understand their own lives. (Hamilton 2007, 32)

Nevertheless, hagiography was "one of the dominant literary genres in Europe from Late Antiquity to the end of the Middle Ages" (Lee 2009, 25). Early collective lives of canonical figures are representative of biographies that continued to celebrate success and promote the lives of famous and powerful men.

In *The Lives of the Most Eminent Painters, Sculptors, and Architects* (1568), Giorgio Vasari seeks to promote the work of artists, although he too argues that his book is designed to do more than celebrate the lives of the great and successful. He hopes that it will "keep the arts alive, or at least ... give them every possible encouragement. In this way, my good intentions and the work of outstanding men will, I hope, provide the arts with support ... they have been lacking hitherto" (1965, 47). An objective for biographers since the sixteenth century has been to play a key role in promoting the literature, arts and culture of a particular historical period, broadening understanding about the life and work of artistic and literary figures, and promoting the work of those who are forgotten or lost.

Lee notes that biographical writing has taken many forms across the centuries. In the seventeenth century, it covered a

> wide, contemporaneous range of subjects—rulers, magistrates, worthies, artists, poets, churchmen, thinkers—and took many forms. There were

individual Lives, collective group Lives, biographical dictionaries, obituaries, "memoirs, diaries, epistolary collections, hagiographies, character sketches and royal lives". Praise and eulogy were mixed with criticism and satire, universal types with curious individuals, formal rhetorical patterns with eccentric deviations. (2009, 34)

Izaak Walton in *Walton's Lives*, "written and much rewritten between 1640 and 1678, fused together a number of the available ways of thinking about 'good men'" (Lee 2009, 34), including hagiography and portraiture. John Aubrey's *Brief Lives*, four hundred or so biographical sketches dating from the late seventeenth century, were "a mixture of anecdotes, gossip, memories, and observations" (36). Lee suggests that biography continues to mix together the contradictory strains of "the epic and the absurd, legends and gossip, the elegiac and the anecdotal, gravity and foolishness" (2009, 38). In a 1683 essay introducing an edition of *Plutarch's Lives*, John Dryden suggests that "here you are led into the private Lodgings of the Heroe: you fee him in his undrefs, and are made Familiar with his moft private actions and converfations" (1683, 94). Dryden was interested in the character of his subjects and details about their private lives, including indiscretions. He places these day-to-day aspects of life within the wider reaches of history and philosophy:

> there is alfo room referv'd for the loftinefs and gravity of general Hiftory, when the actions related fhall require that manner of expreffion. But there is withal, a defcent into minute circumftances, and trivial paffages of life, which are natural to this way of writing. (94)

This is another early passage about the interdisciplinary nature of biography and its focus, at times, on the everyday. Tension between the promotion of exemplary lives based on significant historical events and an interest in the domestic, private and mundane in the lives of canonical or less famous biographical subjects can be seen in the work of a small number of writers throughout the genre's history.

In the seventeenth century, the word 'biography' came into general use. It was John Dryden in 1683 who first referred to biography "as a collective noun" (Hamilton 2007, 81). However, Hamilton suggests that a definition of biography that focuses on written lives "did scant justice to three thousand years of the depiction of real individuals, in every conceivable medium" (2007, 82). Lives have continued to this day to be reflected in many different forms. Recent trends on social media, including Twitter and blogs, written narratives about the lives of objects and places, and the role of fiction, film and performance are only a few of the alternative forms available for exploring lives.

Then, of course, came the eighteenth century and James Boswell's canonical life of Samuel Johnson, published in 1791. Other 'Great Men' of the period had their sayings written down, but Lee notes that "Boswell was unusual in turning 'ana' [sayings] into a whole biographical narrative, while keeping the fragmentary quality of an anthology. He was pioneering as one of the first to publish private conversations so fully and candidly" (2009, 46). Underpinning his approach was an understanding of biography as a kind of 'copartnership'. As Lee argues, "we want to see how the asexual but tender attachment between the biographer and his subject develops" (51) in this biography. Boswell describes what he means by copartnership when writing about a journey he undertook with Johnson to Scotland: "I looked on this tour to the Hebrides as a copartnership between Dr. Johnson and me. Each was to do all he could to promote its success" (1848, 360), which included entertaining local people on Skye. He believes that he was "fortunate enough frequently to draw ... [Johnson] forth to talk, when he would otherwise have been silent. The fountain was at times locked up, till I opened the spring" (360). In these scenes, Boswell becomes Johnson's sidekick, in which it is the role of the travelling companion and biographer to get his subject talking. This suggests an image of Johnson's biographical narrator also empowering him to speak in his own biography, almost bringing him to life and providing him with an opportunity to offer another performance that will impress his audience. An understanding of the nature of performance in biography is an aspect of the genre to which this book returns. Lee notes this feature in Boswell's narrative, as Johnson becomes "the man of letters as epic hero" (2009, 51), and "Boswell gives Johnson spiritual victories, disciples, intellectual influence, and a good death" (52). This is more than a type of hagiography promoting the nature of a good life, because the "presentation of identity in the Life is complicated, subtle, and new" (52):

> In the dance of conversation and copartnership between the two, the figures seem to move about, talk, and think in front of us, embodied and immediate, though so long vanished into the past. (Lee 2009, 52)

This sense of a biographical subject coming to life in biography, the influential role of the biographer and the nature of the conversation between biographer and subject are important aspects of contemporary biography. Late twentieth and early twenty-first century British biography is understood in this book as a conversation and copartnership in which the self-fashioned nature of a biographical subject and the character of the narrator are explored.

Boswell "believed—as Johnson did—that the point of life-writing was to be truthful and realistic ... Fidelity to the subject should not be a process of loyal concealment, but of accurate characterization" (Lee 2009, 46). According to Johnson, in a seminal essay published in *The Rambler* in 1750, "The Dignity and Usefulness of Biography", a biographer must be careful if he is writing about someone he knows, in order to remain faithful to the facts—what Johnson calls "fidelity" (1888, 84)—and to avoid influences that might "tempt him to conceal, if not to invent" (84). Lee suggests that Boswell's biography "reads like a realist novel of its time" (2009, 50), full of the performance of its leading character and comic scenes, "with Boswell as stage-manager" (49) directing the action and giving his own character as narrator a significant role. The performance of the narrator and the storytelling qualities of this biography are part of its strength. Boswell's belief that biography should be truthful and realistic, and Lee's comment about the performative nature of his writing, highlights one of the pervading tensions across the genre that troubles some historians and critics. When it is written as a nonfiction form, how can biography maintain the fidelity important to Johnson as well as the copartnership and conversational tone important to Boswell without jeopardising authenticity? Concerns about the form and style of biography inform debates about the genre across recent decades, as biographers explore whether to write cradle to grave narratives, or to experiment with chronology, focus on particular scenes or anecdotes in a life, make their own views as narrator clear, and balance what we know about someone's life with what we think we know about their motives and feelings. Martin Stannard makes a distinction between the different approaches to biography by Boswell and Johnson, who wrote his own biography of the poet Richard Savage, *The Life of Richard Savage*

(1728), and the extent to which this can be traced in the work of contemporary biographers:

> The Boswellian biographers, writing a form of fiction in which their 'presence' is crucial ... comfort us with the assumption that their hero or heroine is both 'knowable' and likeable ... The Johnsonian version is cooler. Here the biographer is equally in the position of persuasion, but rather more in the role of entertaining barrister than that of autobiographer or novelist. A certain distance is preserved. (1996, 39)

Romantic biographer Richard Holmes describes Boswell's biography as a study of a friendship and in his view, "There are few experimental techniques that Boswell has not already tried" (2005, 367). For Holmes, "he is our prophet" (367). Other biographers adopt a more Johnsonian tone.

Adam Sisman argues that Boswell "deliberately downplayed his own role in selecting and shaping ... In organizing and shaping his material, Boswell aimed to create a unified and coherent narrative" (2006, 174) that communicated his vision of Johnson. This would be based, Boswell hoped, as much as possible on Johnson's own voice: "Boswell planned to let Johnson speak for himself" (Sisman 2006, 171). In doing so, Sisman suggests that Boswell reinforced "the sense of dialogue between the two men" (172). Sisman sees Boswell as both a ventriloquist and a character himself in this biography.[3] The storytelling ability of a biographer and the dialogues between biographers and their subjects are key themes in this reading of the genre.

Johnson and Boswell both believed, in common with Dryden, that it "was the 'minute particulars' that gave biography its usefulness" (Lee 2009, 46). Johnson comments in the essay for the *Rambler* in October 1750 that we "are all prompted by the same motives, all deceived by the same fallacies, all animated by hope, obstructed by danger, entangled by desire, and seduced by pleasure" (1888, 81), and the "business of the biographer is often to pass slightly over those performances and incidents, which produce vulgar greatness, to lead the thoughts into domestick privacies, and display the minute details of daily life, where exterior appendages are cast aside" (82). In his view, there are "many invisible circumstances which ... are more important than publick occurrences" (82), and anecdotes about these types of details are an essential part of contemporary British biography. Johnson is also interested in the distinction between hagiography of exemplary public figures and biography about all sorts of different people:

> there has rarely passed a life of which a judicious and faithful narrative would not be useful. For ... there is such a uniformity in the state of man ... that there is scarce any possibility of good or ill, but it is common to human kind. (1888, 81)

Life-writing narratives about less canonical subjects has been a key trend in recent publishing. Johnson's perspective here emphasises that, in understanding something about the lives of others who lead more ordinary lives, we have an opportunity to learn about our everyday selves, and in doing so life-writing, including biography, becomes a genre in which public and private aspects of people's lives are central to the form, whether the subject is famous or not.

The Fortune of Francis Barber (2015) by Michael Bundock tells the story of Samuel Johnson's servant and the experience of black people in eighteenth century England. James Boswell knew Barber and draws on his experience for his biography of Johnson. We hear a rare example of Barber's own voice in Boswell, as noted in Bundock's biography:

> Barber told James Boswell that "he lived with Dr. Johnson from 1752 to about 1757—when upon some difference he left him and served a Mr. Farren Apothecary in Cheapside for about two years." (2015, 71)

Bundock's biography is both a story about Barber's life and the friendship between Johnson and Barber, whose life has played a small part in narratives about Johnson. Bundock suggests that Barber's life "has a wider significance: it opens up a window" (6) to the forgotten lives of thousands of black Britons in the eighteenth century. We only know of Barber's life because of his connection with Johnson and, as a result, he "appears, at least passingly, in many accounts of the period" (6). Bundock associates Barber's life with the places he lived and, in an image which resonates with Johnson's friendship with the poet Richard Savage and is discussed in Chap. 6, Bundock opens the biography with Johnson and Barber walking through London together: "On a summer's day in 1752, two conspicuously odd figures are making their way through the hubbub and grime of London's Fleet Street ... these two stand out" (1). In Barber's case, this is because he is black.

Novelist Caryl Phillips has written about Francis Barber's life in *Foreigners: Three English Lives* (2008), a book, as his title suggests, about three black men who come to Britain to live. His other subjects are twentieth century figures, Randolph Turpin, Britain's first black world-champion boxer, and David Oluwale, a Nigerian stowaway. This is a fictional narrative that recounts Barber's life through the voice of an unnamed fictional peer of Johnson's who, in this story, knew Barber when he was living with Samuel Johnson, attended Johnson's funeral with him and speaks to Barber shortly before he dies. The fictional narrator recounts Barber's fall into poverty despite a generous legacy from Johnson. The narrative draws attention to the extent to which Barber may have been exploited after Johnson's death. The fictional narrator has a conversation with Barber's impoverished wife in which she comments that "there were those who cheated us. Lots of them" (2008, 44). Barber is reported, in this fictional account, to say as he lies dying in a workhouse hospital:

> My master provided me with many advantages yet I still find myself in these circumstances. I sincerely wish that he had used me differently ... Perhaps it would have been more profitable for me to have established for myself the limits of my abilities rather than having them blurred by kindness, dependence, and my own indolence. (2008, 58)

Johnson gave Barber opportunities to expand his education and to live in circumstances that were better than many of his peers, but Barber's identity was scripted by Johnson's expectations. Twice in his life, Barber ran away from Johnson but found himself back living with him. The type of liberty he experienced staying with Johnson was perhaps not the opportunity he needed to find the freedom of a life lived on his own terms. The voice of similar men and women can be heard in life-writing narratives from the eighteenth century, such as *The Interesting Narrative of the Life of Olaudah Equiano or Gustavus Vassa, the African* (1789) by Olaudah Equiano, and from the nineteenth century, including *Twelve Years a Slave* (1853) by Solomon Northup and *My Bondage and My Freedom* (1855) by Frederick Douglass, but the voices of many black people from these periods remain hidden.

Biographers have been criticised for exposing too much about the lives of their subjects. William Godwin's memoir about his wife, Mary Wollstonecraft, published five years after Boswell's biography, was widely criticised for revealing his wife's previous affair with Gilbert Imlay and the birth of their illegitimate child, Fanny. Australian biographer Barbara Caine notes that this public outcry "pointed to a new concern about the limits on what could be discussed in biography and the need for discretion, especially when it came to questions about personal and domestic life" (2010, 34). In the case of Godwin, his focus on Wollstonecraft's private life damaged his wife's reputation. In comparison, Caine suggests that Boswell omits "many aspects of … [Johnson's] personal and emotional life" (33), in particular his relationships with women. Biographers walk a tightrope between revealing too little or too much about the personal and domestic aspects of a life and what we consider to be private today will be different in the future.[4]

Lee suggests that in the early part of the nineteenth century, as in the seventeenth century, life-writing took many forms, and that this connects with the experimental nature of recent autobiographical narratives and biographies:

> Conversation, friendship, collaboration, quarrels; letters telling of personal feelings and encounters, of work in progress and political opinions; confessional narratives of addiction, love, and weakness; journals of domestic life; manuscripts circulating between small groups: early 19th-century literature was criss-crossed with a spider's web of life-writing. 'Self-fashioning' took many forms. (2009, 54)

She also notes that, "The emphasis in life-writing was on empathy" (55). Writing about biography became more significant during the nineteenth century. In another essay, Lee suggests that Thomas Carlyle, "was passionately interested in biography" (2005, 1):

> [His] idea of life-writing as the creation of intimate links between the dead and living, his insistence on sympathy as the motivating force, his interest in the rescuing of lives, however obscure, from oblivion, and his belief in the power of small anecdotes and little details … to bring a whole life home to us: all this still has value. (2005, 2)

In an early book about biography by James Field Stanfield, *An Essay on the Study and Composition of Biography* (1813), Elinor Shaffer identifies the same contemporary perspective that "biography should assist us in understanding human character" (2004, 115). Shaffer highlights G.H. Lewes's biography of Goethe as a notable example of a biography that was sympathetic, although Lewes "did not mince words" (122). A concern with the nature of empathy, the role of anecdotes and hidden lives are features of late twentieth century biography.

According to Shaffer, the role of tone "in lulling, misleading, and smoothing over uncomfortable matters in biography as in autobiography became a major one in Victorian life-writing" (123). In the case of much nineteenth century biography, the tone is elegiac, eulogising and often hyperbolic. As Lee makes clear, these biographies are a form of memorial and the "impulses of sympathy and veneration that dominated much 19th-century biography often solidified into hagiography" (2009, 57). This mainly focused on the public, professional life of a biographical subject, written by an admirer or family member. For others, Lee argues, the genre was seen as representative of a low culture, as "journalistic intrusion, the beginnings of celebrity culture, and the ever more shaky dividing line between private and public, gave rise to debates uncannily like our own" (2009, 68).

A particular exception to the hagiography of the nineteenth century was J.A. Froude's biography of Thomas Carlyle. He was widely condemned for highlighting the unhappiness of Carlyle's marriage to his wife Jane.[5] Other notable examples of less formulaic biographies from this period, include John Gibson Lockhart's biography of his father-in-law, Sir Walter Scott, which exposes some of his failings, and Elizabeth Gaskell's *The Life of Charlotte Brontë* (1857), which laid the foundations for the Brontë myth and the image of Charlotte as a victim of her circumstances and the constraining influence of her father. Gaskell's biography shows Charlotte's virtues but fails altogether to acknowledge her friendship with, and passion for, her married Belgian teacher, Monsieur Heger. For Shaffer, this biography "has all the qualities of a novel, the sustained building of suspense, the powerful empathy with the central character, the creation of a milieu in intimate detail; and it commands the complete absorption of the narrator, the character and the reader" (2004, 131). This is a biography that shares the passion of Boswell to offer a partisan and moving portrait, rather than a more measured portrayal.[6]

The development and popularity of Victorian hagiography gave an opportunity for the profession of biographer to grow. Lee argues that, by the end of the century, a "self-consciousness was developing about the practice of the craft" (2009, 71). She suggests that the dividing lines between the tomes of nineteenth century biography and the move to a more creative, less reverent form in the early twentieth century can be over-emphasised and that "Cultural shifts get over-simplified" (73). Nevertheless, the balance did change in this period as biography moved to use "fictional tactics, irony, parody, and caricature ... [and] biography aimed to uncover the inner self behind the public figure" (72). There are various strands in the development of biography at this point, including a more self-reflexive approach to its writing, new forms that challenge a life and times format, and the development of psychoanalytic approaches. Laura Marcus provides an overview of the characteristics of the 'new biography'; in this period, there emerged

> a new equality between biographer and subject, by contrast with the hero-worship and hagiography of Victorian eulogistic biography; brevity, selection, and an attention to form and unity traditionally associated with fiction rather than history; the discovery of central motifs in a life and of a 'key' to personality, so that single aspects of the self or details of the life and person came to stand for or to explain the whole; and a focus on character rather than events. (2004, 196)

Influential figures in the development of this 'new biography' in the early twentieth century were Virginia Woolf, Lytton Strachey, Harold Nicolson, Edmund Gosse and Desmond MacCarthy. Harold Nicolson makes a distinction between scientific and literary biography in *The Development of English Biography* (1927), and sees the future of imaginative literary biography in fiction, whilst what he calls scientific biography will focus on facts. A closer look at Nicolson's approach identifies issues that remain at the heart of contemporary debates about the genre.

He argues that biography "must be a truthful record of an individual and composed as a work of art" (1959, 8). By truthful, he means, as did Johnson, that important facts about someone's life should not be hidden, as was common in Victorian hagiography, and Nicolson goes on to argue that biography must also be "well constructed" (12). His description of what this means is Aristotelian in nature. In his definition of biography, sympathy and pity will be stimulated, intricate associations will be evoked ... There must be result for the reader, an active and not merely a passive adjustment of sympathy; there must result for him an acquisition not of facts only but of experience; there must remain for him a definite metal impression, an altered attitude of mind. There must finally be a conscious-ness of creation. (13)

Nicolson is concerned if biography becomes hagiography or seeks to promote a particular theory, or if the biographer exhibits undue sub-jectivity, rather than detachment; although he comments that to a "cer-tain extent a subjective attitude is desirable and inevitable" (10). Here lies one of the tensions that has haunted biography and its critics ever since. A biographer needs to come close to, but remain at a distance from, her subject to help re-create an authentic portrayal. Nicolson pro-motes Boswell as an ideal of biography, although his view that Johnson's biographer "does not obtrude unnecessarily" (104) would perhaps not be a perspective shared by more recent critics. He makes a distinction between the kind of biography he is promoting and life and times biog-raphy, which, in his view, "is less a study of an individual than a study of history expressed in and through an individual" (140). Nicolson dis-misses Gaskell's *Charlotte Brontë* because it omits key facts about her life, is sentimental and falls "under the heading of historical fiction" (140). So, at this time, an influential view was that biography must not be too close to fiction. Nicolson describes modernist concerns about the generic boundaries of biography in terms that anticipate later debates about the balance between form and content in the genre and the omniscient pres-ence of the biographer in some biographies. He argues that "the form of a biography is less important than its content" (144), but he thinks that there is a central problem of content versus form in biography: "it is on the rocks of this problem that [what he calls] pure biography is doomed to split" (144), into scientific or what he calls applied biogra-phy, and fictional forms. In his view, biography will develop in two direc-tions—scientific biography "will insist ... on all the facts" (154), and is more like the life and times biography he describes, whilst literary biog-raphy "demands a partial or artificial representation of facts" (154) and will develop as fiction. This tension between documentary, scholarly biography and a more self-reflexive form marks an important moment in metanarratives about biography. If the genre is to move away from the hagiography of the nineteenth century, questions about subjectivity, the role of the narrator, the use of material and facts, tone, style and form in the narrative are important. In future writing about the genre, applied biography is associated with the idea of biography as a form of scholarly chronicle or critical academic analysis, whilst Nicolson aligns a more self-reflexive literary form with fiction. As Chap. 3 illustrates, there has certainly been a significant growth in fictional biographies, or hybrid narratives that are closer to fiction.

Desmond MacCarthy famously suggests that the biographer "is an artist who is on oath, and anyone who knows anything about artists, knows that that is almost a contradiction in terms" (1953, 32). In his view, biography "is undoubtedly an art. But if it is an art, how are we to define it? I think the simplest way is to say that a biography must aim at being a truthful record of an individual life, composed as a work of art" (32). In doing so, "the biographer cannot invent those circumstances which might illustrate best the character he is depicting" (32). For the biographer,

> All he can do is arrange facts as effectively as possible … And yet he must impose some pattern on the disorder of life, or his book will only be a quarry from which some other man may be able some day to construct a building. (1953, 33)

Some biographies are rich and valuable quarries on which others draw for their less scholarly writing. Indeed, many popular biographers acknowledge the huge debt they owe to scholars from whose work they take significant knowledge and information. MacCarthy's definition is very close indeed to Nicolson's, which states that biography is "a truthful record of an individual and composed as a work of art" (1959, 8). However, there is clearly a crucial distinction between them. MacCarthy encourages the biographer to "*aim* at a truthful record" (my emphasis), a more pragmatic expectation. The suggestion that a biographer may arrange facts and impose a pattern on the disorder of a life is less prescriptive and perhaps more achievable. It accepts that biography is messy, fluid and open to different narrative strategies. Critics will continue to disagree with the patterns presented by individual biographers but that, MacCarthy might say, is inevitable. In *The Brontë Myth* (2001), a meta-biography about how the lives of the three sisters have been rewritten, Lucasta Miller brings this debate into the twenty-first century and argues that literary biography is "an amphibious art form, which ideally has *both* to obey the constraints of evidence *and* to respond creatively to the challenge of making shape, form and meaning" (2002, 169).[7] In this analysis, the form becomes one in which integrity is central and rigour will be open to debate, as it is in academic and many other forms of writing.

Caine comments that Virginia Woolf's view about the importance of inner thoughts and emotions "has been a driving force in the writing of biography across the twentieth century" (2010, 40). In her seminal essay, "The Art of Biography" (1942), Woolf offers her own overview of biography's development: "Interest in our selves and in other people's selves is a late development of the human mind. Not until the eighteenth century in England did that curiosity express itself in writing the lives of private people. Only in the nineteenth century was biography fully grown and hugely prolific" (1967a, 221). She comments that "the art of biography is the most restricted of all the arts ... The novelist is free; the biographer is tied" (221) to the facts of the life she is writing about. Woolf argues that towards the end of the nineteenth century there was a change in attitudes to biography and the biographer "won a measure of freedom" (222):

> Froude's Carlyle is by no means a wax mask painted rosy red. And following Froude there was Sir Edmund Gosse, who dared to say that his own father was a fallible human being. And following Edmund Gosse in the early years of the [twentieth] century came Lytton Strachey. (222)

Edmund Gosse broke new ground. He describes his book about his relationship with his father, *Father and Son: A Study of Two Temperaments* (1907), as "a struggle between two temperaments, two consciences and almost two epochs" (1989, 35), and he is keen to emphasise that it "is not an autobiography" (217). However, it is in part a study of "the consciousness of self" (55), and in writing this memoir about his difficult relationship with his father, Gosse found "a companion and a confidant in myself" (58). Gosse is keen to emphasise to his readers that his book "is scrupulously true" (33) and should be understood as having a wider relevance as a "*document*, as a record of educational and religious conditions which, having passed away, will never return" (33), and as not in any way fictional. His memoir is only 'true' from his point of view and it relies on his memories. Lee describes it as a novelistic memoir (2009, 75). Gosse's book, as Caine suggests, "anticipated later developments in its criticism of Victorian values and assumptions, especially those concerning the duties that children owed parents, however unreasonable parental demands might be" (2010, 39). Gosse not only draws attention to early twentieth century issues about the paternalism of family life and the influence of religion and the church, but, as he experiments with the form, he also explores the nature of authenticity in autobiographical narratives and memoirs.

Lytton Strachey's approach to biography in *Eminent Victorians* (1918), discussed further in a later chapter about the writing of Michael Holroyd, broached new ground not only in relation to the content of his lives, which challenged the paternalism of Victorian biography, but also in his narrative style and tone. Caine argues that Strachey offered "an example of a new approach to biography in the brevity of his treatment, his crisp literary style and his often ironic tone, but also in his open criticism and his interest in hidden and sometimes unconscious motives" (2010, 39). Marcus places Strachey's influence within the historical context of this period as "*Eminent Victorians* was perceived as the first text of postwar England, opening up to ridicule the workings of power and the blind submission to God and Country which had led to the mass slaughter of World War 1" (2004, 197). Strachey's purpose in *Eminent Victorians* (1918) is "to illustrate, rather than to explain" (1986, 9) the lives of: Cardinal Henry Manning, "an ecclesiastic" (9); Florence Nightingale, "a woman of action" (9) and "a rock in the angry ocean" (122); Thomas Arnold, headmaster of Rugby School and "an educational authority" (9); and General Charles George Gordon, "a man of adventure" (9), who led armed forces in China and Sudan. His method is to "examine and elucidate certain fragments of the truth which took my fancy" (9). This contrasts with other forms of hagiography, which in his view include "ill-digested masses of material" (10), a slipshod style and a "tone of tedious panegyric" (10). He believes that the biographer must "maintain his own freedom of spirit" (10). There is a note of irony here as the biographer gives his perspective on selected facts—in other words, only those that he chooses to highlight. There is a wry tone throughout Strachey's book that is reflected in both his content and style.

Woolf makes a distinction between the short sketches in *Eminent Victorians* and Strachey's full-length biographies *Victoria* (1921) and *Elizabeth and Essex: A Tragic History* (1928). She argues that the longer works throw "great light upon the nature of biography" (1967a, 223), and she shares some of Nicolson's concerns. Her perspective is that Strachey's biography of Victoria is successful and treats biography as a craft, whilst his biography of Elizabeth I treats biography as an art and "flouted its limitations" (223). The Victoria biography "used to the full the biographer's power of selection and relation, but ... kept strictly within the world of fact" (224); yet, in the biography of Elizabeth I, Strachey was "urged to invent" (225), particularly as facts are missing. As a result, Woolf is concerned that in this biography there is a "sense of vacancy and effort, of a tragedy that has no crisis, of characters that meet but do not clash" (225). Like her peers, Woolf argues that nonfiction biography must be based on verifiable facts because without them biography may be doomed to fail and the authentic picture of a biographical subject becomes merely the vision of the biographer. She famously wrote in another seminal essay about the genre, "The New Biography", that

> On the one hand there is truth; on the other there is personality. And if we think of truth as something of granite-like solidity and of personality as something of rainbow-like intangibility and reflect that the aim of biography is to weld these two into one seamless whole, we shall admit that the problem is a stiff one. (1967b, 229)

She praises the granite-like qualities of Strachey's biography of Victoria, whilst criticising the more fictional approach he takes in his biography of Elizabeth I. Woolf's view of this tension in biography has been very influential, but it does perpetuate the idea that facts have an intrinsic granite-like quality, whilst many do not. Facts may reflect something that happened, but different people may well see an event or relationship from very different points of view.

Woolf's Bloomsbury Group contemporary Desmond MacCarthy argues that Strachey should be understood as "an artist in biography" (1932, 90). In his view, for Strachey, "biography was interpretation, and therefore the record, not only of facts, but of the biographer's deepest responses to them ... His preoccupation was with human nature itself, and only incidentally with the causes of events or of changes" (92). For MacCarthy, "what is most interesting from a biographical point of view, is precisely the interplay of the private and public life" (92), and he believes that Strachey covers both "the dramatic rhythm of certain lives" (98) and "the tone and aspect of their times" (98). As this book goes on to discuss, more recent biographers have also sought some kind of freedom to write versions of a life—focusing on human nature and imposing some pattern on the facts, writing in the context of wider historical and cultural events, interweaving both public and private aspects of lives and sometimes taking a thematic approach, although without the harsh partisan style adopted in Strachey's debunking. It explores the extent to which some late twentieth century British biography can be understood as addressing the tension between granite and rainbow in longer biographical narratives and, in doing so, creating a form of the pure, or what will be called here personal biography, that Nicolson thought might be impossible, although not everyone will agree with the patterns and the connections they make. To varying degrees, they are in tune with MacCarthy's idea of the biographer as "an artist on oath", albeit that the tune is more passionately rendered in some biographies than others.

An interesting feature of Strachey's short life of Florence Nightingale is the extent to which it makes clear the importance of the role that colleagues played in her professional life. Biographies may be criticised for being too individualistic, focusing on the life of a single subject and excluding the significance of anyone else in that person's life. However, late twentieth and early twenty first century British biography pays more attention to the lives of others in the story of a biographical subject, or subjects, and this is touched on in Strachey's approach to Florence Nightingale. Sidney Herbert MP saw her almost daily for many years and had the power and influence that she needed: "he devoted the whole of his life with an unwavering conscientiousness to the public service" (Strachey 1986, 138) and was appointed Secretary of State at War several times between 1845 and 1859. Dr. John Sutherland was her private secretary for more than thirty years and "surrendered to her purposes literally the whole of his life" (141). These men and others helped Nightingale achieve some hard-earned reforms in health care for the army and were long-serving public servants. If one looks past the fiery woman portrayed in Strachey's sketch, one can also see a study of a towering crusader who had to work closely with others to achieve her ambitions, although in this vignette their lives are primarily seen as abutting on to her own and they are understood as servants to her aims. This is a picture of a woman known for her achievements and then beaten down in old age by the scourge of senility. In the later years of the twentieth century, the life of Florence Nightingale was linked to that of nurse Mary Seacole, voted the greatest black Briton in 2004 and whose first full-length biography, by Jane Robinson, *Mary Seacole: The Charismatic Black Nurse Who Became a Heroine of the Crimea*, was not published until 2005. Ron Ramdin notes, "Given that Victorian Britain was securely founded upon a combination of race, class and colour, it was incredible that Mary got as far as she did" (2005, 123). Since her death, her life and achievements, particularly during the Crimean War, had been hidden for too long.

In addition to modernist writers and critics, the theories of Freud and the field of psychoanalysis have been influential in twentieth century biography, supporting the growth of a specialist category of biography: psychobiography. Marcus proposes that the "growing impact of psychological and psychoanalytical theories on literary creation and criticism clearly played a central role in shaping the 'new biography', and its emphases on identity rather than event or action" (2004, 205). Freud's essay, *Leonardo da Vinci, A Memory of His Childhood* (1910) was particularly influential. Later in the twentieth century, Leon Edel, biographer of Henry James, is an important figure in the development of this new biography. He believes that a study of a subject's unconscious, including their dreams, could enable the biographer "to recognize the existence of a series of possibilities" (1987, 63) in each subject. Edel calls his approach 'literary psychology', which is "the study of what literature expresses of the human being who creates it" (1982, 12), given that "a literary work is never impersonal" (12):

> What literary psychology proposes is nothing less than the exploration of man's way of dreaming, thinking, imagining and behaving—and the exploration is conducted on the terrain of man's imaginative creations. (19)

In *Writing Lives* (1987), Edel proposes four principles for the new biography. The biographer must analyse "the manifestations of the unconscious as they are projected in conscious forms of action" (29); should not identify too closely with their subject, or "fall in love with them" (29); must look for deeper truths, for the private mythology of their subject (29); and must find an appropriate form for their biography, which need not be chronological (30). In the 1990s, psychiatrist Anthony Storr recommends to biographers that because "Writers are so notoriously prone to recurrent depression and to manic-depressive illness … every aspiring literary biographer ought to know something about these conditions" (1995, 84). On the other hand, Malcolm Bowie reflects on Freud's approach and is concerned about the danger of reductive analysis in biography, including psychobiography, which Storr's approach implies. He warns that "Freud is at once a powerful critic of identification and a helpless victim of its seductions" (2004, 192) in his own biographical writing. He debunks Freud's life of Da Vinci as "a fantasy of intellectual omnipotence and a series of all too falsifiable conjectures" (188) that produces "a perfectly disreputable biography of a great man" (188). In his view, it is a clear case of the biographer imposing a theory on his subject to suit his own purposes. As Lee makes clear, "Psycho-biography is out of fashion now", certainly in Britain (2009, 87), although it influenced much mid-twentieth century biography. Caine notes that "it is in the United States that there has been the deepest interest in linking psychoanalysis, biography and history. Discussion amongst both biographers and historians about the importance of psychoanalysis has continued up to the present" (2010, 95), whilst in Britain there remains considerable scepticism about its application to history and biography. This reflects a wider scepticism in British biography about the use of theory in the writing of lives.

Nevertheless, Lee comments that both modernist experiments and Freudian biography have "fed into a thriving, rich, popular Anglo-American tradition of professional biography in the mid to late 20th century. Large-scale, realistic, thoroughly historicized Lives were energized by strong characterization and description, humour, candour, and intimacy" (2009, 90). These biographies respond to modernist practice in their "belief in truth-telling, humour, and realism" (Lee 2009, 91), plus an interest in childhood, and "explorations of inner lives as much as public achievements" (91), and in a reluctance "(with a few notorious exceptions) to moralize, take sides, or cast blame" (91). Whether some are more open to the experimental approaches of Boswell and Strachey than others is a rich source of discussion for readers and critics alike. Lee distinguishes these from other more quarry-like contemporary biographies that are

> solid, thoroughly researched professional and academic biographies of writers, artists, thinkers, politicians, scientists, and national leaders … these monuments to hard work and careful investigation are not self-consciously crafted, but set down, as fully and as accurately as possible, a chronological account of a significant life. (91)

Here we perhaps have a definition that comes close to Nicolson's understanding of what he calls applied or scientific biography, more commonly known today as scholarly, documentary or chronicle biography. They are an important source for popular re-creative biographies, other hybrid forms and biographical novels.

The tension between biography as an art or as a science is discussed by American Paul Murray Kendall in the mid-twentieth century. He draws on Woolf's metaphor about the nature of biography as a form which encompasses both granite and rainbow: "biography is an impossible amalgam: half rainbow, half stone. To exist at all, it must feed upon the truth of facts, and yet to exist on its highest level, it must pursue the truth of interpretation" (1985, first published 1965, xii), it must "build with stone instead of rainbow" (9). Kendall argues that the "highest biographical art is the concealment of the biographer" (12), which, surprisingly, he argues is the practice of Boswell. Biography is more than a record, but it is not a story, because in his view this suggests fiction. He proposes his own definition:

> Considering that biography represents imagination limited by truth, facts raised to the power of revelation, I suggest that it may be defined as "the simulation, in words, of a man's life, from all that is known about that man". (15)

Kendall argues that biography "works through effects" (15) and is "an art with boundaries" (15), and that this puts limitations on how a life can be written when evidence is missing and a biographer is inclined to speculate. What Kendall calls the rhythm of a biography must be in tune with the pace of key moments in a life.[8] He is an advocate of strict chronology: "Biographical time and novelistic time do not mix" (25), and "thematic groupings cannot be permitted" (26). In his view, a biographer can interpret a life, but he or she cannot do so outside the boundaries of the historical movement of a life; so, "the biographer cannot leap from his own time into his subject's time" (28). The boundaries that Kendall places around biography have been challenged and broken by late twentieth century biographers, who do write thematically and shift the rhythm of time in their writing, seeking to make connections between the past of the biographical subject, or subjects, and the present of the biographer. The tensions implicit in Nicolson's arguments have not been fully addressed by Kendall in 1965. He dismisses both literary storytelling, which makes some biography comparable to fiction, and the voice of the biographer, thereby overlooking the copartnership, collaboration and conversation inherent in such a dialogic discourse.

For American literary scholar Richard Altick, also in the mid-twentieth century, Johnson was the first important theorist of biography and "an able practitioner of the art" (1966, 46), as well as "the subject of the greatest biography" (46). He was the "first great advocate of personal, as opposed to public, biography" (48) in which the private life and the details of daily life are as important, or in some cases more important, than the professional or public life of a biographical subject. Altick's use of the term personal biography is perhaps a more helpful alternative to Nicolson's description of pure biography, and is referred to further in this book. It is hard to think of anything in life that might be described as pure, and certainly the life of any human being is unlikely to fit the bill. The biographers discussed in this book adhere to Dryden's and Johnson's view that by exploring both the public or professional and domestic or private lives of their subjects, looking for details and compelling anecdotes, a biographer might be able to say something important about someone's life.

In 1986, American biographer Stephen Oates identifies three types of biography: the critical biography that adopts an academic approach, is intellectual, engages our minds not our hearts, and does not bring the biographical subject to life but instead engages "in critical discussion, not in art" (x); "the scholarly chronicle [which] is a straightforward recitation of acts" (x), read for information; and the 'pure' biography, identified by Nicolson. The critical biography may be concerned with the professional, publishing and social contexts that shaped an influential author's writing. However, as boundaries between fiction and nonfiction are blurred in contemporary biography, it is becoming unnecessary to make such rigid distinctions between different types of biography. Nevertheless, a critical biography is less likely to be read by general readers than the more popular personal biography, and it is this wider market that many biographers, including academics, want to reach. Oates identifies the key characteristics of his version of pure biography, as the subject takes

> the whole stage, with just enough historical backdrop for us to understand the subject in proper context. Functioning as "the hidden author," to use Wayne Booth's term, the pure biographer makes his subject come alive through graphic scenes, telling quotations, apt details, character development, interpersonal relationships, intellectual and emotional struggle, and

dramatic narrative sweep. To give a sense of life unfolding, the pure biographer is careful to tell his story sequentially, never topically. (1986, x)

The 'pure' biographer may have psychological insights, but he or she
must not lapse into critical commentary or psychoanalytical speculation,
and "hopes to engage our hearts as well as our minds" (xi). Reading
such material is a cathartic experience, which encourages us, as readers,
to come to our own conclusions about the lives we read about in biography. This type of biography humanises history and allows the reader
to witness "another's long journey through the vicissitudes of life" (xi),
suffering personal dilemmas like our own. It may be a narrative that has
literary qualities, without being about literary lives, and it could include
biographies "that seek to illuminate universal truths about humankind
through the sufferings and triumphs of a single human being" (xi).
Oates's book discusses the views of ten American biographers about the
narrative art of biography. He identifies a number of essential characteristics on which they all agree:

> the function of biography is to evoke and dramatize a life through nov-
> elistic techniques but not invention itself, and … it should emerge from
> painstaking research … and intimate familiarity with the places where
> the subject lived and died. All would agree that the writer of lives must
> be selective in his choice of details, must eschew psychological jargon and
> write "in the language of literature," must let the subject "have the whole
> floor" and "speak in his own words and stance," must present a portrait
> that is "dramatically and psychologically coherent" and that makes the
> subject live in a living world. (xiii)

There are points in this description that could apply to the biographies
discussed in this book, which do use the rhetorical skills of literature, are
based on extensive research and are often familiar with the places important to a biographical subject or subjects. Details about a life are carefully
chosen, a pattern is imposed upon them within the biographical narrative and we can often hear the voice of the subject arising from the story
being told. Views may vary about how much historical context is appropriate, and this will be determined by a range of factors, including the
extent to which the life, or lives, in question are understood as representative of a wider group of peers and a particular historical moment,
or not. However, other aspects of Oates's analysis are not applicable to

contemporary biographies. Late twentieth and early twenty-first century British narrative nonfiction popular and personal biography does not offer a unified portrait of any one person, given that we are all made up of many different selves that we show to the world in different circumstances. Biography may be dramatically coherent but cannot offer a psychologically unified portrayal. In a biography, it may be possible to hear both the voice of the subject and that of the biographer, or at least the character of the biographer in conversation with his or her subject. The haunting presence of the biographical author in the narrative may well be important, as narrator, and in fact be something to celebrate. The biographer as author may offer a point of view and may speculate, particularly where evidence is missing, and can still leave it up to readers to make up their own minds about the available evidence and the version of a life, or lives, on offer in any particular biography. As Victoria Glendinning notes, biographers are often in the "lies and silences business" (49), and a biography may offer a counterfactual story about what might have happened in someone's life. Finally, biographies are increasingly not told sequentially but take a thematic approach. This reader will not offer an alternative description or definition of recent British biography in response to Oates or Kendall. My readers are invited to develop their own, but they may find that each time they read a biography it will need to be amended.[9]

In a study of African biography, Esperanza Brizuela-Garcia is critical of Oates's approach, arguing that "biographies are often a complex combination of life description, literary account, and historical analysis, and whose potential and appeal reside precisely in this multifaceted nature" (2007, 64). She is interested in cases of African historiography which, she argues, blend the forms of analytical and 'pure' biography described by Oates: "This synthesis reveals the dialectical connections between individual agency and historical process" (67). The time frame of any life or lives is much shorter than that of society or political history, and the life of any one family or professional network will also ebb and flow differently; so, in some biographies "biographical narrative demands a reconsideration of accepted chronologies and periodization" (69). In these types of biographies, Brizuela-Garcia describes the historical process "as organic as well as chronological in the sense that the links between the past and the present can be found outside the temporal line defined by historians, in the subtle attempts of individuals to establish meaningful connections to their own historical environment" (80). She proposes a redefinition of agency that "does not necessarily depend on the notions of exceptionality or representativeness" (68); lives can be both "exceptional and representative, demonstrating that these notions are relative and should not be used a priori when it comes to defining or justifying a biographical account" (79). They are determined as much by internal motivation and individual needs as historical contexts. Brizuela-Garcia's emphasis on the organic nature of history and lives helps to unfetter biographical narrative from rigid chronology and reductive definitions.

Biography increasingly places the lives of an individual or group within the wider context in which they lived. Caine proposes that

> Richard Holmes, Victoria Glendinning, Michael Holroyd and Claire Tomalin, for example, all place their biographical subjects within their social and literary worlds with extreme skill, offering insights also into the ways in which added depth can be brought to their inner lives and emotional registers by an understanding of the wider world in which people lived. (2010, 117)

For Caine, recent developments suggest that an individual life has the capacity to both "show in detail the experiences and the impact of historical developments on a particular individual and, through this study, to gain a wider understanding of social and historical change" (2010, 123). A further important influence in recent biography has been the recognition that biography should be concerned with the lives of ordinary people and with minority voices. More lives are being written about non-canonical figures who are special in part because they are representative of a wider group or community. They are important because "they can illustrate how differences of wealth and power, of class and gender and of ethnicity and religion have affected historical experiences and understanding" (Caine 2010, 2). Moreover, a growing number of biographies have been concerned with group lives, such as those of scientists and industrialists, as well as families, friends and professional peers. Writing in 1981, American biographer Margot Peters believes this illustrates that success achieved by an individual is often "a composite effort" (1981, 43) involving a range of people, including overlooked figures in the life of someone famous. For Peters, group biography "sees that the course of human events depends less on individualism than upon the endless ramifications of human interaction, much of which is beyond control or even consciousness" (44). More and more group biographies and biographies about relationships, friendships and hidden lives have been published over the last thirty years or so. Changes in biography have been part of the growing field of life-writing that, as Caine suggests, encourages "the notion that many, and indeed potentially all, lives are of interest and worth writing and reading about" (2010, 67), as Johnson suggested. The growth of biographies about women, hidden voices and group biography in the late twentieth century has significantly increased the range of people's lives portrayed in biography, challenging the status of traditional single life biography. Chapter 3 brings the history of the genre up to date and discusses examples of biographies that are representative of these and other significant developments.

It is important to acknowledge the huge impact that feminism has had on the genre, as a discussion of Claire Tomalin's work illustrates in a later chapter. Feminists in the late twentieth century challenged what they saw as a male dominated genre and envisaged the potential for biography, in partnership with autobiography and other forms of life-writing, to provide a voice for noncanonical subjects, including women, in their roles as both subject and biographer.[10] In 1999, American biographer Paula Backscheider notes that there have been growing numbers of biographies published about the lives of women. Biography now considers 'ordinary', private and domestic aspects of people's lives as important, and supports the recognition of the personal as political. These changes have led to the use of different types of evidence in life-writing, such as photographs, which can "highlight themes that might be overlooked" (1999, 155). One of the major shifts in biography achieved by feminist approaches has been a move away from a focus on professional and public careers, and a turn to the domestic and private in women's lives, and of those around them. This refocusing came to be thought of in the 1990s as a revisioning of individuals' lives and of history. For American biographer Linda Wagner-Martin, the "aim, of revising history—or at least women's personal history—is shared by all biographers of women subjects" (1994, 162), as the lives of women are often hidden from view and constrained by repressive social conventions.

How biographers struggle to reconcile their writing with the expectations of a subject's family and literary estate has been the basis of a number of complex and salutary tales about the life of a biographer. Perhaps two of the best known are Ian Hamilton's experience of writing a biography of J.D. Salinger and the aftermath following the publication of Sylvia Plath and Ted Hughes biographies.[11] *In Search of J.D. Salinger* (1988) is a metabiography about Hamilton's attempts to secure the agreement of Salinger to answer questions about his life and writing, and to publish an experimental biography.[12] Hamilton knew when he first approached Salinger that he would struggle to gain his agreement and he planned his biography, *J.D. Salinger: A Writing Life*, as a quest so that the anticipated rebuffs "would be as much part of the action as the triumphs ... The idea ... was to see what would happen if orthodox biographical procedures were to be applied to a subject who actively set himself to resist, and even to forestall, them" (1989, 4). He was interested in the idea of Salinger: "he was a fictional character, almost, and certainly a symbolic one" (7). Hamilton also makes a distinction between himself and the character of his biographer, "my sleuthing other self" (7). He grapples with the moral issues that dealing with a reluctant subject involves, whilst his "biographizing alter ego" (9) was "merely eager to get on with the job" (9). He writes about "we" throughout his book, tussling with his "companion" who is more unscrupulous. Hamilton also writes about Salinger's different selves, and how he found the author's letters to be performances depending on who he was writing to and why.[13] Hamilton and his "companion" are primarily interested in "Salinger the writer" (133) and Hamilton reads Salinger's fictional self in his fiction. His character, Buddy Glass, "is presented as having almost everything in common with his author" (156). Hamilton hopes that his "invented biographer figure" (189), his own self-fashioning, would help to lure Salinger "into the open" (189) so that at the end of his biography "there might even be some sort of amusing confrontation, a final scene in which *he* would try to outsmart *us*" (189). Hamilton submitted his manuscript for his biography in 1985 and Salinger took objection to his use of quotations from unpublished letters. Legal action followed and Hamilton was unable to publish. *In Search* is a story about his quest to do so and the type of biography it might have been. Rather than the ghostly conversation that Hamilton had hoped for between the fictional character of Salinger and his biographer alter ego, he regrets that it is as "litigants or foes, in the law school textbooks, on the shelves of the Supreme Court, and in the minds of everyone who reads this, the 'legal' version of my book" (212) that their relationship will be remembered. Their conversation is available in a very different written narrative from the one for which he had hoped.[14]

The lives of Sylvia Plath and her husband Ted Hughes have been the subject of battles about authenticity and biographical entitlements since her suicide in 1963. Wagner-Martin has written about her struggles to deal with the constraints placed on her by the Plath estate.[15] Janet Malcolm's *Silent Woman* (1994), about the literary and personal heritage of Sylvia Plath, suggests that the "transgressive nature of biography is rarely acknowledged, but it is the only explanation for biography's status as a popular genre" (1994, 9). Her book is a study of the myths surrounding Sylvia Plath and of Plath's biographers and the huge impact they had on the lives of her husband, Ted Hughes, and his sister and literary executor, Olwyn Hughes. It also becomes a study of the pitfalls of biography itself. Malcolm makes the case that, "Writing cannot be done in a state of desirelessness. The pose of fairmindedness, the charade of evenhandedness, the striking of an attitude of detachment can never be more than rhetorical ruses" (176). In Malcolm's view, it is not possible for a biographer to have an objective, detached perspective; the authenticity of biographical narrative is always open to question, except perhaps in the case of a rigorous scholarly chronicle that only focuses on presenting facts. The version of a life re-created by a biographer may be just wrong if facts are misused or mislaid, or are biased in such a way that would be considered inappropriate. The key challenge for any biography is to be accepted as an authentic and credible account of a life or lives at a particular point in time, based on rigorous research, an adherence to the facts, and bearing in mind the approach to storytelling taken by each biographer. The balance between the pattern of facts re-created and the nature of storytelling in popular biography will influence each portrayal.

Finally, storytelling is part of human existence and, according to Hanna Meretoja, "the role of narratives ... has both an epistemological and an ontological dimension" (2014, 6) concerning notions of subjectivity and identity within dialogic and relational social contexts:

> storytelling is a creative, constructive and selective activity of foregrounding and connecting certain aspects of experiences and events while ignoring others; it is a process of producing meaningful order through *reinterpretation*, which does not necessarily have to be a matter of imposition. (19)

Nevertheless, it is important to recognise varying power relations in the ways in which the stories about people's lives are told and how this process will impact on different people's sense of themselves and their ability to influence their own lives. An understanding of biography as nonfiction storytelling reflects the perspective of a range of biographers since the late 1960s. American biographer Diane Middlebrook argues that "biography has never functioned simply as an arrangement of facts; it is a narrative, with a point of view" (1990, 159). She defines issues about authorship as an "awareness that both author and subject in a biography are hostages to the universes of discourse that inhabit them" (165). Not unlike his British peers, Martin Stannard believes that we "tell stories to try to make sense of our lives. We read stories for the same reason. The story of someone else's life, particularly that of a story-teller, is a self-reflexive exercise which should be acutely sensitive to the fragility of truth" (1998, 16). Claire Tomalin comments, "What you look for when you are thinking about a biography are the stories in somebody's life … I think the impulse behind writing biography is the same as the impulse that lies behind most writing. It's the ability to see stories, to tell stories" (2004, 92 and 94). Lee's definition of biography as, "the story of a person told by someone else" (2009, 5), that is "a form of narrative, not just a presentation of facts" (5), is inclusive and could cover all sorts of forms. She qualifies this by adding that biography could be "the story of several lives … [and] might tell the story of an animal or a thing rather than a person" (6). Examples of this type of biography are discussed in Chap. 3.

British biography is alert to questions about the nature of storytelling, the social nature of biography, feminism, the genealogical nature of history and the flexibility of form of which nonfiction narratives can make use. This can be seen in the work of Michael Holroyd, Hermione Lee, Richard Holmes and Claire Tomalin, whose writing embraces experimental and non-traditional approaches in their style and form. These biographies interrogate the nature of authorship and the habitat of storytelling, exploring the reading and writing life of both biographer and his or her subject. Jenny Uglow, in her 1993 biography of Elizabeth Gaskell, describes this habit:

> Gaskell herself said she could never express herself so well as through stories … Then … I began to see storytelling less as a habit than a habitat, subject to its own evolutionary laws. Our ways of reading, like Gaskell's

writing, have their roots in the mental landscapes of our age ... we may accept 'the death of the author', but the habit of stories does not die. (x)

This habitat of storytelling is a useful way to sum up the huge range of life-writing that has emerged since the late twentieth century, whatever the subject matter or the form. Life-writing tells stories about real people but the form they take is increasingly varied.

Philip Holden offers a note of caution that "it is impossible to draw a line between texts that are primarily critical and scholarly in nature, and those that exploit narrative techniques fully to entertain an audience at the expense of scholarly accuracy" (2014, 924). There is certainly no attempt to draw such a rigid line here. Biographies have been and will continue to be written very differently and the genre is flexible, often confounding the law of genre. Some British biographers have taken on Nicolson's challenge to rescue pure or personal biography from oblivion, whilst others have written hybrid forms or opted for fiction, as Nicolson predicted. This is distinct from biography as a form of history or micro-history described by Nicolson as "a study of history expressed in and through an individual" (1959, 140).[16] This book is most certainly not trying to be prescriptive about how biography has been written. Rather, it aims to highlight the distinct characteristics of each biographer's writing, and means to avoid any suggestion of a neat chronological development of the genre over the last fifty years given that discourse is inherently dialogic and in collaboration with both the past and the present. Echoes of Boswell and Johnson, Woolf and Strachey can be found in the work of their contemporary peers and they continue to be in conversation—with each other and with us as their readers.

Chapter 3 discusses examples of contemporary British biography that break some of the genre's more traditional conventions and has experimental characteristics. These hybrids and metabiographies have opened up conversations across different disciplines. As well as changes in the form of biographies, there has been a growth of academic interest in what has come to be called life-writing within British universities, one which encompasses, among others, biography, autobiography, journals, diaries, letters and memoirs. As Lee has noted, "the word 'biography' literally means 'life-writing'" (2009, 5) and biography, based on written narratives, has become part of a wider and more fluid understanding of form and subject matter within life-writing in British academic research and teaching. This growth is now based on an interdisciplinary approach which includes oral history, film, drama and performance, new media, dance, and the study of the body, science and medicine, memory, place and objects. Specialist journals such as *Biography*, *Life Writing* and *a/b: Auto/Biography Studies* now publish academic articles about life-writing. Other journals of interest are the *European Journal of Life Writing* and the *Journal of Medical Biography*. The *Lifewriting Annual: Biographical and Autobiographical Studies* publishes regular issues too. There have been developments both in the number of life-writing courses for practicing and aspiring biographers, including postgraduate courses at the University of East Anglia and the University of Buckingham, and in the development of life-writing centres within British universities, including the Oxford Centre for Life-Writing, the Centre for Life History and Life Writing Research at Sussex University, and the Centre for Life-Writing Research (CLWR) at King's College, London.

In a 2016 conversation, I discussed with Clare Brant, Director of the CLWR, some recent trends in life-writing. There are tremendous developments in digital life-writing, including blogs, Twitter and online platforms. The digital world is a very important place in the twenty-first century for writing about people's lives, and life for many is partly online. This is challenging notions about 'literature' and how we understand narrative. It both encourages global thinking and can give more focus to the local, from the perspective of communities and families. It also makes available more subjects and offers wider opportunities for research to larger numbers of people. There has been a huge growth of interest in the lives of migrants and displaced persons, as well as in genealogies, family history and the exploration of roots, for example in terms of black history and women's history.

In addition, life-writing is increasingly interested in the lives of people in relation both to visual life-writing, including portraits, advertising, biopics and film studies, and to places and different types of spaces, such as houses and graveyards and pilgrimages to specific sites. There is also an interest in how lives connect with nature, such as our relationship with rivers and the lives of objects. Oral history and audio versions of life-writing, including radio, also have a lot of potential to provide life-writing narratives. Biography can be modest as well as canonising and can offer vignettes or particular anecdotes, make the everyday more familiar, and show how fragmentary lives can be. There may be more biographies about biography, in other words, about how the lives of some people have been told at different times by different biographers and what cultural and historical themes these can illustrate. The growth in biofiction and more inventive forms of biography continues. [17]

Finally, Brant and I discussed how the place of life-writing within higher education is growing, and how it is gaining a foothold in post-graduate teaching and becoming increasingly interdisciplinary, joining literary studies to other disciplines. In other disciplines, some scientists are being thought of as life-writers, for example by keeping diaries on their explorations. Life-writing has also helped to link literary studies with medical humanities, for instance in treating case histories as life narratives, or scientists' diaries as autobiography.

NOTES

1. Lee, *A Very Short Introduction*, 29.
2. The Centre for Life-Writing Research at King's College, London, was established in 2007, and is now part of the Arts & Humanities Research Institute. It enables experts and students to share research and exchange ideas with a wider audience. It works on all sorts of topics and periods covering a wide range of genres—biography, autobiography, autofiction, diaries and letters, memoirs, digital life-writing including social media, blogs, audio and video, the visual arts especially portraiture, poetry and medical narratives, including case histories.
3. Sisman, Adam, *Boswell's Presumptuous Task: Writing the Life of Dr. Johnson* (2006), xvii.
4. Several essays in *Mapping Lives: The Uses of Biography* (2004), edited by Peter France and William St Clair, cover the history and development of biography in Antiquity, the Italian Renaissance, seventeenth century England and eighteenth century France, while others cover German and Russian literature and biography. Also see descriptions of the history of biography in Hughes, Kathryn, "Lives in Institutions" *a/b: Auto/Biography Studies* 25.2 (2010) and Brown, Andrew, *A Brief History of Biographies: From Plutarch to Celebs* (2001). Richard Altick (1966) offers his historical perspective from the mid-twentieth century. David Novarr provides an overview of theories about biography in *The Lines of Life: Theories of Biography, 1880–1970* (1986).
5. Elinor Shaffer gives an interesting overview of nineteenth century objections to Froude's biography much of which resonates with contemporary debates about the nature of historical authenticity (2004, 124–30).
6. Jenny Uglow also empathises with Gaskell and the lives of women "who find that … they must rely on their own strength, not the illusory strength of father or husband. They have to learn to step out from the

shadow and speak and act for themselves" (1994, 25). In Uglow's biography of Elizabeth Gaskell, her subject's story resonates with women today as she makes connections that touch on our own experience:

> From the beginning Gaskell's stance was both radical and feminist, and she continued all her life to make use of these Gothic conventions to link the cruel repression of wives and daughters to the pressure of history and the patriarchal power of the aristocracy. (120)

Other biographies of women writers often cover the public world in which their subjects lived, their professional lives and the constraints placed upon them in their domestic and intimate lives.

7. In 2014, Miller reflects on her experience as a biographer. Miller's hindsight twelve years after the publication of her group biography about the Brontës is written against the "broader backdrop of contemporary developments in life-writing" (2014, 255), which has moved "towards more experimental or interrogative forms" (256), and a move away "from traditional cradle-to-grave lives of much-written-about subjects" (256). She credits developments in life-writing from the 1980s with concerns about "the nature of narrative, ideology, subjectivity, textuality and hermeneutics" (256).

8. Kendall, *The Art of Biography*, 20.

9. Ben Pimlott offers another useful overview about the nature of popular biography: "Biography is itself. What a biography ought to be like is of course an unanswerable question, although biography in the modern sense operates within fairly tight rules—attention to accuracy, avoidance of suppressio veri most important among them, and a recognition that there is no such thing as a 'true' biography: however scrupulous the research, nobody has access to another's soul, and the character on the page is the author's unique creation. One aspect of the creativity is the subject-in-context ... far from underplaying social factors, the good biographer highlights them, to give added precision to the story. Good biography is flexible, making unexpected connections across periods of time" (2004, 169).

10. Catherine Parke distinguishes between majority and minority biographies, identifying several characteristics that make them different from each other: "(1) the subject being or not being a member of the dominant culture ...; (2) the author being or not being a member of the dominant culture; (3) the subject being or not being a conventional candidate for biography i.e. one whose importance and interest go without saying; (4) construction of the subject's identity [is] different from majority biography, often with greater emphasis on group contexts in which the subject lived and worked; and (5) [in minority biography there is] implicit or

explicit cross-examination of the manner, methods, and assumptions of majority biography" (2002, xvii).

11. Here are just a few other examples. David Lodge has written about Martin Stannard's experience of writing a biography of Muriel Spark whilst she was alive in "A Tricky Undertaking", an essay in *Lives in Writing* (2014). Also see Fiona MacCarthy's experience of dealing with Eric Gill's literary executor, Walter Shewring, in "Baptism by Fire" (*The Guardian* 24 July 2004). Nigel Hamilton comments that "Brenda Maddox was forced to omit large chunks of material from her print biography *Nore: the Real Life of Molly Bloom* at the behest of Joyce's quixotic grandson Stephen" (2007, 247).

12. Edward Saunders discusses differing definitions of metabiography in "Defining Metabiography in Historical Perspective: Between Biomyths and Documentary" in *Biography* 38.3 (2015): 325–342.

13. Hamilton, *In Search of J.D. Salinger*, 68.

14. Nigel Hamilton notes that in 1995 the European Union extended the period of copyright over any work to the author's lifetime, plus seventy years "during which no biographer could quote more than a few lines of a published document, and even less from an unpublished letter, memo, or conversation without the express permission of the subject's legal inheritors" (2007, 244), and "Congress then passed the Sonny Bono Copyright Term Extension Act (1998) to keep the United States in parallel with the European Union directive" (245). This is a restriction that has influenced subsequent biographies.

15. See "Reflections on Writing the Plath Biography" by Linda Wagner-Martin, in *Literary Biography: Problems and Solutions* (1996), edited by Dale Salwak.

16. For a recent historical approach to biography see Renders, Hans and Binne de Haan, eds, *Theoretical Discussions in Biography: Approaches from History, Microhistory and Life Writing* (2014), and Renders, Hans, Binne de Haan and Jonne Harmsma, eds, *The Biographical Turn: Lives in History* (2017). They define what they describe as the biographical turn as "a methodological and theoretical turn" (2017, 3) that understands biographical research as part of scholarly historical methodology, particularly microhistory: "Biographical research complies with the research procedures of the microhistorian, which are based on the study of source materials and the principles of verifiability" (5). Its focus is on understanding the past and "shaping both current public and historical debates" (6).

17. Just a few examples of biographical novels are *Woolf Hall* (2009) and *Bringing Up the Bodies* (2012) by Hilary Mantel, *The True History of the Kelly Gang* (2011) by Peter Carey, *Black Water* (1992) and *Blonde* (2000) by Joyce Carol Oates and *In the Time of the Butterflies* (1994) by Julia Alvarez.

REFERENCES

Altick, Richard. 1966. *Lives and Letters: A History of Literary Biography in England and America*. New York: Alfred A. Knopf.

Backscheider, Paula R. 1999. *Reflections on Biography*. New York: Oxford University Press.

Boswell, James. 1848. First published in 1791. In *Boswell's Life of Johnson, Including Their Tour to the Hebrides*, ed. John Wilson Croker. London: John Murray.

Bowie, Malcolm. 2004. Freud and the Art of Biography. In *Mapping Lives: The Uses of Biography*, ed. Peter France and William StClair, 177–192. Oxford: Oxford University Press.

Brizuela-Garcia, Esperanza. 2007. The Part Never Stays Behind: Biographical Narrative and African Colonial History. *Journal of Historical Biography* 2: 63–83.

Bundock, Michael. 2015. *The Fortunes of Francis Barber: The True Story of the Jamaican Slave who Became Samuel Johnson's Heir*. London: Yale University Press.

Caine, Barbara. 2010. *Biography and History*. New York: Palgrave Macmillan.

Dryden, John. 1683. The Life of Plutarch. In *Plutarch's Lives: Translated from the Greek by Several Hands*, Plutarch, 1–128. London: Jacob Tonson.

Edel, Leon. 1982. *Stuff of Sleep and Dreams: Experiments in Literary Psychology*. New York: Harper & Row.

———. 1987. First published in 1959. *Writing Lives: Principia Biographica*. New York: Norton.

Glendinning, Victoria. 1988. Lies and Silences. In *The Troubled Face of Biography*, ed. Eric Homberger and John Charmley, 49–62. New York: St Martin's Press

Gosse, Edmund. 1989. First published in 1907. *Father and Son: A Study of Two Temperaments*. London: Penguin.

Hamilton, Ian. 1989. First published in 1988. *In Search of J.D. Salinger*. London: Heinemann.

Hamilton, Nigel. 2007. *Biography: A Brief History*. Cambridge, MA: Harvard University Press.

Holden, Philip. 2014. Literary Biography as a Critical Form. *Biography* 37 (4): 917–934.

Holmes, Richard. 2005. First published in 2007. *Sidetracks: Explorations of a Romantic Biographer*. London: Harper Perennial.

Hughes, Kathryn. 2010. Poetry in Motion. *The Guardian*, May 1: 7.

Johnson, Samuel. 1888. The Dignity and Usefulness of Biography, the Rambler Saturday October 13, 1750. In *The Essays of Samuel Johnson: Selected from the Rambler 1750–1752, The Adventurer 1753 and the Idler 1758–1760*, ed. Stuart Reid, 79–84. London: Walter Scott.

Kendall, Paul Murray. 1985. First published in 1965. *The Art of Biography*. New York: Garland.

Lee, Hermione. 2005. *Body Parts: Essays on Life-writing*. London: Chatto & Windus.

———. 2009. *Biography: A Very Short Introduction*. New York: Oxford University Press.

Lodge, David. 2014. *Lives in Writing: Essays*. London: Harvill Secker.

MacCarthy, Desmond. 1932. Lytton Strachey as a Biographer. In *Life and Letters Volume 8: March, June, September and December 1932*, ed. Desmond MacCarthy, 90–102. London: J.Curwen & Sons.

———. 1953. Lytton Strachey and the Art of Biography, Circa 1934. In *Memories*, ed. Desmond MacCarthy, 31–49. London: MacGibbon & Kee.

Malcolm, Janet. 1994. *The Silent Woman: Sylvia Plath and Ted Hughes*. London: Picador.

Marcus, Laura. 2004. The Newness of the 'New Biography': Biographical Theory and Practice in the Early Twentieth Century. In *Mapping Lives: The Uses of Biography*, ed. Peter France and William StClair, 193–218. New York: Oxford University Press.

Meretoja, Hanna. 2014. *The Narrative Turn in Fiction and Theory: The Crisis and Return of Storytelling from Robbe-Grillet to Tournier*. New York: Palgrave Macmillan.

Middlebrook, Diane Wood. 1990. Postmodernism and the Biographer. In *Revealing Lives: Autobiography, Biography, and Gender*, ed. Susan Groag Bell and Marilyn Yalom, 155–165. Albany: University of New York.

Miller, Lucasta. 2002. First published in 2001. *The Brontë Myth*. London: Vintage.

———. 2014. Lives and Afterlives: The Brontë Myth Revisited. *Brontë Studies* 39.4: 254–266.

Nicolson, Harold. 1959. First published in 1927. *The Development of English Biography*. London: Hogarth Press.

Oates, Stephen. 1986. Prologue. In *Biography as High Adventure: Life-Writers Speak on Their Art*, ed. Stephen Oates, ix–xiii. Amherst: University of Massachusetts Press.

Parke, Catherine N. 2002. *Biography: Writing Lives*. New York: Routledge.

Peters, Margot. 1981. Group Biography: Challenges and Methods. In *New Directions in Biography*, ed. Anthony Friedson, 41–51. Hawaii, Honolulu: University of Hawaii.

Phillips, Caryl. 2008. *Foreigners: Three English Lives*. London: Vintage.

Pimlott, Ben. 2004. Brushstrokes. In *Lives for Sale: Biographers' Tales*, ed. Mark Bostridge, 165–170. London: Continuum.

Renders, Hans, and Binne De Haan. 2014. *Theoretical Discussions of Biography: Approaches from History, Microhistory, and Life Writing*. Leiden: Brill.

Renders, Hans, Binne De Haan, and Jonne Harmsma. 2017. *The Biographical Turn: Lives in History*. London: Routledge.

Ramdin, Ron. 2005. *Mary Seacole*. London: Haus Publishing.

Robinson, Jane. 2005. *Mary Seacole: The Charismatic Black Nurse Who Became a Heroine of the Crimea*. London: Constable & Robinson.

Shaffer, Elinor S. 2004. Shaping Victorian Biography: From Anecdote to Bildungsroman. In *Mapping Lives: The Uses of Biography*, ed. Peter France and William St Clair, 115–133. New York: Oxford University Press.

Sisman. 2006. First published in 2000. *Boswell's Presumptuous Task: Writing the Life of Dr. Johnson*. London: Harper Perennial.

Stannard, Martin. 1996. The Necrophiliac Art? In *The Literary Biography: Problems and Solutions*, ed. Dale Salwak, 32–40. Basingstoke: Macmillan.

Stannard, Martin. 1998. A Matter of Life and Death. In *Writing the Lives of Writers*, ed. Warwick Gould and Thomas F. Staley, 1–18. Basingstoke: Macmillan.

Storr, Anthony. 1995. Psychiatry and Literary Biography. In *The Art of Literary Biography*, ed. John Batchelor, 73–86. New York: Oxford University Press.

Strachey, Lytton. 1986. First published in 1918. *Eminent Victorians*. London: Penguin.

Tomalin, Claire. 2004. Starting Over. In *Lives for Sale: Biographer's Tales*, ed. Mark Bostridge, 90–95. London: Continuum.

Uglow, Jenny. 1994. First published in 1993. *Elizabeth Gaskell*. London: Faber and Faber.

Vasari, Giorgio. 1965. First published in 1568. *Lives of the Artists*. Middlesex, England: Penguin.

Wagner-Martin, Linda. 1994. *Telling Women's Lives: The New Biography*. New Brunswick, NJ: Rutgers University Press.

Wagner-Martin, Linda. 1996. Reflections on Writing the Plath Biography. In *The Literary Biography: Problems and Solutions*, ed. Dale Salwak, 47–55. London: Macmillan.

Woolf, Virginia. 1967a. First published in 1927. The Art of Biography. In *Virginia Woolf Collected Essays 1882–1941*, vol. 4, ed. Virginia Woolf, 221–228. London: Hogarth Press.

———. 1967b. First published in 1927. The New Biography. In *Virginia Woolf Collected Essays 1882–1941*, vol. 4, ed. Virginia Woolf, 229–235. London: Hogarth Press.

CHAPTER 3

A Habitat of Stories

In describing experimental biography and biographies that challenge the conventions of traditional cradle-to-grave narratives, one is in danger of identifying another form of 'new' biography when there have been several moments in which the genre has been identified as new over the last century already. The characteristics of the 'new biography' in the 1920s and 1930s, reflected in the title of Virginia Woolf's essay, "The New Biography" (1927), and described by Marcus in an essay with the title, "The Newness of the 'New Biography'", echo the writings of Strachey and Freud, who were, in Marcus's view, "the two primary influences on biography in the 1920s" (2004, 216). From the mid-twentieth century into the 1980s, American biographer and critic Leon Edel developed a theory of biography, which he similarly called the 'new biography', in *Writing Lives: Principia Biographica* (1987). A collection of essays about biography called *New Directions in Biography*, edited by Anthony Friedson, who was based at the University of Hawaii, was published in 1981. Moving into the 1990s, *The Seductions of Biography* (1996), edited by Mary Rhiel and David Suchoff, argues that the contributors have been called 'New Biographers' because they challenge traditional forms, explore the development of biography as a popular genre, and provide a voice for those not heard before, becoming "a way of calling established cultural history into question" (1996, 2). For these writers, it was important to provide a voice for women and those of others whose lives have previously been hidden and undervalued; 'new' biographers "question whether traditional forms of self-telling neutralize or vocalize

© The Author(s) 2017
J. McVeigh, *In Collaboration with British Literary Biography*,
DOI 10.1007/978-3-319-58383-9_3

the claims of cultural difference" (2). Linda Wagner-Martin makes her commitment to the new biography explicit in the title of her book about the lives of women, *Telling Women's Lives: The New Biography* (1994). She describes biography as "the enactment of cultural performance" (1994, 8) and says that a biographer must work with the "performative identities" (8) of her subjects. American Jo Margadant edited *The New Biography: Performing Femininity in Nineteenth Century France* (2000), which looks at the life-stories of eight famous women who became public figures. J.R. Mulryne, in 2006, makes a further claim to establish new directions in biography: "a new liberty has ushered in an era of what one could call biographical self-fashioning. Whilst conscious, in the best cases, of the constraints of detailed and more general scholarship, the new biography invites the reader to approve or reject the offered biographical account not so much in terms of fact as of vision" (2006, 3). The visions of some British biographers and the self-fashioning and performance of both the biographer and his or her subject in their work are an integral part of the discursive nature of these narratives.

In 2009, Canadian Elizabeth Podnieks introduces a collection of essays, 'Introduction: "New Biography" for a New Millennium', suggesting that

> the two greatest changes notable in biography arise both from technologies that allow for radical new ways of producing, disseminating, and theorizing the genre and from an expansion of the definition of what constitutes biographical expression so that when we think of biography we mean not only written but also (tele-)visual, graphic, digital, and performed lives, for instance. (2009, 2)[1]

All these approaches described as the so-called new biography—and there have been others—including the growth of biofiction, hybrid fiction and nonfiction forms, and stories in a range of oral, written and visual media about previously lost and undervalued lives, have influenced late twentieth century and early twenty-first century biography in Britain.[2] So, it may be wise at this point to approach the definition or description of different types of experimental biographies based on their particular characteristics, rather than trying to claim that they are new. As the history of the genre discussed in Chap. 2 has identified, it can be difficult to trace a neat linear development across the genre.

Recent narrative nonfiction biographies, in addition to the publication of single lives, have been concerned with friendships, group biographies of peers, communities and families, and partial lives concerned with particular periods in, or aspects of, a life, as well as with the lives of more ordinary people, some of whom may have had a significant part to play in the life of a canonical figure. Biographies have also approached someone's life from the perspective of objects that seem to represent something about a life, as well as about the historical period and society in which someone lived; and the object may have its own life-story to tell. There has also been a trend to write about places, producing biographies that are more than travel guides or histories and help bring to life the people who live there. Metabiographies about the myth that surrounds a particular person, studies in comparative biography, and books by biographers about their approaches to the genre have been other trends in recent years. A very small number of British examples of these alternative forms are discussed in this chapter. There is no attempt to claim that any one of these biographies is more experimental than another, or that those books not discussed here are not equally important.[3]

There are multiple versions of the life of Charlotte Brontë and a brief overview of just a few of them illustrates a range of experimental forms, including metabiographies, object and group biographies. The Brontë sisters' lives have been understood through a study of objects in Deborah Lutz's *The Brontë Cabinet: Three Lives in Nine Objects* (2015), a title which alludes perhaps to the nineteenth century image of a cabinet of curiosities, a small collection of extraordinary objects that attempted to tell stories about the world. The scenes were intended to work like plays or stories, representing particular themes or ideas. Lutz collects in her cabinet a number of objects that can be related to different aspects of the Brontë family's life and experience. A walking stick sets their life in Haworth in the context of their rural home and the nineteenth century interest in walking: according to Lutz, "Walking as an aesthetic pursuit, as a taking in of nature to spur creativity, may have come naturally to Emily and her siblings, but it was also a practice they learned from the English Romantic poets" (2015, 74). Another chapter discusses the dog collar worn by one of Emily's pet dogs and this introduces an overview of other pets which "filled up the Brontë household" (116) and were an important part of their domestic life. Lutz suggests that in the novels of Anne and Charlotte, "Characters are judged by the way they treat animals" (119). A description of the sisters' small writing desks or boxes give an insight into their writing lives and are "unremittingly average" (163), which is suggestive of lives that were modest, unglamorous and hidden from view.

Juliet Barker's *The Brontës* (1994) is a group biography. She argues that taking "one of … [the sisters] out of context creates the sort of imbalance and distortion of facts that has added considerably to the Brontë legend" (2010, xviii). Her book aims to decentre the stories told in single-life biographies and emphasises the relational and social nature of the Brontë sisters' experience. Lucasta Miller's *The Brontë Myth* (2001) studies the mythology surrounding the Brontës. This is a myth founded on the first biography, *The Life of Charlotte Brontë* (1857) by Elizabeth Gaskell. Miller argues that Gaskell's "tragic vision" (2002, 57) reinforced a history of the Brontës that was then transformed into story. She understands that part of Gaskell's legacy is "to make the public mistake life for literature" (63), although we might indeed mistake biography for literature. Miller notes that Barker's intention was of "setting the factual record straight" (167), and that "Barker is one of the most trustworthy Brontë biographers: from the documentary viewpoint her work will prove a lasting achievement. But it is far less certain that she gets to the core of Charlotte's genius" (168). On the other hand, in Miller's view, Lyndall Gordon's biography, *Charlotte Brontë: A Passionate Life* (1994), "is most convincing when exploring the inner workings of the creative life" (168), compared to Barker's "meticulous amassing of detail" (168). She understands Barker's biography as more of a chronicle, rather than a biography that can tell us what the Brontës were like and how their circumstances and what happened to them influenced their writing lives, whilst Gordon's has the passion of a Boswellian narrative, as her biographer empathises with her subject. Miller argues that all life-writing "is a paradoxical process whereby the fragmentary business of lived experience is moulded into a formal literary structure and given an artificial sense of direction" (64). This notion of the paradox underpinning biography is interesting—it reminds us that a coherent narrative may portray fragmented and messy lives. Different readers will read any one biography from their own point of view and biographies of the same subject place that life, or lives, within the context of the biographer's time. As Miller suggests, future generations will need to "tell their story from a new perspective" (169). Her study offers us as readers an opportunity to compare existing versions of the Brontë's lives.[4]

Paula Byrne's *The Real Jane Austen: A Life in Small Things* (2014) is a metabiography that not only seeks to understand Jane Austen's life in the context of specific objects but, in doing so, places her work and life within a wider historical and cultural context. She challenges some of the prevailing myths about Austen's personality. Clearly, as in Lutz's metabiography, this is not a chronological narrative, but it creates connections that tell a partial story about some aspects of Austen's life set within a wider cultural landscape. In a chapter about a card of lace, we learn that Jane Austen liked to shop (2014, 154), and indeed, claims Byrne, there "is every reason to believe that she enjoyed urban life" (166). In her biography, *Jane Austen: A Life* (1997), Claire Tomalin suggests that Austen modestly took advantage of a visit to her brother in London:

> She enjoyed being on her own in London, and driving about in her rich brother's open carriage: "I liked my solitary elegance very much ... I could not but feel that I had naturally small right to be parading about London in a Barouche." (2000, 240)

The opening of a chapter in Byrne's book about the barouche starts with a paragraph describing a carriage itself, the next gives an example from an Austen story in which carriages and larger coaches feature and, according to Byrne, "it reveals [Austen's] knowledge of the many varieties of road transport vehicles available in the late Georgian era" (2014, 110). The third paragraph moves on to discuss descriptions of travel in Jane Austen's novels and a fourth clinches the argument and comments that it "should not therefore come as a surprise that Austen herself was a very well-travelled woman. In thinking about the forces that shaped her imagination, we should add to her family and her books her experience of the road and of different places" (110). Byrne's book closes with Cassandra Austen's portrait of her sister Jane, although her face is turned away, and Byrne speculates whether this was undertaken when the pair visited Charmouth, where key scenes in her novel *Persuasion* (1817) are set. This is one reader's analysis based on imaginative speculation and it is up to us, as other readers, to reflect on Byrne's reading.

In another metabiography, Claire Harman writes about the myth surrounding Jane Austen in *Austen's Fame: How Jane Austen Conquered the World* (2009), and the way that the status of her work has changed, given "what it has stood for, or been made to stand for, in English culture over the past two hundred years" (2009, 7). She suggests that Austen is "a brand, a product … [a] myth" (244) and inspired "the boom in 'chick-lit' books and romantic comedy films of the 1990s" (252). This is a metabiography that considers how an author has become disembodied and commodified, as a mythical version of Jane Austen becomes a function of the commercial and entrepreneurial production consumed by her readers, including those who know the plots of her stories but may never have actually read the novels.

Biographers have increasingly placed single lives within wider historical, cultural and political perspectives. In his biography *Keats* (1997), Andrew Motion wants to explore his subject's political and social concerns, as well as his poetic influence as a Romantic:

> Examining his liberal beliefs, I have tried to show how they shaped the argument as well as the language of his work … My intention is not to transform Keats into a narrowly political poet. It is to show that his efforts to crystallise moments of "Truth" combine a political purpose with a poetic ambition, a social search with an aesthetic ideal. (1997, xxv)

This aim to set Romantic poetry within a wider context is also carried out in some group biographies, such as *Young Romantics: The Shelleys, Byron and Other Tangled Lives* (2010) by Daisy Hay, which explores the networks surrounding Shelley and Leigh Hunt, including Byron, Mary Shelley, Claire Clairmont, Benjamin Haydon and others, or *The Godwins and the Shelleys: A Biography of a Family* (1991) by William St Clair.[5] Hay argues that the Romantic poets were principally influenced by their friendships. Kathryn Hughes, in a review of Hay's biography, suggests that her study strips away "the old myths about solitary romantic genius creating timeless works of art, and what you find is a busy network of creative people doing what they have always done" (2010, 7). For Hughes, Hay's story "comes closer to the way these things mostly get done—in a hurry, accidentally, and with several people's sticky fingerprints on the finished product" (7), and, in dealing with the evidence in this fashion, Hay challenges prevailing myths and allows "fresh emphases to emerge in the process" (7).

A move away from a focus on genius and single-life biography has also been explored in biographies of friendships. This is a trend that has been recognised by Richard Holmes, amongst others: "The monolithic single Life is giving way to biographies of groups, of friendships, of love-affairs"

(Holmes 2008, 140). In *The Friendship: Wordsworth and Coleridge* (2006), Adam Sisman concentrates "on the friendship itself, at its most intense when both men were young and full of hope" (2006, xxiii) and they shared a "joint mission, to fulfil the hopes of a generation disappointed at the failure of the French Revolution" (xxiii). This is not a cradle-to-grave biography but focuses on the particular period of their lives when they knew each other intimately and culminates with Wordsworth's rejection of poems by Coleridge for the second edition of *Lyrical Ballads*, published in 1802. The third and final part of the biography, about the period after this moment in their relationship, is less than a quarter of the book. The inference of this rejection seems clear: Wordsworth's action not only damaged their relationship but had a hugely painful impact on Coleridge's life as a poet: "Though the friendship remained warm a long time, it could never recover the same closeness ... Wordsworth had eclipsed his friend, and afterwards Coleridge would always be in his shadow" (Sisman 2006, 325). Frances Wilson, in *The Ballad of Dorothy Wordsworth* (2008), approaches the lives of these poets from a different perspective with another partial biography about the memoirs of Wordsworth's sister, Dorothy, and the importance to her of her relationship with her brother.

Dorothy was also a good friend of Coleridge, and Wilson sees her as a bridge between Wordsworth and their close mutual friend:

> In *Lyrical Ballads*, Wordsworth and Coleridge agreed that there would be two depictions of nature: Wordsworth would observe and describe the common things of rural life, and Coleridge would direct his "endeavours" to "persons and characters supernatural, or at least romantic". Dorothy stands on the threshold between these two natures. (2008, 172)

The *Grasmere Journals* written by Dorothy Wordsworth are at the heart of Wilson's book. They cover only two-and-half years and the journal ends shortly after Wordsworth's marriage in October 1802, a shattering blow for Dorothy, and the moment when "Dorothy Wordsworth ceases to be" (Wilson 2008, 213). Wilson frames the journal as a way to make "motionless the world in which she lived, defending it from mutability and change" (12), describing "what she sees rather than what she feels" (211) in a record of her life spent with her beloved brother. It is an elegy to their daily life together. Wilson identifies Wordsworth's wedding day as a peak in his life, which marked the start of nearly fifty years of marriage, and as an ending for Dorothy, as their intimate life together came to a close. Dorothy's nature leaves her vulnerable and her health seriously deteriorated in later life. In this partial life, Wilson not only emphasises the importance of Dove Cottage in both their lives, she also brings Dorothy—a figure often lost in Wordsworth's shadow— into the centre of the reader's view. This is a book-length anecdote that helps to explain a key moment in both their lives. Wilson argues that:

> It is not unusual to think of this or that moment in the lives of ourselves or of others as representing a beginning, end or turning point, or to see a certain experience as signalling either a high or a low mark, a peak or a trough. (14)

Much of the storytelling in biography is built on each biographer's approach to these anecdotes or moments in a life, or lives. A single-life biography draws together many examples to give a version of a life, whilst partial biography focuses on a particular event, period of time, or aspects of intellectual culture and history, whilst a friendship or group biography emphasises the collaborative nature of life and lives, bringing some people out from the shadows.[6]

Comparable biographies have been published about other canonical writers, and some books about William Shakespeare's life have taken an anecdotal and partial approach.[7] American biographer James Shapiro focuses on two years in Shakespeare's life in *1599: A Year in the Life of William Shakespeare* (2005), and in *1606: William Shakespeare and the Year of Lear* (2015). In *1599*, Shapiro wants to explore both "what Shakespeare achieved" (2005, xv), including the writing of *Hamlet*, and what "Elizabethans experienced" (xv) in this particular year. His book is concerned with "the familiar desire to understand how Shakespeare became Shakespeare" (xviii), the project about the nature of authorship that lies at the heart of much literary biography, but in this case Shapiro sets this squarely amidst "a sense of how deeply Shakespeare's work emerged from an engagement with his times" (xxii). This is a partial life of the writer, how the writer Shakespeare became the writer he was, rather than a biography about what Shakespeare was like, set within the historical context of his time. Not only does Shapiro consider wider events from that year, he also "read almost all of the books written in 1599 that Shakespeare might have owned or borrowed or come upon in London's bookstalls" (xxii), albeit that he acknowledges that a good deal of how he suggests Shakespeare uses scholarly information "remains speculation" (xxiii). So, this is a study of the reading and writing of both biographer and subject in which biography becomes a form of cultural history.

Shapiro comments on Shakespeare's use of *Plutarch's Lives* in *Henry V*, which "made available to him a model for conveying interiority" (2005, 150). *1599* discusses the creation of soliloquies for *Hamlet* in which "Shakespeare finally found a dramatically compelling way to internalize contesting forces" (337). In *1606*, Shakespeare is shown to finish *King Lear* and write *Macbeth* and *Anthony and Cleopatra*; again, Shapiro is interested in the extent to which these plays were written "in dialogue" (2015, 15) with Shakespeare's time. This partial biography, like its predecessor, is a form of cultural history in which, for example, Shapiro explores Shakespeare's own reading and discusses the extent to which he draws on a range of sources for his play *King Lear* (1608), including: an anonymous play, *The True Chronicle History of the life and death of King Leir and his three Daughters* (1605); Raphael Holinshed's writing about the story of King Lier in *Holinshed's Chronicles;* and Sir Philip Sydney's *Arcadia* (1590), that provides material for the subplot about the Earl of Gloucester and his two sons, Edgar and Edmund.[8] Finally, Shapiro suggests that whilst "we will never know in what ways the Gunpowder Plot and its aftermath affected Shakespeare personally, it's nonetheless possible to recover some of the traces that it left on his work" (150), in particular in *Macbeth*. It is not a question for Shapiro of primarily writing about Shakespeare's genius, or of understanding the extent to which his work draws on that of others and how it is set within the historical and cultural context of his time; his aim is to encompass all of these contexts. He does not and cannot know what Shakespeare's intentions were, but he can make connections between his work and the wider cultural and historical context in which he lived.

Charles Nicholl *The Lodger: Shakespeare on Silver Street* (2008) is another partial life which covers a period when Shakespeare lived with a family called Mountjoy in the early seventeenth century. Nicholl is interested in "recreating the physical and cultural circumstances of a period of Shakespeare's life. The plays he was writing at the time are part of those circumstances" (2008, 34). Nicholl suggests possible connections between Shakespeare and the lives of the Mountjoys, particularly Mary, the Mountjoy's daughter:

> Her life touches Shakespeare's in … [a] circumstantial way, but seems also to touch his imagination. She is betrothed to a reluctant husband, as Helen is in *All's Well*; she is banished 'dowerless' by her father, as Cordelia is in *King Lear*; she is lodged in the house of a pimp, as Marina is in *Pericles*. She is not the 'model' for these characters … but there are traces of her in them. (2008, 270)

The traces that Nicholl seeks are connected with Shakespeare's home and those who lived there.

Jonathan Bate also acknowledges how difficult it is to know Shakespeare the man. In *The Genius of Shakespeare* (1997), a meta-biography about the genre as much as a biography, Bate argues that Shakespeare's genius is connected with his power as a disembodied figure, on the basis that "'greatness' should be thought about in terms of effects, not causes" (1997, 321). He is not primarily interested in the life of the man, but in the construction of an author who is representative of a historical and cultural moment. We may not know Shakespeare the man, but we know what he has come to embody for us—although this will be different for different people depending on their experience as a reader, audience member, performer, writer, director, stage designer, literary tourist or academic. Bate understands his author through "a body of words and stage-images which live because they were originally Shakespeare's modifications of the words and stage-images of his predecessors and because they have subsequently been modified again and again in the guts of successive generations of the living" (1997, viii). This is an ongoing discourse of reading, writing and performing in which the author is understood as both reader and a writer, and the general reader has an important role to play. Bate is interested in understanding Shakespeare's work and to think about where it came from by avoiding what he calls, drawing on William Empson, either/or analysis: "A story about where the sonnets came from is necessary for an understanding to their nature, but not sufficient for an appreciation of their complexity" (44). Bate argues that

> Shakespeare has proved himself peculiarly adaptable to a world of ambiguity, uncertainty, and relativity. Like the fittest organisms in the natural world, he survives. He is a triumph of evolution, mutating in order to cope with a changed cultural environment … The evolutionary potential of the plays is proof of their genius. (1997, 316)

Here we have a metabiography concerned with the wider social and historical context of which Shakespeare was a part that is based on both the past and the transformations of Shakespeare, or at least his works, over time. Shakespeare and his genius becomes what we have made him. As noted in the introduction, Bate suggests that "the genius of Shakespeare is not a factual hypothesis, but a truth function of the difference it makes to the lives of those who maintain it" (1997, 325). Bate argues that we maintain Shakespeare's genius through performance each time his work is read or dramatised, filmed or watched. Each time we do so, our experience of his work will be different. The fact that "Shakespeare is changed by being performed does not mean there is no Shakespeare. The plays do not mean anything and everything just because they mean many things" (Bate 1997, 336). He argues that the genius of Shakespeare "is the process of Shakespeare, that which is performed by the performance ... the working through does not *lead to a conclusion*, it *performs the point*" (336). Bate is suggesting that the genius of Shakespeare and the different possibilities of his life can be understood in our reading and performance of his work. Put simply, if no one read or performed his work, Shakespeare could not be a genius. This places the subject at the heart of a discursive view of biography, because the subject is inherently relational, performative and social in nature. Each reading or performance depends on the reader or audience, some of whom may be biographers, and in such readings the nature of this genius is fluid and re-created in each performance or reading. This suggests a different perspective from the 'is this fact true or not' critique of biography, and a move towards one concerned with understanding why we care about any particular biographical subject or subjects. It suggests that one way to think about what is authentic about Shakespeare, or any other life, is to consider the impact he has had on the lives of others and the extent to which his life has in turn been fashioned by them. This is relevant to the life of any person, famous or not. In doing so, myths will be created, but it does acknowledge that biography becomes a form of remembrance in which our memories of people we have lost remain with us, albeit that we may conflate some facts and anecdotes about the past, which we revisit in different forms as we relive or perform aspects of their life and work.

In *Soul of the Age* (2009), Bate is again keen to understand Shakespeare in the context of his age. He seeks to comprehend his subject by considering the cultural context at key phases in his life, what he calls his seven ages, as Shakespeare's thinking loops backwards and forwards throughout his life. Bate argues that

> the mind does not obey the same rule of time as the entropic human body. In writing a life of Shakespeare's mind that looks "before and after", we might just be able to escape not only the deadening march of chronological sequence that is biography's besetting vice, but also the depressingly reductive narrative ... discerned in the life when it is told in the traditional way. (2009, 5)

Bate emphasises that Shakespeare can be understood by making connections, but only if these are not treated in a reductive way. He suggests that his characters are not based on particular people he knew, rather he was "a snapper-up of trifles of personality traits from hither and yon" (318). Similarly, the 'Dark Lady' may be "an embodiment of Venus" (209), rather than someone he knew, and the 'fair youth' "does not *have* to be a real person" (209). This encourages the reader not to look for direct connections between events in the life of the man and his work, but to think of them as an indication of a fertile mind at work roaming here and there, taking what he needs from wherever he can and transforming it in his writing. This is not a form of biography that suggests what Shakespeare was like but rather one about what may have been on his mind at different points in his writing life. Other recent biographies also 'play' with both the nature of chronology and aim to avoid reductive storytelling.

Other examples of partial lives include those about the hidden lives of women lurking in the background behind more canonical figures, and who are brought into the foreground in these biographies. *Charles Dickens and the House of Fallen Women* (2009) by Jenny Hartley focuses on Urania Cottage, a home developed by Dickens to support the rehabilitation of prostitutes and women who had been in prison. This home is an example of innovative social reform, but in Hartley's book it is also understood as a performance space, a world that Dickens was able to control (2009, 24). It becomes like "Dickens's stage set" (32), a theatre. After all, comments Hartley, "he adored being part of the drama himself" (35) and the "stage manager of the make-over show" (43). The women are supported, but their time in the home is highly regulated. They have little influence on decisions about their lives, including the deportation Dickens arranges for the women he sees as the most compliant. "Generalissimo Dickens" (99) used the lives of these women in his fiction (131), as

> they insinuated themselves ever more deeply into his imagination. They swarm through the fiction of the late forties and fifties, to make *David Copperfield* the great novel of servants, *Hard Times* the great novel of education ... he experimented with their voices on the pages of *Bleak House* and *Little Dorrit*. (157)

In this story, we come to know something about Dickens as a social reformer and influential community figure, and as a man keen to have his own way.

Mrs Woolf and her Servants (2008) by Alison Light is both a study of the lives of servants in the early twentieth century, "still the largest single female occupation" (2008, xv), and of the individual lives of women who worked for Virginia Woolf, Nellie Boxall in particular. Her book has a wider reach, as she decentres the life of Virginia Woolf and demythologises the "fantasy of independence, the idea of the fully self-directed, autonomous individual" (xx). Light argues that "there is no such thing as an individual, only the social relations by which we know ourselves and our limits" (xxi). This is the case for all forms of biography, although in the case of single lives only the voices of a small number of people may be heard and lives apart from the main subjects might be undervalued. Light makes connections between Virginia Woolf's writing and her day-to-day domestic life as "the figure of the servant and of the working woman haunts Woolf's experiments in literary modernism" (xviii), including her writing in *The Years* (72), *Night and Day* (75) and *The Waves* (202), although Light emphasises that "Virginia's public sympathy with the lives of poor women was always at odds with private recoil" (203). What both these biographies suggest is the complexity of encompassing the multifaceted and social nature of individual and collective lives.

A notable recent example of a biography that deals with a noncanonical and vulnerable subject is *Stuart: A Life Backwards* (2005) by Alexander Masters. This biography challenges conventional chronology as it opens with the biographer and his subject in conversation. The opening line makes the view of Masters's subject, a homeless man called Stuart, clear: "Stuart does not like the manuscript" (2006, 1). The book is a story about Stuart's life that begins close to its end, as

Masters journeys with his subject through the later part of his life and talks to him about his past; and it includes parts of Stuart's diary. His story is representative of the experience of homeless men and the impact of abuse. It sets Stuart talking in conversation with his biographer. As Holroyd comments, "the book was created by the subject and the writer together" (2017, 17). This biography is an example of the copartnership in biography initiated by Boswell.

Wainewright the Poisoner (2000) by Andrew Motion and *John Aubrey: My Own Life* (2015) by Ruth Scurr are examples of recent hybrid life-writing that subvert the balance between fiction and nonfiction and are based on creative invention, as are novels. These books ask questions about the form of experimental biography as well as telling fascinating stories about their subjects. Motion invents a confession by his forgotten Romantic poet, aiming to bring him to life. He argues that his work is experimental and "contains a mixture of different forms—some imaginative, some factual—they all share a common purpose. They are dedicated to rescuing Wainewright from obscurity, and to bringing him back to life as a plausible and dynamic force" (2000, xviii). He makes the case that the "great majority of scenes and encounters in the Confession, all the friendships, and all the main events, actually happened" (xviii). Similarly, Scurr's book is an invented diary of the seventeenth century biographer John Aubrey and is based on the facts of his life. These innovative experimental texts rooted in fiction defy the laws of conventional genres.

Both Peter Ackroyd's *Dickens* (1990) and Kathryn Hughes's *The Short Life and Long Times of Mrs Beeton* (2005) are examples of non-fiction biography in which the balance between fiction and nonfiction identifies them as experimental. They introduce, in Michael Benton's phrase, "fictional interludes" (2015, 37). In her biography of Mrs Beeton, Hughes is interested in the representative nature of her subject's famous book and the extent to which this acts as a "mirror to our most intimate needs and desires" (2005, 16) by representing the 'home' where we go to be loved and fed. As Hughes's title suggests, Beeton's life may have been short, but her influence on both her time and ours has been long, although this biography questions whether this influence draws on the life of a real woman, or a character constructed by publishers, including her husband Sam Beeton. Hughes introduces sections called "Interludes" between chapters of her biography, although these are not identified in the contents page. These short sections, of two to three pages each, discuss the impact that

Isabella Beeton's *Book of Household Management* (1869) had on middle-class values and conventions, including changes in the timing of regular meals, dinner planning, healthy eating and the roasting of turkey. Their focus is on social and cultural influences and reinforces an understanding of Mrs Beeton as a commodity or brand for a successful product. The biography explores the extent to which this famous book about cookery is inherently intertextual, as the original version drew on many sources for recipes and other material and later versions published after Isabella Beeton's early death are different from the original. The nature of authorship is questioned throughout this biography.

Fashions change, and reviews by Hughes reflect the trends in re-creative, fictional and hybrid biographies. Reviews of biographies offer an interesting perspective on trends within the genre and are in conversation with it. In *This Long Pursuit* (2016), Romantic biographer Richard Holmes notes that reviews still tend "to consist of a lively critical *précis* of the whole life, with perhaps one brief mention of the actual author of the book, tucked away somewhere in the penultimate paragraph" (2016, 54). The reviews of late twentieth and early twenty-first century British biographies, when not focusing on details about the life, or lives, in question, or revealing new facts, tend to discuss the scholarly attributes of the research on which the biography is based, the point of view taken by the biography, and whether the voice of the narrator can be heard above that of his or her subject. Reviews are more critical when questions are raised about the quality of research, the way in which autobiographical or other evidence has been used, and if the biography speculates about some aspect of the biographical subject's life when factual evidence is limited or missing. They are also more critical if the biography has a point of view with which the reviewer disagrees, or has a form and style that the reviewer considers inappropriate. There is a tendency in some academic reviews to question the scholarly nature of popular biography, particularly in relation to the use of footnotes to verify evidence, and the critical and analytical abilities of a biographer, particularly when they are not academics or experts in the field covered by the biography. Reviewers may also comment on the extent to which a biographer sympathises with his or her subject and whether they adopt a descriptive approach, leaving it up to the reader to decide on key points. In recent years, experimentation, such as in fictional biographies, has been welcomed, but any attempts at fiction—by which I mean inventing any material—within nonfiction narratives may still receive short shrift from reviewers. When a new biography takes a fictional and explicitly experimental form, reviews are interested in their style.[9] Criticism may also ensue if a biography provides too many facts and the biography is long or, indeed, if too few facts are provided and the book is too short. Whether a nuanced and objective biographer is preferred may depend on reviewers' approaches to the storytelling ability of the biographer in question.

In addition to teaching biography and creative nonfiction at the University of East Anglia and her work as a biographer, Kathryn Hughes has written many reviews of biographies, as well as on many other subjects, including memoirs, social and cultural history, and visual art.[10] These reviews, by someone who is a British critic, academic and a biographer herself, offer a distinctive conversation with other biographers and readers about the nature of recent biography in Britain. As well as providing a synopsis of some of the key facts about someone's life, in her reviews, Hughes is alert to the different versions of a person's character that are explored in a biography. Her reviews may discuss the extent to which a life is set within a historical context, of which the life or lives portrayed in a biography may be representative. She explores issues related to both the public and private aspects of people's lives and the lives of those who have been forgotten or hidden from view. They may comment on length and the use of evidence or facts about a life or lives, particularly when speculation by a biographer invites comment. The issue of length may reflect a biography's approach to balancing storytelling and scholarly research based on verifiable evidence. Hughes is interested in the extent to which a more traditional biography takes a thematic approach, and subverts the use of chronology. Biographies may create new myths about canonical subjects, or challenge those of the past, and Hughes's reviews are interested in those that do so and revisit the way that stories about particular events have been retold.[11] Hughes also comments on the growth of group biographies of families, friends and peers, of biographies about people who were significant in the lives of canonical figures but may have been forgotten or undervalued in the past, on the growth of metabiographies about "the cultural afterlife of the [biographical] subject" (2009, 8), and on other new trends, such as biography as nature writing, and biblio-biography about personal histories of reading.[12] Finally, Hughes may comment on biographies that adopt more experimental forms by looking closely at objects or places.[13]

In a conversation in 2016 about her reviews, Hughes suggested that her number one priority is to write a piece that is interesting and pleasurable to read. Other reviewers often use reviews as a way of retelling a life-story and Hughes also comments on the facts about the lives of people featured in biographies covered by her reviews. Yet, she also wants to do more and tell people a story about how different biographies connect with those written in the past about the same subjects. Connections can be made with other forms of biographical narrative, such as films, and she is interested in how some biographies have focused on particular themes. This approach situates each biography reviewed within the biographical tradition that relates to that person or people, and the historical period they come from. In doing so, she is keen not to be too directive. Her aim is rather to try and situate her reviews within a larger conversation about her subjects and the world in which they lived. Each review is based on extensive research, including several readings of each biography and thorough fact-checking. A well-written review will inevitably be based on in-depth research. Hughes comments that, "Ideally, I hope that I will reach some readers through my reviews who might not have been interested in a particular subject before." She does not have an overarching sense of what her reviews are trying to do, each one is different and some will be much more light-hearted than others. However, this reader did find that they are in tune with contemporary concerns about different forms and subjects for biography. They offer a revealing litmus test of recent experimentation with both fact and fiction.

The 1990 publication of Ackroyd's biography, *Dickens*, has two complete texts running in parallel. One is a more traditional biography of Dickens, the other is fictional and has seven chapters interweaving with the main account. This is a hybrid biography in which nonfiction and fiction rest side by side within the same narrative. The series of seven fictional chapters is a parallel book, to some extent a haunting of the main biography and in conversation with it, and with its readers. The imagined biography may be a fiction, but it is also a metabiography about biography placed within a more traditional biography. It is a meditation about the author, Charles Dickens—a narrative construct that suggests that it is in both the real and the unreal that one can find connections between the man and the work that embodies his power.

The penultimate fictional section is an interview with the fictional biographer, who is influenced by scholars and decides he must include footnotes, recognising "how much cannot be known. Cannot now be recovered" (941) about his subject. He questions whether it is a fault or a virtue to "often imply more certainty and assume more authority than in fact I possess?" (942). This biographer is self-effacing and very much aware of the tensions in his work. We do not know what the man, Peter Ackroyd, really thinks; it is only the biographer, as a character in this biography, who reveals what he believes. He is looking at connections between small details of a life that can be traced back into a writer's work, although he recognises that "I have sometimes imposed a pattern where no pattern really exists" (943), and filled in gaps where there was instead discontinuity. In doing so, he wonders if biographies are like novels:

> I never really believed it. It just sounded good at the time. The only real connection between the two, as far as I am concerned, is in the need to make the narrative coherent. To impose a pattern upon the world. (946)

Ultimately, only "the reader has the answer" (946). This fictional character is a self-reflexive biographer who questions the veracity and authenticity of his work and knows its limitations. It is the form that is coherent, not necessarily the story that it tells, and the influential role of the reader is revealed. In the final section, the character of the biographer dreams of Dickens and he turns to him and smiles as he leaves the train they are sharing: "And, when he smiled, I knew that it truly was Charles Dickens. That, in some sense, he had not died. I never saw him again" (1120). One has a sense that the writing of this biography and the biographer's journey with his subject have been completed. In this fictional interlude, the biographer experiences "the phantom of the presence of Dickens" (1119). The character of Dickens and his biographer are hauntingly brought to life in the fictional interludes of Ackroyd's biography. The nature of this haunting is a feature of writing by Hermione Lee and Richard Holmes and is discussed in Chap. 4. Biography becomes a form of haunting as we as readers, and biographers as both readers and writers, are close to, and yet distant from, the lives of others.

Ackroyd draws attention to the relationship between fiction and fact in biography in his study, *Albion: The Origins of the English Imagination* (2002). He suggests that the "novel and the biography are aspects of the same creative process. In fact it might be suggested that the greatest writers are those ... who effortlessly transcend the limitations of genre" (2002, 347). Furthermore, for Ackroyd the "imagination is the secret of

Boswell's art" (351). Ackroyd argues that "The radical reshaping of a life is primarily the imperative of the artist who must fashion the narrative to accord with his or her own personal vision" (351). Boswell mythologises the figure of Johnson as "the first 'romantic' hero" (353) and, in doing so, Ackroyd believes that "Out of artificial material a great truth was born; romance, epic, fiction and drama come together to form biography" (353). Elizabeth Gaskell does something similar in her biography of Charlotte Brontë, which echoes Gaskell's writing as a novelist: "the mingling of character and landscape expresses a great truth, and out of this essentially fictional intuition by Elizabeth Gaskell have sprung a myriad books and literary pilgrimages" (Ackroyd 2002, 354). Ackroyd posits the notion that Gaskell, "inspired by the imaginative vision of her novels, re-created Charlotte Brontë" (354). For Ackroyd, "it is precisely because it is 'like a novel' that … [Gaskell's biography] has created an enduring impression upon successive generations of readers" (355). This is also important to Ackroyd in his writing about Dickens. As Philip Holden stresses in another discussion about this biography, Ackroyd also "returns to a process of reading: to the biographer as both writer and reader, and to the reader of biography" (2014, 931). This book is interested in this process of reading and the nature of haunting in Ackroyd's and other biographies that also read and rewrite the lives of their subjects and imaginatively re-create stories about other lives as romance, epic, tragedy or comedy. In the context of all this experimentation, the biographers discussed in this book have transformed the way that they write biography. They continue to re-create the lives of their subjects in a form of narrative nonfiction that challenges traditional forms and embraces the rhetorical features of literary narratives and powerful storytelling.

NOTES

1. Two special issues of the journal *Biography* consider developments in online life-writing: "Writing Online Lives" *Biography* 26.1 (2003), and "Online Lives 2.0" *Biography* 38.2 (2015).
2. More recent fictional forms include those by David Lodge who writes biographical novels, "which uses fictional techniques to represent real lives" (2014, 232). These are

> based on documented facts about historical persons, and does not invent any action or event with significant consequences for

> them, but uses fictional methods to explore and fill the gaps in our knowledge, which is primarily the subjective experience of the persons involved and their verbal interaction. (239)

He distinguishes this type of novel from those that draw on the life of a living person, but do not stick to the facts and invent material about their characters. Novels about biographers are also other versions of the type of biography envisaged by Harold Nicolson, of which *Possession* by A.S. Byatt (1990) and *Flaubert's Parrott* (1984) by Julian Barnes are notable examples. These types of narratives are an important field of life-writing research.

3. An eclectic collection of essays, *Writing the Lives of People and Things, AD 500–1700: A Multi-disciplinary Future for Biography* (2016), edited by Robert Smith and Gemma Watson, brings together examples of recent developments in the genre and includes pieces on the lives of objects, understanding a life through objects and books, forgotten lives and group lives.

4. Another form of rereading lives is emerging in the bibliomemoir, which Joyce Carol Oates describes as "a subspecies of literature combining criticism and biography with the intimate, confessional tone of autobiography" (2014, BR1) in a review of recent books, including *My Life in Middlemarch* (2014) by American writer Rebecca Mead. British examples include *Out of Sheer Rage: Wrestling with D H Lawrence* (1997) by Geoff Dyer and *To the River* (2012) by Olivia Laing, which combines her reading of Virginia Woolf, memoir and both nature and travel writing.

5. Haydon features in an early group biography, *A Sultry Month: Scenes of London Literary Life in 1846* (1965) by Alethea Hayter, which explores the lives of several literary figures in June 1846, including Robert Browning, Elizabeth Barrett Browning, Charles Dickens, Alfred Tennyson and William Wordsworth, as they touch on the life of the artist, Benjamin Haydon.

6. In Hackstaff, Karla B., Feiwel Kupferberg and Catherine Negroni, eds, *Biography and Turning Points in Europe and America* (2012), Kupferberg argues that a turning point can mark not only a milestone, but also the need to meet a challenge or face a 'last straw' (2012, 232). He makes a distinction between objective or realist approaches to life narratives and subjective, constructivist or narrated aspects of lives, in which a turning point can be understood as an epiphany. Kupferberg argues that "a combination of a realistic and a constructivist approach might be what the biography researcher should be aiming at. We need the realistic (objectivistic) approach in order to emphasise that we are dealing with factual narratives or 'lived experience', but we also need the constructivist (subjectivistic) approach in order to study in more detail how such lived experience is narrated" (2012, 234).

7. In "'Author! Author!': Shakespeare and Biography" (2009), Graham Holderness discusses versions of Shakespeare's biography. Also see Bevington, David, *Shakespeare and Biography* (2010) and Ellis, David, *The Truth about William Shakespeare: Fact, Fiction and Modern Biographies* (2013).

8. Holinshed's *Chronicles*, also known as Holinshed's *Chronicles of England, Scotland, and Ireland*, was published in several volumes and two editions, the first in 1577, and the second in 1587.

9. For example, see Kelly, Stuart, "Enter John Aubrey" in the *Times Literary Supplement* (25 February 2015) discussing Ruth Scurr's *John Aubrey* (2015).

10. The MA in Biography and Creative Non-Fiction at the University of East Anglia is for anyone seeking to develop their writing in the increasingly diverse and exciting genre of nonfiction. As this chapter has discussed, literary nonfiction is currently undergoing rapid change and reformation. Instead of the old 'cradle-to-grave' narratives of well-known literary or political figures, writers are now experimenting with new forms and subjects. Nature writing, the personal essay, food journalism, art criticism and memoir are all part of the emerging mix.

11. For examples see Hughes's reviews in *The Guardian* of: Ophelia Field's *The Favourite: Sarah, Duchess of Marlborough* (2002), 22 June 2002; *Byron: Life and Legend* (2002) by Fiona MacCarthy, 16 November 2002; *Perkin: A Story of Deception* (2003) by Ann Wroe, 19 April 2003; *Douglas Jerrold: A Life (1803–1857)* (2002) by Michael Slater, 14 December 2002; *Last of the Dandies: The Scandalous Life and Escapades of Count D'Orsay* (2003) by Nick Foulkes, 14 June 2003; *William and Lucy: The Other Rossettis* (2004) by Angela Thirlwell, 3 January 2004; *Dick Turpin: The Myth of the English Highwayman* (2004) by James Sharpe, 31 January 2004; *Sentimental Murder: Love and Madness in the 18th Century* (2004) by John Brewer, 6 March 2004; *Bombay to Bloomsbury: A Biography of the Strachey Family* (2005) by Barbara Caine, 19 February 2005.

12. See reviews by Hughes in *The Guardian*: "From major to minor", 16 September 2006, and "Six Facets of Light by Ann Wroe—a mesmerising hybrid of biography, memoir and nature writing", 16 April 2016. Another example of this type of biography is *London Fog: The Biography* (2015) by John Carey.

13. See Hughes's reviews in *The Guardian* of Hollingsworth, Mary, *The Cardinal's Hat: Money, Ambition and Housekeeping in a Renaissance Court* (2004), 22 May 2004, and Tindall, Gillian, *The House by the Thames* (2006), 29 April 2006.

14. Hughes made this comment in an interview for this book in 2016.

REFERENCES

Ackroyd, Peter. 1999. First published in 1990. *Dickens*. London: Vintage.
———. 2002. *Albion: The Origins of the English Imagination*. London: Chatto & Windus.
Barker, Juliet. 2010. First published in 1994. *The Brontës*. London: Abacus.
Bate, Jonathan. 1997. *The Genius of Shakespeare*. London: Macmillan.
———. 2009. First published 2008. *Soul of the Age: The Life, Mind and World of William Shakespeare*. London: Penguin.
Benton, Michael. 2015. First published in 2009. *Literary Biography: An Introduction*. Chichester, West Sussex: Wiley Blackwell.
Byrne, Paula. 2014. *The Real Jane Austen: A Life of Small Things*. London: William Collins.
Edel, Leon. 1987. First published in 1959. *Writing Lives: Principia Biographica*. New York: Norton.
Gordon, Lyndall. 1994. *Charlotte Brontë: A Passionate Life*. London: Chatto & Windus.
Harman, Claire. 2009. *Jane's Fame: How Jane Austen Conquered the World*. Edinburgh: Canongate.
Hartley, Jenny. 2009. *Charles Dickens and the House of Fallen Women*. London: Methuen.
Hay, Daisy. 2010. *Young Romantics: The Shelleys, Byron and Other Tangled Lives*. London: Bloomsbury.
Holden, Philip. 2014. Literary Biography as a Critical Form. *Biography* 37 (4): 917–934.
Holderness, Graham. 2009. Author! Author!: Shakespeare and Biography. *Shakespeare* 5 (1): 122–133.
Holmes, Richard. 2008. *The Age of Wonder: How the Romantic Generations Discovered the Beauty and Terror of Science*. London: Harper Press.
———. 2016. *This Long Pursuit: Reflections of a Romantic Biographer*. London: William Collins.
Holroyd, Michael. 2017. A life less ordinary. *The Guardian*, February 4: 17.
Hughes, Kathryn. 2005. *The Short Life & Long Times of Mrs Beeton*. London: Fourth Estate.
Hughes, Kathryn. 2010. Poetry in Motion. *The Guardian*, May 1: 7.
———. 2009. The Leftovers of a Life: Review of Jane's Fame: How Jane Austen Conquered the World by Claire Harman. *The Guardian*, April 4: 8.
Kupferberg, Feiwel. 2012. Conclusion: theorising turning points and decoding. In *Biography and Turning Points in Europe and America*, ed. Feiwel Kupferberg, Catherine Negroni, and Karal B. Hackstaff, 227–259. Bristol: The Policy Press.
Light, Alison. 2008. First published in 2007. *Mrs Woolf and her Servants*. London: Penguin.

Lodge, David. 2014. *Lives in Writing: Essays*. London: Harvill Secker.

Lutz, Deborah. 2015. *The Brontë Cabinet: Three Lives in Nine Objects*. New York: W.W.Norton.

Marcus, Laura. 2004. The Newness of the 'New Biography': Biographical Theory and Practice in the Early Twentieth Century. In *Mapping Lives: The Uses of Biography*, ed. Peter France, and William StClair, 193–218. New York: Oxford University Press.

Margadant, Jo Burr. 2000. *The New Biography: Performing Femininity In Nineteenth Century France*. Berkeley: University of California Press.

Masters, Alexander. 2006. First published 2005. *Stuart: A Life Backwards*. London: Harper Perennial.

Miller, Lucasta. 2002. First Published in 2001. *The Brontë Myth*. London: Vintage.

Motion, Andrew. 1997. *Keats*. London: Faber and Faber.

———. 2000. *Wainewright the Poisoner*. London: Faber and Faber.

Mulryne, J.R. 2006. Where We Are Now: New Directions and Biographical Methods. In *Shakespeare, Marlowe, Jonson: New Directions in Biography*, ed. Takashi Kozuka and J.R. Mulryne, 1–19. Aldershot, Hampshire: Ashgate.

Nicholl, Charles. 2008. First published in 2007. *The Lodger: Shakespeare on Silver Street*. London: Penguin.

Oates, Joyce Carol. 2014. "Deep Reader." *New York Times Sunday Book Review*, January 26: BR1.

Podnieks, Elizabeth. 2009. Introduction: "New Biography" for a New Millenium. *a/b: Auto/Biography Studies* 24 (1): 1–14.

Rhiel, Mary, and David Suchoff. 1996. Introduction. In *The Seductions of Biography*, ed. Mary Rhiel, and David Suchoff, 1–5. London: Routledge.

Shapiro, James. 2005. *1599: A Year in the Life of William Shakespeare*. London: Faber and Faber.

———. 2015. *1606: William Shakespeare and the Year of Lear*. London: Faber and Faber.

Sisman, Adam. 2006. *The Friendship: Wordsworth and Coleridge*. London: Penguin.

Smith, Robert F.W., and Gemma L. Watson. 2016. *Writing the Lives of People and Things, AD 500–1700: A Multi-disciplinary Future for Biography*. Farnham, Surrey: Ashgate.

Tomalin, Claire. 2000. First published in 1997. *Jane Austen: A Life*. London: Penguin.

Wagner-Martin, Linda. 1994. *Telling Women's Lives: The New Biography*. New Brunswick, NJ: Rutgers University Press.

Wilson, Frances. 2008. *The Ballad of Dorothy Wordsworth*. London: Faber and Faber.

Woolf, Virginia. 1967. First published in 1927. The New Biography. In *Virginia Woolf Collected Essays Volume 4 1882–1941*, Virginia Woolf, 229–235. London: Hogarth Press.

CHAPTER 4

Haunting Conversations

In a lecture for the Oxford Centre for Life-Writing in February 2014, Romantic biographer Richard Holmes suggested that in using what he calls the biographical eye/I to write about a life, biography becomes a type of ghost story.[1] In the opening of an essay about M.R. James, an author of ghost stories in the early twentieth century, he suggested that "he wanted to set the scene as if it was a ghost story".[2] But there is a dearth of studies which make a case for this approach in biographical writing.[3] This chapter considers three ways of looking at biographies as haunted narratives, as suggested by the work of Hermione Lee and Richard Holmes. First, that biography can be understood as ghost stories, stories concerned with the ghosts that we find within narrative and in our reading. In these stories, we find the haunting presence not only of the biographical subject but of the biographer. This supports the perspective that biography can be understood as collaborative, a conversation and a process of exchange between different voices, in this case the haunting presence of the biographical subject and his or her biographer. Second, biographical narratives explore our inheritance and its contemporary relevance. In doing so, the narrator bears witness to history and gives a voice and speech back to people from the past. The biographer gets a subject talking about his or her life. The narrative becomes an interview, a dialogic discourse outside time. Third, this conversation is often associated with places, in particular houses and homes, visited by the haunting presence of the biographical subject and his or her biographer.

© The Author(s) 2017   73
J. McVeigh, *In Collaboration with British Literary Biography*,
DOI 10.1007/978-3-319-58383-9_4

For Hermione Lee, at the heart of biographies "is always the desire to get a vivid sense of the person, or people, who are the subject ... we always greedily want moments of intimacy, revelation, immediacy, and inwardness" (2015, 125). This is often achieved through the telling of anecdotes, particularly those that record a turning point in someone's life: "For a biographer, such moments can reveal a great deal about the people involved" (127). Lee is particularly interested here in "how these momentary encounters are remembered and narrated" (127) by the witnesses involved who tell their own story. She suggests that, in what she calls "encounter narratives" (139), the people involved "make each other up" (139), and in them the reader can latch on to "the traces of something real" (139). Lee describes such encounter narratives as ghost stories haunted by the voices of the people involved.[4] This chapter builds on this idea of biographies as haunted stories and draws the biographer him- or herself into the haunted narrative, suggesting a form of literary encounter and conversation within biographical narrative between the biographer and their subject.

Virginia Woolf's writing is filled with the ghosts of her past and, in like manner, Woolf becomes a haunting presence in Lee's own writing. Lee's approach, in her biography of Woolf, suggests a relationship in which the author as subject and the biographer are both writers, a feature of, and a construction in, their own writing and in conversation—haunting each other. As an author writes they can become a character in their writing, and similarly a biographer also creates a haunting presence in her own writing; the biographer becomes a character in her own work. We as readers find the character of the narrator constructed by the biographer in her biographical writing. It is not the voice of the actual biographer we hear but her haunting presence as a writer in conversation with her dead subject. In other words, assuming that we cannot know the intentions of the actual biographer, the narrative voice in a biography is a construction created in writing, which offers a version both of the biographical subject and the biographer.

In her biography *Virginia Woolf* (1997), Lee suggests that after her death Katherine Mansfield, a contemporary writer and a rival, haunted Virginia Woolf, "as we are haunted by people we have loved, but with whom we have not completed our conversation, with whom we have unfinished business" (1997, 400). Perhaps biography is similarly a story about unfinished business with people who continue to haunt our imagination and with whom we have not completed our conversation. Despite being concerned with reconstructing the past of an individual life, the nature of haunting in these biographies is essentially a dialogic discourse in which both biographee and the biographical narrator are in conversation. This is primarily a literary, rather than a historiographic, process through which we learn as readers, as in all storytelling, about both the lives of others and our connection to them. In the case of literary biographies by Hermione Lee and Richard Holmes, their biographical subjects certainly seem to haunt their imaginations, as well as our own. These biographies encourage a reading of the biographical figure as a spectre, as the other who returns and dominates the biographical narrative, haunting the biographical imagination of his or her biographer, and our experience as readers of biography. They may also draw our attention to the experience of haunting in the life of this figure, as some experiences and relationships with other people follow them like spectral shadows throughout their lives. The biographer becomes an advocate, whether they like their subject personally or not, drawing our attention to both the work of his or her subject, whatever work that might be and, in the case of literary biography, to this author's writing, reading and day-to-day life. As a result, we come to understand not so much the work itself but the extent to which the life and work are inseparable. Yet, like all ghosts, the biographer may be unwelcome and uninvited, as the often difficult relation between biographers and estates or living subjects has proven; and critics may reject a biographer's version of a life.

In his metanarrative about his experience as a biographer, *Footsteps* (1985), Holmes describes the growth of an imaginary relationship with a non-existent person, often a dead one, in biography: "In this sense, what I experienced ... was a haunting ... an act of deliberate psychological trespass, an invasion or encroachment of the present upon the past, and in some sense the past upon the present" (1995, 66). He describes this haunting as the essential process of biography which involves firstly the gathering of facts and "the assembling in chronological order of a man's "journey" through the world" (66), and secondly, "the creation of a fictional or imaginary relationship between the biographer and his subject" (66) that results in

> a continuous living dialogue between the two as they move over the same historical ground, the same trail of events. There is between them a ceaseless discussion ... It is fictional, imaginary, because of course the subject

cannot really, literally, talk back; but the biographer must come to act and think of his subject as if he can. (66)

As part of this process, the other of the biographical figure comes to life within the biography and becomes what Holmes describes in one example as "a true history of my time in Shelley's company" (2005a, ix). So, one version of the truth lies in the history of the writing of the biography, with one particular biographer at one particular moment in time, rather than in the life of the subject. This history makes a connection between our own inheritance and the past. Holmes has suggested that "the past is not simply 'out there', an objective history to be researched or forgotten, at will; but ... it lives most vividly in all of us, deep inside, and needs constantly to be given expression and interpretation" (1995, 208). Holmes follows in Shelley's footsteps; he travels to Italy where the poet lived for the last years of his life. As he becomes closer and closer to his subject, this pursuit becomes dangerous as Shelley's haunting can at times take over Holmes's sense of self:

> my outward life took on a curious thinness and unreality that I find difficult to describe. It was almost at times as if I was physically transparent, even invisible ... I gazed into mirrors above small washbasins with no plugs and did not see myself properly. (1995, 136)

In this biography, Holmes draws a specific connection between his own life and that of his subject, as he sets Shelley's death at sea with friends in the context of one of his own life experiences: "My own personal connections with Shelley hauntingly remain. In 1991 I was wrecked in a 28-foot sailing boat in the North Sea, but was pulled to safety with my two companions by an Airsea Rescue helicopter" (2005a, xii). Holmes is "looking *outwards* from within Shelley's life rather than the more usual attempt to look inwards from the outside—the view *from* the window, rather than the view of the window in the façade" (1995, 178). So, we have a sense of the biographer and subject sharing the same view, at a risk to the biographer's sense of identity as he haunts and witnesses his subject's life and at times understands it in connection with his own. As Lee comments, "the living make sense of their life through their thoughts of the dead" (1997, 401). Other biographers have expressed similar views. Michael Holroyd suggests that literary biographers are what he calls messengers, who "can stretch out a hand to his subject and invite him, invite her, to write one more work, posthumously and in collaboration" (2003, 19). American biographer Brenda Wineapple agrees that "Biography is a discourse with the dead (1997, 439), and "a form of public mourning" (448), in which "the past is not past, the dead shall live again" (445). The biographer rehabilitates his or her subject and helps to ensure that they are not forgotten.

For Holmes, a direct historical connection with the past is a vital element of his biographical writing. Shelley's political vision corresponded to what the younger Holmes, in the 1960s, "had myself seen and witnessed, what my whole generation had seen and witnessed ... I had a unique chance to follow and reinterpret Shelley's life, almost from the inside" (1995, 143), and he believes that this is part of Shelley's importance as a representative figure of his time and as such his life "seems more a haunting than a history" (2005a, xvii). Holmes suggests that biographical evidence is witnessed not only by those who knew the biographical figure and provide evidence about his or her life but also by the biographer haunting the life of his subject, who "witnesses ... daily human affairs in a special and privileged perspective" (1995, 174), bringing a view of the past into the present and re-creating a pattern: the biographer "sees every act as part of a constantly unfolding pattern" (174). In this analysis, a biography becomes a work of mourning and a form of remembrance. In learning about the life of someone else, we learn about ourselves as biographers and as readers.

A biography may do more than encapsulate a life, or lives, within a series of facts and anecdotes; whilst also asking questions about these lives and making connections, they offer a version that can be understood as a countersignature and this is another way to describe the copartnership important to Boswell in biographical narratives. This suggests that biography, in writing something different about a life or lives, can be faithful to the facts of someone's life, whilst re-creating a version of them that portrays characteristics of the fidelity important to Johnson. It is not that the biographer becomes a ventriloquist speaking his or her own words through the inert embodiment of the biographical subject but that the biographer creates a version of another life, or perhaps lives, that is faithful to the facts of that life, assembling them in some sort of order, although not always chronologically, whilst at the same time creating a new narrative, a version of a life in which the presence of both subject and biographer can be felt and heard. As Brenda Wineapple comments, as biography "enters the far-off realm of imagination, where the dead remain quixotically undead" (1997, 445) it arouses the reader's imagination "as it roused, and comforted, ours" (1997, 445).

Holmes offers a version of Shelley's life, which he sees as an attempt to write literary biography "as a form of modern epic" (2005a, ix) in which Shelley becomes a heroic figure, "which continues so vividly into the present day, a restless and demanding presence for each younger generation to encounter" (ix). In his biography of Coleridge, Holmes is quite explicit that he wants to understand what made him such an extraordinary man and to make his subject live, move, talk and "invade your imagination (as he has done mine)" (2005b, xiii). Holmes defines biography as "an art of human understanding, and a celebration of human nature" (2003, 25). He believes that the study of biography provides an opportunity "above all, *to exercise empathy*, to enter imaginatively into another place, another time, another life" (2004, 17), and that we "make sense of life by establishing 'significant' facts, and by telling 'revealing' stories about them" (2004, 17). This is a form of biography in which the biographical imagination seeks to stimulate our empathy by invoking very personal images and versions of our inheritance. By saying something different, Holmes creates his own countersignature about his subjects whilst also respecting the uniqueness of Shelley and Coleridge. It is not so much that the biographer identifies directly with the subject to such an extent that he or she is only really writing about themselves but that the biography, as Holmes argues, offers a narrative through which the voice of someone else—the biographical subject—can be heard once more. Admittedly, it is one version of his or her voice, but it can nevertheless sound authentic, whether we as readers agree with the voice presented is a different point.

Holmes wants "to summon up for one moment a living breathing shape, to make the dead walk again, to make the reader *see* a figure and *hear* a voice" (2005c, 136). This approach is very explicit, in particular, in his biography of Samuel Coleridge which aims "to set Coleridge *talking*" (2005b, xvi) to such an extent that ideally Coleridge's voice will dominate, as indeed many would argue that it should. For this biographer, even after the biography has been completed "Coleridge's life continues in one's head … This is the peculiar music of biography, haunting and uniquely *life-like* for a moment … sending out many echoes into the future" (1999, 561). It is these echoes that haunt biographies and readers' remembrance of particular people.

Holmes goes so far as to see a ghost during one of his journeys in search of his subject. He writes about his pursuit of Shelley as he retraces his steps by visiting the houses where the poet lived in Italy. At one house, Casa Bertini, Holmes takes a photograph; months later he looks at it and sees a ghost:

> It was a boy, aged between three and four, almost dwarfed by the trees, up to his ankles in leaves, and with a pair of dark eyes fixed on the camera. A faint tingling sensation passed over the top of my scalp. I felt I was looking at a photograph of little William, Shelley's dead son. (1995, 149)

Holmes was "astonished by the presence" he had "conjured up" (150) but moments later realises that the actual boy in the photograph lives in the house that Holmes is visiting. For Holmes, the photograph represents what biography can achieve: "It should summon up figures like a magic photograph plate, and hold them through time, at ten foot to infinity, with the soft shock of recognition, perfectly alive" (150). The photograph made Holmes ask questions about what this image "might mean as a symbol of some larger imagination at work" (151), not only a biographical imagination which creates and transforms connections between the present of the biographical narrator and the past of his subjects but also a wider historical imagination that reaches out into our inheritance from the past.

Virginia Woolf's writing is filled with the ghosts of her past and, in like manner, Woolf becomes a ghostly figure in Hermione Lee's own writing life. Lee writes about her visit to Woolf's childhood holiday home, Talland House, at the very end of her biography:

> No convenient ghost is going to appear, casting her shadow on the step. However, looking away from the house, over the buildings of the twentieth century, at the distant view from this island look-out, I can allow myself to suppose that I am seeing something of what she saw. My view overlaps with, just touches, hers. (1997, 772)

Lee's approach emphasises the re-creative nature of life-writing, in which the author as subject and the biographer are both writers, a feature of, and a construction in, their own writing, and in conversation, haunting each other. It is not the voice of the biographer we hear, but her haunting presence as a writer in conversation with her subject.

A theme in Lee's biography is the importance of houses and holiday homes in Virginia Woolf's life; this is also true of her biography of Edith Wharton.[5]

Lee suggests that Wharton's views on writing fiction "were very like her views on house design ... Novels, like houses, should have a firm outline, a sound structure, and a quality of inevitableness" (2008, 182), and both novels and houses can be haunted. Lee argues that "to visit her houses is ... to understand her character and her way of life" (2004, 31). Lee is clear that "Wharton always characterises families and societies through the decoration of houses" (2008, 18), and when she does so "she is writing about behaviour and beliefs" (28). In this context, Wharton's writing about architecture and decoration becomes, in *The Custom of the Country* and in other writing, a "stand in ... for morality and personal values" (426). Books and libraries can also inform a biographer's understanding of a writer's life.

Wharton took great care with the binding and presentation of her books: her "novels and stories are full of book-lined studies and discriminating collectors. Private libraries are the place where friendships are made or started" (2008, 132), and books "do not just provide evidence of her life story, they were also protagonists in it, and the equivalent of old friends" (670). Wharton haunts her libraries and the houses visited by her biographer. Moreover, in her writing about these places, the biographer can leave traces of her conversation with the haunting presence of her biographical subject.

Lee suggests that *To the Lighthouse* "is a kind of ghost story, a story of a haunted house" (1997, 482) and the title of the chapter in her biography which focuses on this autobiographical novel is simply called "A Haunted House".[6] The biography argues that "Virginia Woolf's lifelong argument with the past took its central images from the leaving, and the memory, of the Victorian house" (47). Woolf returns repeatedly to the memory of the family house in her writing as it represents her own family history and a Victorian world which has passed.[7] Talland House was where she spent memorable days in her childhood, and as an adult her return to this house "haunted her" (44). Also, Lee notes that a London home, Hyde Park Gate, "came to stand for all of Victorian domestic life and for the whole of her family history" (1997, 35). Following her move to Tavistock Square in 1924, Woolf "felt haunted" (1997, 474) by her new experience of living in London, given everything that had happened to her since she had last lived there.

A short story by Woolf, "A Haunted House", is based on Asheham, where she lived with her husband Leonard. The story "imagines a ghostly couple revisiting the house, half-sensed by the couple living there" (1997, 318), and "the present inhabitants seem as insubstantial as the ghosts, the ghosts' marriage more vivid than that of the living sleepers" (318). In her biography of Woolf, Lee writes at five key moments of opening and closure in the text about ghosts and haunting and the key place that houses and homes played in her life: at the beginning and end of her first chapter, called "Biography"; in the opening of the second chapter; at the end of the last chapter; and, finally, at the end of an additional section, called "Biographer".

The first chapter, titled "Biography", sets the scene for Lee's approach and discusses Woolf's concerns about life-writing. The biography opens with a question about the genre as a whole: "'My God, how does one write a Biography?' Virginia Woolf's question haunts her own biographers. How do they begin?" (1997, 3). Lee not only opens by acknowledging a relationship between the biographer and her subject, both of whom are asking the same question about biography, she also reaches out as a biographer to her predecessors, 'they', emphasising that she shares this dilemma with practitioners across the genre. The question also draws attention to an understanding of biography as a conversation. Lee's conversation is also with readers of the biography who are haunted by Virginia Woolf: "It began to seem that everyone who reads books has an opinion of some kind about Virginia Woolf" (3). Some readers may understand Woolf not as a person or writer, but rather as a disembodied figure based on who they think she was and what she came to represent. Those who do not even read her books have an opinion about her, "even if derived only from the title of Albee's play, *Who's Afraid of Virginia Woolf?*" (3). Here, Lee draws attention to the extent to which we bring our own mythologised view of Woolf's private life to our reading of her character and what we think we know about it.

At the end of this opening chapter, Lee suggests that Woolf makes "lives vivid through scenes and moments" (20) from her past:

> This, she tells us, is how her autobiography is written. Again and again, she marks the past by returning to the same scenes, the rooms, the landscapes, the figures of her life, like the ghosts revisiting their haunted house in her story of that name. Back she goes to the scenes of childhood: the blind tapping on the window of the bedroom at St Ives, the lighthouse beam going round, the sound of the waves breaking on the shore. (20)

This introduces a section in the biography which highlights the autobiographical nature of *To The Lighthouse* (1927), in which the central characters, Mr and Mrs Ramsey, are connected to her memories of her parents and the childhood holidays she shared with them. The second chapter of Lee's biography opens with the house from her childhood, Talland House, to which Virginia Woolf returns as an adult with her siblings, Thoby, Vanessa and Adrian, after the death of both of their parents. Lee notes Virginia Woolf's diary entry after this visit: "We hung there like ghosts in the shade of the hedge, & at the sound of footsteps we turned away" (21). Lee imagines "the four 'ghosts', tall, silent, similar" (21): "This revisiting would ... be the source of the emotion and the plot of *To the Lighthouse*, the novel that comes from this house ... We can take the ghosts, turning them back into children" (22). We have a sense here of a complex conversation, in which Virginia Woolf pays tribute to her childhood and brings her parents back to life in one of her novels and Lee becomes a guest, perhaps uninvited, on her visit to Talland House. This is like the character of Lily Briscoe in the novel, who returns to the house near the lighthouse some years after Mrs Ramsey has died and where the "waves sounded hoarse on the stones beneath" (1970, 229). She seems to see a ghostly image in a window of the house like some "wave of white ... over the window-pane" (229). Lily cries out to Mrs Ramsey, remembering her happy visits to the house in the past and Mrs Ramsey casting "her shadow on the step" (1970, 230). Similarly, Lee discusses her experience of actually visiting the places where Virginia Woolf lived, which "embody my sense of her as at once distant and close" (1997, 770), and gave her an opportunity "to see and do some of what she did" (770). Lee closes her book with these lines, directly echoing the end of the opening "Biography" chapter: "I stand in the garden [of Talland House], feeling like a biographer, a tourist and an intruder ... No convenient ghost is going to appear, casting her shadow on the step" (772), unlike Lily Briscoe's haunting experience on her return visit. Nevertheless, Lee comments that, "The view, in fact, seems to have been written by Virginia Woolf. The lighthouse beam strikes round; the waves break on the shore" (772). This makes a connection between the past of Virginia Woolf, her novel and the haunting of her life by her biographer. It suggests the integral connection between the writing and personal lives of both women. In the penultimate sentence above, Lee highlights the connections between her view of the house and her reading of Virginia Woolf's work and life. In part, this is an understanding of biography as a shared way of seeing, of making connections across time between individuals and the wider context in which they live. No convenient ghost of Virginia Woolf may appear on the step but perhaps we experience the haunting of her ghostly presence in her novels and in Lee's biographical narrative.

Lee's extensive biography ends, in chapter forty, with Virginia Woolf's suicide. She does not write a separate chapter on Woolf's afterlife but closes with a comment that predicts what is to come. The very last lines of the formal biography are:

> As she had once said of her own dead friends, she went on living and changing after her death:
>
> So we discuss suicide, and the ghosts as I say, change so oddly in my mind; like people who live, & are changed by what one hears of them. (767)

But Lee's biography does not end here, there is a further section, which is not identified as a chapter and labelled forty-one, nor is it identified as an appendix; it just has the title "Biographer". In this last section, Lee responds directly to a key aspect of Virginia Woolf's approach to life-writing, which seems to reflect Lee's own and echoes the ending of chapter forty. She comments,

> I have been reading a Virginia Woolf who has greatly changed … Posthumously, it feels as if she has generously, abundantly opened herself up to such retellings, as if in an echo of her joking phrase to John Lehmann: "You are hereby invited to be the guest of Virginia Woolf's ghost." Virginia Woolf's story is reformulated by each generation. (769)

At the end of both chapter forty and the chapter called "Biographer" are spectral images of lives to which Virginia Woolf paid tribute in her fiction and of her own life, as well as the haunting presence of her biographer. Virginia Woolf herself comments that in telling stories about the lives of others what we believe we know about them is changed but at least they are not forgotten and to that extent we remain faithful to their memory.

Finally, Lee discusses other connections with Virginia Woolf's childhood and emphasises that her adult life was influenced in part by her family and her roots. According to Lee, "Inheritance interests Virginia Woolf very much: her fictions are full of it" (1997, 50); her biographer is similarly interested in the extent to which her family, as well as her family homes, were integral to her subject's life and writing. Virginia Woolf often rewrites her experience of her parents, and their influence on her writing pervades throughout her life: "it is probable that her writer's life was driven by the desire to say 'look at me!' to those two exceptional and critical parents" (95). Lee believes that Woolf "used … [her father] for her politicised arguments against patriarchy in *The Years* and *Three Guineas*. When she began planning *To the Lighthouse*, in which he was at first going to be the central figure, she called it 'The Old Man'" (68). Woolf's mother was also a hugely important influence on her life and, to some extent, her writing life becomes a work of mourning, given that "laying this ghost to rest, is one of the secret plots of Virginia Woolf's existence" (79), as seen in *To The Lighthouse* in particular. Her childhood "turned into a macabre ghost story, her feelings about her mother were distorted, and Hyde Park Gate became a haunted house. Like Katharine Hilbery, the daughter in *Night and Day* … she would often feel that she belonged to the world of the dead: 'She seemed to herself to be moving among them, an invisible ghost among the living'" (Lee 1997, 133). If *To the Lighthouse* (1927) is a kind of ghost story, a sort of haunted house, and Woolf herself experienced haunting in her own life, perhaps Lee's biography can be understood in the same way.

In *Penelope Fitzgerald: A Life* (2013), Lee returns explicitly to an experience of haunting. She describes how she came to meet her subject and to write her life. She allows herself to think that "If, like her, I believed in ghosts, I would think of her looking on with reluctance as I trawled through her private papers, her annotations in her books, her notebooks and her manuscripts" (2013, 434). Lee's and Holmes's approaches are suggestive of this sense of haunting, which becomes a conversation, sometimes more of an interview, and of different ways of seeing, as biographical subject and biographer draw on their experience, and on their reading and writing lives. In these biographies, we can trace a version or countersignature of a life which is unique, albeit that the actual biographer may be apprehensive about what we make of it.

NOTES

1. Hermione Lee is Director of the Oxford Centre for Life-Writing (OCLW), a research centre based at Wolfson College at the University of Oxford, designed to support those who write auto/biography and those who undertake research on different forms of life narratives. Life-writing involves, and goes beyond, biography. It encompasses everything from the

complete life to the day-in-the-life, from the fictional to the factional. It embraces the lives of objects and institutions as well as the lives of individuals, families and groups. Life-writing includes autobiography, memoirs, letters, diaries, journals (written and documentary), anthropological data, oral testimony, and eye-witness accounts. It is not only a literary or historical specialism, but is relevant across the arts and sciences, and can involve philosophers, psychologists, sociologists, ethnographers and anthropologists.

2. Richard Holmes gave a Weinrebe Lecture for the Oxford Centre for Life-Writing, "The Biographer's Other I", on 18 February 2014.

3. Kathryn Hughes was surprised by the nature of her subject's haunting: "During my apprentice years as a biographer, I could never quite understand this business of literary haunting" (2004, 150), but this changed when she wrote her biography of George Eliot. She felt that Eliot had chosen her to write the book: "without that central, pulsing madness, how else could anyone give up five years of their life to living with an imaginary friend whom only they can see?" (153).

There have been some recent life-writing studies which consider the notion of spectrality and haunting in relation to trauma narratives and postcolonial analysis, such as Gabriele Rippl et al., eds, *Haunted Narratives: Life Writing in an Age of Trauma* (2013), and a special issue of the journal *Biography* 36:1 (2013).

4. Lee, "Literary Encounters and Life-Writing", 141.

5. Some critics have questioned the relationship that biographers and other literary tourists have with the houses haunted by their literary subjects. Nicola Watson suggests that at one extreme of the practice "tourists actively seek out the anti-realist experience of being 'haunted', of forcefully realizing the presence of an absence" (2006, 7). One could argue that visiting a place important to someone else creates a form of performance space within which we can reimagine our understanding of their lives, a haunting that is based on our reading of someone's life and work.

6. She also places this novel within a wider historical context, adding that *To the Lighthouse* is "a twentieth century post-war novel, concerned with the English class structure and with the social and political legacies of the war as much as with family memory" (1997, 482).

7. *Virginia Woolf*, 49.

References

Holmes, Richard. 1995. First published in 1985. *Footsteps: Adventure of a Romantic Biographer*. London: Flamingo.

———. 1999. First published in 1998. *Coleridge: Darker Visions*. London: Flamingo.

———. 2003. Inventing the Truth. In *The Art of Literary Biography*, ed. John Batchelor, 15–25. Oxford: Oxford University Press.

———. 2004. The Proper Study. In *Mapping Lives: The Uses of Biography*, ed. Peter France and William St Clair, 7–18. Oxford: Oxford University Press.

———. 2005a. First published in 1974. *Shelley: The Pursuit*. London: Harper Perennial.

———. 2005b. First published in 1989. *Coleridge: Early Visions*. London: Harper Perennial.

———. 2005c. First published in 2000. *Sidetracks: Explorations of a Romantic Biographer*. London: Harper Perennial.

Holroyd, Michael. 2003. First published in 2002. *Works on Paper: The Craft of Biography and Autobiography*. London: Abacus.

Hughes, Kathryn. 2004. Fever. In *Lives for Sale: Biographers' Tales*, ed. Mark Bostridge, 150–153. London: Continuum.

Lee, Hermione. 1997. First published in 1996. *Virginia Woolf*. London: Vintage.

———. 2004. A Great House Full of Rooms. In *Lives for Sale: Biographers' Tales*, ed. Mark Bostridge, 31–37. London: Continuum.

———. 2008. First published in 2007. *Edith Wharton*. London: Vintage.

———. 2013. *Penelope Fitzgerald: A Life*. London: Chatto & Windus.

———. 2015. 'From Memory': Literary Encounters and Life-Writing. In *On Life-Writing*, ed. Zachary Leader, 124–141. Oxford: Oxford University Press.

Watson, Nicola. 2006. *The Literary Tourist: Readers and Places in Romantic & Victorian Britain*. Basingstoke: Palgrave Macmillan.

Wineapple, Brenda. 1997. Mourning Becomes Biography. *American Imago* 54 (4): 437–451.

Woolf, Virginia. 1927. *To the Lighthouse*. Harmondsworth, Middlesex: Penguin (reprinted in 1970).

CHAPTER 5

Hermione Lee by Indirections Finds Directions Out

In Hermione Lee's work, questions about the lives of the people she writes about are closely connected with the process of, what she calls, the making up and making over of the lives of her subjects, both by the biographical narrator and the subjects themselves. This can be understood as a type of fashioning, as we fashion ourselves and others through an ongoing process of rereading and rewriting our own lives and those of others. Lee's approach to the structure and style of a biography contribute to the story she has to tell and to the makeover that the biography re-creates. This makeover is part of the process through which a countersignature is re-created and in which the biographer re-creates her own version of a life or lives. Also, Lee sees the biographer as both reader and writer, openly acknowledging that no work can be definitive or objective, that each biography is a "reading", a product as much of the reading and writing of both biographical subject and her biographer as of fact or new fact. Finally, Lee's writing also becomes a discourse about biography itself as, in rewriting the life of her subjects, she rewrites the way that their stories are told and invites us, as readers, to re-create her subjects through our own reading.

Lee describes her practice as a biographer as "a process of making up, or making over" (2005, 28).[1] She suggests that:

> Since biographers try to compose a whole out of parts (evidence, testimony, stories, chronologies) and arrange it on the page, since they appropriate their subjects and usually attempt to create a new or special version

© The Author(s) 2017
J. McVeigh, *In Collaboration with British Literary Biography*,
DOI 10.1007/978-3-319-58383-9_5

of them … and since they must give a quasi-fictional, story-like shape to their material (or no one will read them), these terms seem to fit. But pulling against "making up" or "making over", both of which imply some forms of alteration or untruth, is the responsibility to likeness and the need for accuracy. (2005, 28)

Lee re-creates a makeover of her subjects that interweaves with the different ways that they make up and fashion a makeover of their own lives, often in their writing. These makeovers are based on a description of important anecdotes and scenes, as well as the professional, public and personal relationships in the lives of Lee's subjects. She points out the contemporary view that biography "is never just the personal story of one life. It always has political and social implications" (2009, 63). Lee suggests that what Virginia Woolf "does with her life, how and what she writes, has to be read as a feature of the dramatic shifts in English cultural history between the 1880s and the 1930s" (1997a, 262). As this chapter discusses, this historical context is also important in Lee's biography of Edith Wharton. Lee suggests that in Wharton's novel *Ethan Frome* (1911),

> The narrator is like a biographer. He collects the evidence, listens to the different versions, and makes up his own story of the past from what he can gather. The characters' imprisonment in their private tragedy pulls against the narrator-biographer's tendency to turn them into a case history of New England life. (2008, 379)

Lee's comment about *Ethan Frome* suggests that writing about a life is not a matter of either a private story or a public, more representative, one, but rather it is both. For this reader, this notion of making up and making over suggests a form of self-fashioning in which the biographer, Lee in this case, explores the ways that someone creates versions of themselves in their writing, professional and private lives, as they 'perform' in front of different audiences at home, in other aspects of their personal and professional lives, and in their writing. The biographer draws on this autobiographical material and also fashions the life of her subject within the context of the historical and cultural period in which they lived.

American biographer Linda Wagner-Martin comments on the nature of refashioning in the context of biographies about the lives of women. She suggests that the "biographer's art is that of refashioning and revising the life narrative, bringing to it more background" (1994, 9). Biography is a search for both the subject's rewriting of public and private identity and experiences, as well as a biographer's rewriting of the same or similar experiences in this life, or lives. In a study about scientific biographies, David Aubin and Charlotte Bigg argue that our sense of self is rooted in place, time and society and in our relations to other people and, as a result, the self "is elaborated, perceived and reflected in a constant process of negotiation" (2007, 65) in which biographical writing should "situate historically the construction of personhood and self" (67).[2] It is this sense of constant negotiation in Lee's biographies that is explored in this chapter. This has both a social and a historical focus, drawing the representation of the past into the context of the present. It illustrates how biography helps to construct social, cultural, historical and individual meaning and identity. Like other biographers, Lee offers different possibilities of her subjects, but no biographer can write about every single possibility. These narratives are not fixed portrayals; rather they are studies of complex, fluid and often contradictory lives. Whilst a biography may give a multifaceted version of someone's life, or the lives of others, it can never cover every single aspect of a life, unless it is a comprehensive chronicle. Therefore, when people ask why other versions of a life are needed, perhaps one response would be to suggest not only that different versions are required for different generations who bring their own perspectives, but that reading and writing are not closed systems—they are fluid and always open to more conversations.

In writing her biography of Virginia Woolf, Lee decided, "Given my subject's own interest in how life-stories can be told[,] ... to point up the artifice of the biographical narrative, and to concentrate on particular aspects of the life, on different 'selves'" (2009, 122). The way that she puts these different perspectives together creates her version or makeover of Virginia Woolf, in her day-to day life, in her reading and in her writing. Lee argues that there "is no reconciling ... [the] contradictions" (1997a, 536) between the different aspects of her personality, feelings or beliefs: "contradictions, of cruelty and kindness, curiosity and snobbery, sympathy and offensiveness, were inextricably mixed together" (574). This is a makeover that reflects the complexity and fluidity of her subject's make up within the coherence of the biographical form. It also subverts some of the conventions of a traditional chronological biography, by taking a thematic approach that, like the work of Virginia Woolf herself, becomes a discourse about the very nature of biographical writing.

Lee suggests that Woolf's life and writing were influenced in part by her family, including the controlling influence of her father, and the early deaths of her mother and brother, Thoby, as well as her experience of mental illness:

> This making of "order" or "wholeness" out of "shocks", is, she says, "the strongest pleasure known to me" … the making of art, in reaction to the blows of life, is both an active, controlling process, in which she orders reality by "putting it into words". (1997a, 173)

In her autobiography, Woolf comments, as quoted in Lee, that "Only by being turned into writing … can these moments be 'made whole' or lose their power to hurt" (1997a, 106). Lee adds that "all her life she gives herself pleasure by finding the 'revelation of some order' through such 'moments of being'. So she masters her memories by structuring them like fictions" (106). Similarly, as Desmond MacCarthy suggests, the biographer creates a makeover of a life based on the patterns that she sees across the many different aspects of the life of her subject, or subjects.

MacCarthy argues, as noted in Chap. 2, that a biographer "must impose some pattern on the disorder of life, or his book will only be a quarry from which some other man may be able some day to construct a building" (1953, 33). This idea of a pattern cannot be fixed or predetermined, but is re-created by each biographer. Ray Monk's view does not force biography into being either a science, or fiction, as discussed in the early twentieth century by Nicolson. Rather, he argues that "biography is not, and cannot ever be, a science, and neither can the understanding of people" (2004, 40); neither is it a branch of fiction. The need for different versions of a life narrated in different forms does not mean—although this may be the case—that facts were missing or misinterpreted in previous versions, instead Monk suggests that "even if *all* the facts of a person's life could be established, there would still be room for several different ways of looking at that life, several different possible ways of writing the biography, and that these different possible biographies could *all* be faithful to the facts, and equally 'objective'" (40), and this is simply because "we see something different, even when what we look at is the same thing" (41). As a Rorschach test proves, we can see things differently depending on how we look at them.

Lee's biography explores how Woolf's family and her Victorian heritage were transformed in her work. *The Years* "made an X-ray of her childhood as a prototype of Victorian patriarchal repression" (96); "*Jacob's Room* is as full of [her brother] Thoby Stephen as *The Voyage Out* is of Virginia's painful adolescence, and *Night and Day* is of her sister's character, her family past, and her decision to marry" (436). However, Lee suggests that "Any display of naked autobiography is carefully suppressed" (436). According to Lee, "*The Waves* ... is the only one of her novels which is not ostensibly concerned with family life or inheritance" (269). Lee emphasises throughout the biography that her subject's writing is a form of rewriting and self-fashioning of her experience of family life.

Woolf's relationships with other people are threaded throughout this biography, so that, although this is a single life narrative, it is full of many different characters, including: members of her family, such as her relationship with her sister, Vanessa, and her brothers; the Bloomsbury group, including Lytton Strachey; her women friends; and other writers, such as Katherine Mansfield, Vita Sackville-West and T.S. Eliot, who all influenced her life to varying degrees, and she theirs. Sackville-West was her lover and "they made each other up" (1997a, 485), as they performed and cast themselves in different characters in their relationship. Woolf "made over" (523) Sackville-West, as "her characteristics are exploited" (523) in Virginia Woolf's rewriting of her as the central character in her novel, *Orlando* (1928). This novel is a significant early example of biography in the form of fiction.

Things and objects are of some significance in Woolf's life and help to make connections between her family's Victorian past and the advent of the modernism that Woolf influenced. Lee's biography of Woolf mentions objects that are an important part of the legacies left to her own, or her parents', heirs. Their physical representations connect with Woolf's memories and her writing: "Julia Margaret Cameron's photographs of Julia Stephens [Woolf's mother] are put up on the walls of Bloomsbury houses; and the Victorian family provides the furniture of Virginia Woolf's modernist novels" (1997a, 47). In terms of her relationship with her sister Vanessa, a painter and designer, Woolf wondered about the connection between "paintings, furnishings ... clothes, forms of social life, domestic arrangements, ways of producing as well as reading and writing books" (371) that encapsulate a "whole style of living" (371). These objects from Woolf's life, associated with her family, childhood and adult life, are representative of her Victorian inheritance and her identity, or at least of the person that she thought she might become.

Jonathan Bate suggests that in "writing a life of Shakespeare's mind that looks 'before and after' … We must by indirections find directions out" (2009, 5). Virginia Woolf explored the nature of her unstable self and "if *she* could find herself out only by indirection, then it was a great deal harder for other people to pin her down. Most of what went on in her internal zoo was invisible to the outsider" (Lee 1997a, 529). Perhaps biography by indirections can look for significant connections across Woolf's different selves and other aspects of her life, although Lee is careful not to make simplified links between Woolf's life and work, but rather to suggest that they represent what may have been on her mind at the time of writing.[3] Thus, in relation to her mental health, Lee believes that, "It seems possible that [Virginia Woolf] may have refashioned the frightening unintelligible mental language of her hallucinations" (196) in *Mrs Dalloway* (1925), but she is very cautious before "attributing to them the kind of coherent biographical meanings which they invite" (197), particularly as "Madness is not her only subject" (194). Lee counsels caution and argues that "we cannot, I think, be sure what 'caused' Virginia Woolf's mental illness. We can only look at what it did to her, and what she did with it" (199). Lee does not want to turn this biography into an illness narrative, making the point that Woolf was "a sane woman who had an illness" (175). It is by indirections that Lee comes to understand some of the ways that her subject 'made over' these experiences in her writing and in her life.

Lee's narrative interrogates the nature of the genre and challenges traditional realist conventions. For any biography, "the opening moves set up the whole approach" (Lee 2009, 125). A close reading of the first short section in her biography of Virginia Woolf, over two pages, in a chapter with the title "Biography", sets the scene for Lee's vision. She does not open the biography in a conventional, chronological way by starting with the birth of Virginia Woolf. Instead the opening draws our attention to the extent to which the story Lee wants to tell and how she tells it are integral to each other. To begin with, there are these sentences, discussed in the last chapter: "'My God, how does one write a Biography?' Virginia Woolf's question haunts her own biographers. How do they begin?" (1997a, 3). Lee's conversation is not only with Woolf, but with other biographers, academics and her general readers.

She makes a direct reference to readers of the biography a few paragraphs on: "I have noticed that in the course of any conversation about this book I would, without fail, be asked one or more of the same four questions … It began to seem that everyone who reads books has an opinion of some kind about Virginia Woolf" (3). These questions relate to the enduring fascination we have with particular aspects of her life: "Is it true she was sexually abused as a child? What was her madness and why did she kill herself? Was Leonard a good or wicked husband? Wasn't she the most terrible snob?" (3). Lee makes us aware that this is a work that is not only about one particular writer, but that it also reflects a wider conversation between biographers and general readers about how we remember her life, what it means to us and the extent to which Virginia Woolf is re-created in our reading and becomes the character that we believe her to be. Questions about Virginia Woolf's life influence how her life is framed and how any telling of it begins.

Lee uses repetition to reinforce the importance of her opening, using the phrase "They can start" (3) five times as she offers different options for the opening of any biography about Woolf. This culminates in a point that highlights something about biography itself, namely that Woolf "is a writer who lends herself to infinitely various interpretation … There is no such thing as an objective biography" (3). Lee does not start her biography with a traditional statement about her subject's birth and parentage (3), immediately subverting the traditional conventions of straightforward chronology found in traditional biography. So, there may be many questions about Virginia Woolf and there can equally be many answers.

Lee questions the extent to which it is possible to re-create an objective and full record of Woolf's life, given how hard it is to get close to her. The huge archival evidence available about Woolf "would allow a really uncompromising biographer to make a record of what Virginia Woolf said, felt, did and wrote on almost every day of her life" (4). But, cautions Lee, they should be fearful about doing so, albeit that they will feel a sense of intimacy with her and "want to call her Virginia" (4). To a biographer she may seem "extremely near, contemporary, timeless. But she is also evasive and obscure … increasingly distant from us in time" (4)—much as Woolf felt herself to be "both near to and utterly distant from her own past" (4). As discussed in Chap. 4, the biographical subject becomes a haunting presence that feels close by and yet out of reach, real and yet only a representation, brought to life and yet intangible and elusive, haunting our experience of reading and writing her life.

All the material about Woolf's life encourages this biographer to feel like she can hear her subject talking in her autobiographical writing: "All readers of Virginia Woolf's diaries ... will feel an extraordinary sense of intimacy with the voice that is talking there" (4). Yet, ultimately, she is a character, a construction within the biographical narrative and becomes 'Virginia Woolf', not Virginia: "Virginia Woolf's 'Orlando', in her 'biography', lives for centuries; so does—so will—'Virginia Woolf'. Meanwhile, as for Orlando, everything changes" (4). In this opening, the biography makes a feature of its subject's name; this is key to Lee's style throughout. She has written elsewhere that a

> still lingering difference between biographies of men and of women is revealed by the matter of naming. Lives are no longer being written of 'Miss Austen', 'Mrs Woolf', or 'Mrs Gaskell'. But because biographies of women have for so long been more protective and intimate than those of great men, a biography of a famous English woman novelist might still refer throughout to Jane or Charlotte, whilst famous male English novelists are not usually called Charles or Anthony. (2009, 129)

On the first page of the biography, Lee's subject is referred to as Miss Stephen and Virginia Stephen, but predominantly she is Virginia Woolf, not Virginia, Mrs Woolf or Woolf. In the opening short paragraph of the biography, her subject is identified as Virginia Woolf six times. This way of naming Virginia Woolf is repeated in every chapter of this biography. Virginia may be used, but this is often because the narrative is referring to the voice of someone who knew her, a friend or relative who would, of course, have called her by her first name, or when the narrative is referring to her private life, or before she became a writer. Lee's subject is known as Virginia Woolf when drawing attention to her life and influence as a writer. For example, in a discussion about the suffrage movement, Lee notes that, "Virginia Woolf's writing was always explicitly on the radical, subversive and modern side" (1997a, 278), followed by the fact that most of the women "Virginia knew who were involved in social work and politics ... were supporters of votes for women" (279), and "Virginia Stephen's participation in the Votes for Women campaign did not last for long" (279). Virginia Woolf was a person but a writer first and foremost and Virginia Woolf is her name as a writer, as a character in this biography and as a representative of the voice of other women writers within her lifetime and up to the present day. We do not really know her, but we believe we know who she came to represent. As Lee points out, we tend to refer to writers and biographers by their surname—Dickens, Milton and Shakespeare are obvious examples. Clearly, Lee would want to avoid any confusion with Virginia's husband, Leonard, but her way of naming her subject as Virginia Woolf throughout her biography seems more significant. Lee understands that in the case of Virginia Woolf "myths have been made" (1997a, 3) about who she really was, and our understanding of her is embodied in her name. We all refer to Dickens, but we refer to Virginia Woolf, as a woman, a writer and a figure about whom we all have an opinion, no matter how much we know about her life or her writing.

There is the presence of the 'I' of the biographer in this story—the first-person pronoun is used throughout the opening section as Lee brings the voice of the biographical narrator out into the open. The final section, "Biographer", opens with statements about Lee's own life, statements which echo her discussion on the limitations of the traditional form of chronological biography in the first chapter of the biography. The opening of this last section establishes a relationship between the biographer of the more recent past and her subject, and places this relationship within a wider historical context: "I was born in February 1948, three years after the end of the war and seven years after Virginia Woolf's death" (768). Lee discusses the different versions of Woolf's influence and character, what she calls reappropriations, and, as a result, "Virginia Woolf as an author will go on changing" (770) and be "touchably close" (770) as different versions of her life and work are re-created in an ongoing performative process of rereading and rewriting that brings her hauntingly back to life.

Lee responds directly to an important aspect of Woolf's approach to life-writing, which reflects her own: "I have been reading a Virginia Woolf who has greatly changed … She herself, as I've said in this book, was intensely aware, from her own reading and theorising of biography, of how lives are changed in retrospect, and how life-stories need to be retold" (769). Woolf's reading and her own reading as a biographer are an essential part of the story that Lee wants to tell, as indeed is the writing life of both Woolf and her biographer. The biography comments that "Her work is permeated with her reading … Her mind is full of echoes" (411). The echoes are heard and passed on to us as readers by her biographer. In "Reading", Lee comments that the "confident enjoyment of the intimacy which comes from reading is one of the main sources of happiness in Virginia Woolf's life. Reading, quite as much as writing, is her life's pleasure and her life's work" (402). Moreover, "Above all, she wanted reading and writing to infiltrate each other" (413) and this becomes another form of making up as she fashions her life and work through reading, as much as writing. In her biography, Lee writes about Woolf's approach to reading, which

> takes the form, often, of what she calls "making up". You make up the author as you might make up the person opposite you in the railway carriage ... Much of the art of reading is "not reading", but a fantasy life carried on behind and during the reading. As she reads, half her mind is on the writer's life, making up the story behind the story. And when she returns to an author ... she will "make him up a little differently at every reading". (1997a, 413)

Then, "When the book is closed, and the 'after reading' begins, 'making up' turns into 'making whole'. (1997a, 413). Lee's writing of her biography is also permeated with her own role as a reader; she opens her biography of Woolf with a comment that she has been "Reading and writing her life" (3).[4] For Lee, as for Woolf in her approach to biography, it is a collaborative and dialogic process of reading as well as writing, as her subject's life and writings are informed by her reading, and in turn the biographer reads and rewrites this woman writer's life and work, which we as readers then go on to read to make up our own version of this life of reading and writing.

In the opening section of *Edith Wharton* (2008), Lee suggests that in many of her fictions and memoirs "Wharton 'made up' versions of herself as a child and of the world she grew up in ... she uses it to describe the most essential activity of her childhood" (2008, 13) as she invents stories that connect with her experience: it was a "ritualistic, solitary, and very physical" process (13). This form of making up goes on into Wharton's adult writing life: "In Paris, the stories she was 'making up' were based—as they would be in future years—on the lives she imagined for 'the ladies and gentlemen who came to dine'" (14):

> "Making up" might be a solitary ecstasy but it was firmly linked to the realities of the physical world, to her relationship with her parents, and to

the social life which she escaped from in order to "make up", but also used for her material. (15)

This is a form of the play acting and making up that any child might enjoy as she creates stories about the adults around her, making her own sense of the world and trying to have some control over it.

In a different form of making up, throughout the biography, we come across different versions of the made up or self-fashioned version of Wharton herself, as we come to know the different selves that make up her character and inform how she lived. In Paris, "we see her ... as an integrated, knowing participant in the literary world" (301). But later, she would spend less time on a busy social life and build around her a close group of supporters: "this dependence on a select, loyal group would set the pattern of her future life" (384). Lee argues that literary biographers "usually try not to split the performing, public, everyday self off from the private writing self, but to work out the connection between them. That is really the whole point of literary biography" (2009, 102). And, in making these connections and writing about them, the biographer creates another form of 'makeover' or version of her subject.[5]

The opening sentence of this biography sets up important themes for the book as a whole—Wharton's heritage and the influence of her parents; the relationship between public events of great historical importance and private lives focusing on a different kind of very personal event; transnational and American experience, planned and unexpected outcomes, and personal wealth and privilege all come together to set the scene: "In Paris, in February 1848, a young American couple on their Grand Tour of Europe found themselves, to their surprise, in the middle of a French revolution" (2008, 3). In this first chapter, Lee goes on to make connections between the past of Wharton's family and her own later life and asks how they could be so different and yet so similar. The revolutionary France of 1848, when her parents visited, and that of 1914 when Wharton was in Paris at the start of the First World War, were very different: "Between these nineteenth and twentieth century American versions of Paris in crisis is the gap of a generation, of historical change, and of widely differing personal knowledge and experience" (6). Wharton "broke with her parents' attitudes and customs ... to construct her own personal and professional revolution" (6), but Lee identifies a key theme in this biography by arguing that, nevertheless, Wharton "followed a family pattern. Though she describes them as at bottom all provincial New Yorkers ... [her family] were forever Europe-bound" (7). Both her mother and two older brothers lived and died in France, having spent their lives there over many years. Lee argues that these connections between Wharton's heritage and her own life underpin much of her writing, and they are an important theme in the biography: "This, then, is the story of an American citizen in France ... who could never be done with the subject of America and Americans" (8). Wharton wrote about

> versions of herself as the daughter of her family and her country. Between 1897 and 1937 Wharton published at least one book almost every year of her life ... In almost every one of them there is a cultural comparison or conflict, a journey or a displacement, a sharp eye cast across national characteristics. (8)

Part of Wharton's making up relates to her heritage and her writing "as a cultural analyst" (23) concerned with the extent to which her family's story is representative of her class and generation, as well as a fundamental influence on her own life.

The second chapter, "Making Up", continues to explore the way that Wharton self-fashions her life-story in her writing. Lee notes that Wharton's "childhood story [in her memoirs] turns, most of all, on the family's move to Europe when she was four ... nothing is the same afterwards" (16). Our attention is drawn to the source of evidence here, her subject's memoirs, based on Wharton's version of her past remembered much later in life. In doing so, the biography interrogates the nature of memory and remembrance as the facts of her life are told by the subject herself. Lee emphasises that these early "formative stories are not told in her memoirs as consecutive factual narrative" (17), and we know that memory can change the tone and detail of the stories we remember. This chapter subverts chronological conventions of linear time and discusses Wharton's childhood from the perspective of her writing looking back and remembered later in life, as described in *A Backward Glance* (1934) and other private memoirs by Wharton. We learn about Wharton's birth from the perspective of her memoir: "What she does not do is start with the birth of a girl on 24 January 1862" (2008, 15). The biography does not start with a description of her birth either—a note of her birth finally appears in the second chapter. Here, Lee is focusing on the voice of her subject, who reimagines and transforms her past by drawing on her memories. In other words, the biography pays attention to how

Wharton has made up her life from the bits and pieces of stories and turning points or key events that she reimagines in her memoirs.

Lee comments that "Wharton's life-story often feels like a cover story, with tremendously articulate activity on the surface, and secrets and silences below" (10). The story of Wharton's life is full of gaps and silences, as she strives for privacy, rewrites her solitary childhood and her parents, particularly her mother, and seeks to ensure that she has control over how her story is made up for future generations: "she preferred not to talk about personal friendships, but ... shapes her life-story as one of solitude, self-education, and self-creation" (40).[6] Wharton rewrites her mother in her fiction; this "is one of the most lethal acts of revenge ever taken by a writing daughter" (Lee 2008, 34). Lee suggests that she "is at pains to describe herself, from her earliest days, as 'making up' another story of her life than the one she had been given" (34). Lee looks into these gaps to see what she might find there and accepts that some evidence is missing.

This is a biography interested in the social self of its subject. Lee partly fashions the version of the Wharton that we come to know in this biography through the many people she knew as friends, relatives and professional colleagues. There are too many to mention here but some stand out as pivotal, such as Walter Berry, Henry James, her lover Morton Fullerton, her domestic staff and her parents—her mother in particular—and her difficult relationship with her husband. Others have smaller parts to play, but are crucial to the themes explored:

> Wharton was ... interested in the ethics of style, whether in the production values of her books, in her house and garden designs, in her appreciation of Europe, or in her theorising of interior decoration. In all these areas, she had mentors or collaborators—editors, literary advisers, travelling companions. (124)

There is much that we do not know and cannot be told in the biography about these relationships, but we nevertheless come to understand Wharton's life in part through them.

Wharton's concern to protect her privacy led to the destruction of many letters, including those from Walter Berry, "the most important person in her life" (10). Henry James was a great friend and destroyed much of his own autobiographical records, including letters from Wharton. At one point, she wrote to him asking for his advice about her affair with Morton Fullerton. We have his reply, but her letters to James are missing and they "cannot be invented" (330), or not at least in this nonfiction narrative. Moreover, we cannot be told the significance of Wharton's relationship with another friend, Egerton Winthrop, "who would play a louder part in Wharton's life-story if the letters between them had not been done away with" (67), as would her friendship with Robert Douglas Norton, "one of Wharton's closest lifelong companions" (249), but no correspondence between them remains. Lee's choice of words is interesting here: 'louder' encourages us to think about the notion of hearing voices in the book, when 'larger' could easily have been used, and 'done away with' is suggestive of a murder or death and reminds us that this biography is peopled with many different voices, some of whom have been killed off when evidence is not available.

Lee is interested in what was on her subject's mind at the time of writing specific works: "The qualities that make Wharton a great writer ... were the product of years of observation, reading, practice and refinement" (346); "she missed nothing of what was going on around her, and would use everything" (45). In Edith Wharton's fiction, "Nothing is lost or wasted from the past" (564): *The Custom of the Country* (1913), "is utterly unautobiographical, though traces of her life are in it everywhere" (424); *The Age of Innocence* (1920), "makes a kind of autobiography, though, as usual, personal emotions are carefully distanced and dressed up" (562); and the story "Roman Fever" (1934) "is one of the best examples of the indirect, rich and surprising ways in which she makes use of her own experiences" (718). Lee considers the extent to which Wharton's love affair with Morton Fullerton can be understood through her writing, including her autobiographical writing in letters and diaries, but is keen not to draw simplistic autobiographical connections. In her early love letters "she turns herself into the heroine of a French erotic novel" (321). Her autobiographical writing becomes a source for her creative writing as Wharton's poems, stories and novels "are waiting to have this material poured into them" (320).[7] However, Lee knows that it "would be a travesty to suggest" that Wharton's writing about marriage, failed love and sexual treachery "issued from her relationship with Morton Fullerton" (346). Nevertheless, "this messy, difficult time in her private and professional life saw some of her finest work" (346). Lee does suggest that Wharton's novel *The Reef* (1912) "was the book that came most closely out of her love-affair" (351), although it looks "not at all like an autobiography" (351). One of Wharton's "great strengths as a writer is her ability to generalise from her own condition" (360), but "she never wrote about her own situation for public consumption" (360); rather, Wharton transforms her experience in her fiction taking from it what she needs to fashion her stories.[8]

Another way that Lee makes up this life-story is "through the symbolic objects that struck ... [Wharton] as a child" (18) and she understands "the fixtures and fittings of her childhood as a collection of solid objects, strong colours and thick textures" (26). The biography discusses some of these, such as an ear trumpet that reminded her of her grandmother and a pair of slippers important to her mother (20). More significantly, Wharton "always characterises families and societies through the decoration of houses" (18), as discussed in Chap. 4, and her life can also be understood through the houses and gardens that she designed, visited, studied and wrote about, and where she lived: "the same mighty energies, appetite for planning, eye for detail, and cogent vision went into her gardening as into the writing of fiction, and as they had into her war-activities and her travels ... She was a writer and a gardener, and her gardens became, for those who saw them and heard about them, as admired as her books" (2008, 527). Libraries and Wharton's passion for not only writing but collecting books are also central to her story.

Wharton's private library "was one of the greatest pleasures of her life, and had its roots in her childhood reading" (Lee 2005, 57); as for Virginia Woolf, "Reading, as well as writing, was one of the most central, essential emotional experiences of her life" (59). She was widely read, having "a lifetime's reading in science, philosophy and anthropology— and a lifetime of translating social history into fiction" (2008, 23). By exploring Wharton's reading, Lee draws our attention to its influence in her writing. Lee's focus on the importance of place, domestic environments and objects are all in tune with contemporary experimentation within the genre and represent different approaches to fashioning and re-creating versions of her subject.[9]

Wharton's life and writing is considered within a wider social and cultural perspective: "Wharton's early story is part of a larger plot in the way it reflected her society's expectations for women of a certain class and type—expectations which would be one of her main subjects" (45). She fashioned her own identity and those of her literary characters in the context of wider social forces that were representative of her time: "Her greatest books would pinpoint the moment at which the complacent habits of a small group are destabilised by the action of larger forces"

(46). Her writing during the First World War became "part of her war-work" (457) and she remained concerned with "the possibilities of—and the obstacles to—cultural cross-fertilisation" (499).

Wharton had many selves and she performed different roles in life—for instance, as a young writer and, in her youth, "as a young debutante, socialite, and wife" (45). In the 1890s and 1900s her "self-creation ... as a woman writer who could not be categorised under 'feminine' or 'sentimental', and a highly cultured author who could also appeal to a big audience, was a remarkable one" (170). Lee describes the many contradictory selves of Wharton:

> She was a woman of dynamic organisational energies, busy and managerial, who also had a profound need for peace and rest. She liked her solitude, and did not enjoy "society", but she could also feel very lonely and wanted her friends around her. She had grown up and lived in big cities, but she preferred the country. She was committed to a life in France, but not to Paris. (519)

Wharton's writing is informed by an identity based on her nationality, her childhood, her class, her European passions and affinities, her friendships, marriage and love affair, being a woman writer, her interdisciplinary interests, her love of houses, gardening and books, her experience of the city and the countryside, and by her role as a representative of the wider domestic experience of war away from the battlefields in the early twentieth century—and, of course, as an American in Paris.

The structure of Lee's Wharton biography is integral to the story that she wants to tell. The first half is about Wharton's life before she left for France, where she lived for the rest of her life, which is described in the second part of the biography. However, the chapters throughout the biography are focused on particular themes, and are not necessarily based on a neat chronological story about Wharton's life. In the first part, chapters relate to the wider social circumstances in which she grew up, the importance of houses and gardens in her life, her interest in the theatre, her relationship with Henry James and other friends who they both knew, as well as sections of literary criticism about her fiction, with one chapter focusing on "the most famous of her novels" (204), *House of Mirth* (1905). This means that the timescale between the chapters is not neatly chronological. Henry James dies at the end of part one only to be alive again in part two. Some chapters may focus on a couple of themes that are representative of particular periods in her life: for example, "There are three energetic strands in her twenties and thirties which are not stories of illness. One is the making of American houses, one is her entry into the literary market-place, and one is her taking possession of Italy" (80). The six chapters that make up the second part of the biography are primarily concerned with: her move to Paris, the friends she made there and her participation in the city's literary life; her affair with Morton Fullerton and the writing inspired by the affair; the state of her marriage to and divorce from Teddy Wharton; literary criticism of her novel, *The Age of Innocence* (1920); and two chapters that focus on her war work in Paris. The development of these themes that help us to understand Wharton's life is central to Lee's approach as a biographer.

However, it would be misleading to suggest that chronological time is not carefully marked out in this biography. The beginning of most chapters pinpoints a particular moment in time and places Wharton within it. Wharton's age is specifically mentioned, often in the opening line, in the first paragraph of ten of the twenty chapters and a date or specific time period is also often mentioned within the first paragraph. Furthermore, the name Edith Wharton provides the first words in six of the chapters and is in the first line in four others (Wharton is used in the first line of three others); in other words, half of the chapters open with Edith Wharton at a specific moment in her life. She is also called Wharton in the biography but at these and other key moments our attention is drawn to Edith Wharton, the writer, the woman, and the self that has been fashioned at this moment in her life.

Lee opens the biography of Penelope Fitzgerald with her subject's own makeover of her heritage, drawing on Fitzgerald's group biography about her father and brothers, *The Knox Brothers* (1977). Her father's family "dominate Penelope Fitzgerald's life-story" (2013, 7) and "left a strong mark on her life and her writing" (7), although within this memoir "she keeps her own story firmly back" (21). As Lee comments wryly, "Looking for Penelope Fitzgerald's autobiography inside *The Knox Brothers* is like bringing invisible ink to light" (21); this is a biography about a very private person who was hard to know. The use of her subject's memories is again interesting in this context. Lee comments that Penelope Fitzgerald's memoir "makes it almost impossible to use any but her words, or think in any but her terms, about her father's family" (7). So, at this point in the biography we hear the voice of the subject being given centre stage—it is the voice of the writer, Penelope Fitzgerald, who we hear most strongly. It is not the voice of a young woman reflecting on her childhood and family, but the voice of a writer refashioning other lives and, in doing so, her own. Again, the life of this writer is fashioned in this biography in part through the self-fashioning she undertakes in her own writing about her heritage.

As in Lee's biography of Wharton, this biography is peopled with Fitzgerald's family, children, friends and publishers, but her relationship with her husband, a man who stands in sharp contrast to her more successful father, seems to share the centre of this book with *The Knox Brothers*. This reader understands the life of Desmond Fitzgerald as a story about the impact of the Second World War on men who survived the battlefield but were broken by what they saw and experienced there. The photographs of Desmond when they married show a handsome man who is almost unrecognisable in later photographs, as his legal career flounders and alcoholism takes its toll on his work and the family's finances:

> He was a hero: but he had been profoundly changed by the war, and, though not physically wounded, came back a different person from the dashing young officer Penelope had married in 1942. He had seen appalling things and lost many men; he had killed a large number of people. He would wake up in the night, screaming. He could never bear fireworks. (87)

This experience changed both their lives forever and the family struggled for many years, living in a houseboat and, via a hostel for homeless families, moving on to a council flat. At the same time as Desmond's legal career reaches a new low when he is charged with stealing money from his chambers' clients, the houseboat sinks, and Penelope and her children are homeless. The measured and understated tone of the biography here, and at other similar moments, seems to mirror the quiet stoicism of Lee's subject, who rarely spoke of these events—although she draws on them in her fiction, and manages to keep her job and her children's lives afloat. Lee describes the sinking of the boat when:

> The cat was found clinging to the mast, and had to be rescued. Most of Penelope's family documents, photographs, letters from her mother, childhood mementoes, were lost, to her great distress. Some books were

salvaged, and remained in her possession, their pages forever crinkled and stained. (158)

It is Penelope, rather than her husband, who clings to what she has left and rescues her family, although, literally and metaphorically, she has lost so much of her heritage and day-to-day life has become another battlefield for Desmond. It is the written and textual narratives about her life and her books that are emphasised here, and it is evidence of her life-story that is lost. This missing evidence often remains hidden in Fitzgerald's self-fashioning of her own life and cannot be recovered in this biography, although the story about how it was lost can be, and part of this loss is the breakdown of her marriage and the loss of her husband's early promise. It is Fitzgerald's ability to create success and art out of this battlefield that is one of the themes in this biography.

It is hard not to notice that only one of her books, a biography of Edmund Burne-Jones, was published before her husband's death and after that of her father, Evoe. In 1975 when it was published, and the family were moving out of their council home, Desmond was already very ill and continually in and out of the Royal Marsden Hospital. The biography notes that in "1969 and 1970, she began to do some research on Edward Burne-Jones. In January 1971, Evoe Knox died" (214); by this point, Fitzgerald's children were adults and her life with her husband had steadied, "there was space in her life now for her to make her own mark, and for her half-century of reading, thinking and learning to be shaped into the books she had always known she would write" (214). Following the death of her father, the death of her husband in 1976 is a crucial turning point when Fitzgerald is nearly sixty. Thus, this is very much a biography of two halves, as her family life and married life becomes a preparation for her writing life.

For much of her life, Fitzgerald is a wife, mother and teacher; then she becomes a writer. The domestic and professional sides of her life are often kept apart. For her eightieth birthday, in an anecdote that again reflects Lee's attention to the use of names, Fitzgerald had two parties, one for her literary circle and the other with her family at which "she was not Penelope Fitzgerald, she was Mops, Ma, or Granny" (413). Lee brings one specific aspect of Fitzgerald's private life into the biography by including copies of her drawings, which highlight her interest in children and the value of domestic life: "The drawings she made all her life for friends were mainly of small children in domestic situations" (34) and they help to bring one small part of what was important in Fitzgerald's life into view. In Fitzgerald's biography, *Charlotte Mew and her Friends* (1984), she wanted to keep illustrations scattered in the book because, in her own words, "I think they help to "tell the story", always a difficulty when you're trying to write about somebody who is not at all well known" (306). Fitzgerald is better known now than Charlotte Mew; nevertheless, perhaps Lee's inclusion of Fitzgerald's drawings in her biography shares her subject's sentiments about the extent to which they say something about her as someone not that well known and also hard to know.

In the first part of the biography, Lee subverts chronology and writes about the books written later in Fitzgerald's life about her early years. She places her discussion of them within the chapters that are about the time of Fitzgerald's life to which they are connected, drawing our attention to the autobiographical influences that inform and are transformed in these stories. Her first group of novels, *The Bookshop* (1978), *Offshore* (1979) and *Human Voices* (1980), draw on Fitzgerald's own life and are discussed in these early chapters. *At Freddie* (1982) was the last of her autobiographical novels:

> It takes off from her own life more loosely and freely than *Human Voices*, *The Bookshop* or *Offshore*, and so it stands at the turning-point between the 'autobiographical' novels of the 1970s and the 'historical' novels (though neither term quite fits) of the 1980s and 1990s. (202)

In her late sixties, Fitzgerald decides "to stop writing fiction that drew directly on her own life" (307), although she continues to transform her experience and what matters to her in her writing:

> her own experiences, feelings and beliefs would, from now on, be metamorphosed into novels set in 1950s Florence, Russia before the revolution, Cambridge in the 1910s and late eighteenth century Germany. The things that most matter to her shaped these historical books just as much as they did her autobiographical novels. (307)

The first book that Fitzgerald wrote was a biography of the Victorian designer and painter Edward Burne-Jones. Lee's biography notes, in a sentence that both seems to paraphrase Fitzgerald's own view and, perhaps, echoes the perspective of Fitzgerald's biographical narrator, that

"It is the job of the biographer to enter the inner life, understand the obsessive images, and see how they become the 'burden' of the works" (225). The 'burden', as Lee's biography quotes Fitzgerald, is "the totality of the given thing which is not complete until it has been understood by a sympathetic attention" (225). This burden is explored in Fitzgerald's life of Burne-Jones and Lee's life of Fitzgerald. In another section about Fitzgerald's views on biography, Lee notes Fitzgerald thinking about the relationship between fiction and biography and commenting that "biographers are madder than novelists" (262), but Lee does not make her own comment in response. At the end of the biography, Lee does comment on her experience of meeting with Fitzgerald. She identifies these meetings and interviews as encounters and they become another version of the "encounter narratives" Lee subsequently writes about in 2015.[10] When Lee's questions attempt "to elicit her life-story and the secrets of her writing life" (433), they "were met, politely and affably, with well-trodden phrases from other interviews … and evasive deflection masquerading as changes of subject" (433). In Lee's interviews with her and in a reading of her life and work, Fitzgerald is hard to know. Following her death, in her archive, Lee feels "the speaking presence of the gaps and silences left in the metaphorical greases between the pages I am reading" (434); she appreciates that in her novels Fitzgerald "both kept herself concealed and gave herself away" (262). Lee recognises that there "are many things she did not want anyone to know about her, and which no one will ever know. I find this frustrating, amusing, seductive, and admirable" (434). Yet, as we peer into what we can see of her marriage and family life and see some of the connections or transformations between her life and her writing that this biography suggests to us, we come to know something about what she was like and, although we will never really know her at all, Lee's sympathetic attention has offered her reading of the burden of her life and work.

Lee draws on the inheritance of her subjects as life, reading and writing are understood as integral to each other. Distinctive features in her biographical writing are a concern with storytelling, the use of a range of literary techniques, including subverting the conventions of chronological time, and an exploration of the self-fashioning of a literary subject in her life, especially her writing. She understands the life of Woolf, Wharton and Fitzgerald in the context of the historical times in which they lived, exploring the different selves and possibilities of her subjects, and not being afraid to let us hear the voice of the narrator. This is a process that needs a special kind of courage in the biographer, who also recognises her subject's courage. On the first page of her biography of Virginia Woolf, Lee expresses her fears about biographical writing:

> There are many times, writing this, when I have been afraid of Virginia Woolf. I think I would have been afraid of meeting her. I am afraid of not being intelligent enough for her. Reading and writing her life, I am often afraid … *for* her. (1997a, 3, original emphasis)

In an essay published shortly after the appearance of the biography, "Am I Afraid of Virginia Woolf?" (1998), Lee explores the nature of this fear as it becomes a trope to explain a biographer's relationship with her subjects and other readers. In the essay, Lee believes that "Courage and fear are vital counter-forces in Virginia Woolf's writing about biography" (1998, 235). Lee places this sense of courage in the context of women's writing as a whole: fearlessness "is an important word for Virginia Woolf when she is talking about other writers" (235), and perhaps it is also important for Lee. Lee found Woolf's approach encouraging and took pleasure "in thinking about the relationship between the word 'encouragement' and the word 'courage'" (236), concluding that "It might be possible for biography to be *about* fear, as well as unafraid" (237). The biographer has to have courage to write about the fear she has of her subject, and perhaps all writers need courage, particularly when they seek to challenge myths and orthodoxy:

> The biographer has to be a pioneer, going "ahead of the rest of us, like the miner's canary, testing the atmosphere, detecting falsity, unreality, and the presence of obsolete conventions". So "There are some stories which have to be retold by each generation." (1997a, 11)

Here, the writer Hermione Lee is quoting the voice of her subject, Virginia Woolf, as this reader is quoting Lee, so we hear both the voices of subject and biographer in this metanarrative about, and conversation with, British biography. My conversation with Hermione Lee continued when we met in 2016 and both our voices, as reader and writer, become part of my ongoing reading of, and writing about, her work, as well as that of her subjects. I was looking for echoes and nuances that would add to my reading not only of her work but of biography, other life-writing and of fiction in general. This body of reading is all part of my fascination with the lives of other people, which always seem to be much more interesting than my own.

In Conversation with Hermione Lee

What, in your view, are the key shifts in biography that are breaking new ground today?
There have been all kinds of changes in biographical traditions in recent years, including treating unexpected subjects, treating them in a different way, using different structures for biography, and experimenting with different kinds of voices. I do see much more versatility and fluidity in the biographical form than, say, in the early twentieth century, and I welcome it.

A biography can now be based on one year in a person's life, or viewed from many aspects. You can also have group lives, a number of short lives in one volume. If you think of a book like Jenny Uglow's *The Lunar Men*, or Alison Light's book about Virginia Woolf's servants, there you have examples of bringing together different lives in complex ways. Obviously, there are great benefits in all these varied forms.

I sometimes feel that I am stuck with the old model of a single life on an individual writer, and that everybody is saying, "Oh you can't do that anymore". But, in fact, I think there is still value in that approach. So, there are as many ways to do biography as there are writers. And I love the fact that there are no fixed rules.

What are you views about Richard Ellmann's view of the social self in biography?[11]
This is one of the things that interests me about biography, and when I gave an inaugural lecture here in Oxford in 1999 for the Goldsmith's Professorship, I took Richard Ellmann's line about the social self as my kicking-off point. The lecture was called "Reading in bed" and it was about women's reading, and how historically it has often been private and secret. Biography also needs to get at "the secret self", to use Katherine Mansfield's phrase, or the private self, or the interior self. What you are constantly doing in biography is to try and balance this seesaw between the social self, as Ellmann describes it, and the interior self, the self that is really hard to get at. And often you can't get at it. One of the things Woolf talks about is how impossible it is for biography to access the private interior self.

History and cultural networks are very much involved with the social self, and of course you have to address that in a biography. But if you don't also try and access the interior self then you have not succeeded.

Do you think it's still helpful to make a distinction between scholarly, chronicle and popular, more personal biography?
There are many different kinds of biography, and they overlap at the edges. So, if you go to one end of the spectrum, you have lives of rock stars and sports people and so on. They will often take the form of ghost-written autobiographies, written when the person is still very young. They are obviously at the very opposite end of the range from something like a long, footnoted scholarly life of Gibbon. But there are of course overlaps. So, biography sits oddly within academic life. Take Roy Foster, the historian who wrote a magnificent two-volume scholarly life of Yeats; he also loves the gossip, he is fascinated by the person and all his idiosyncrasies, and that is what you need to include.

When she set out to write her life of Charlotte Brontë, Elizabeth Gaskell famously put this little notice on her desk saying, "If you love your reader, get anecdotes". And anecdotes are what we are all after. I think hard-line historians sometimes think there is something slightly dubious about biography. Richard Holmes is very good and funny about the idea of biography as being disreputable, which is why it hasn't sat very happily inside academic structures until the last few decades.

I am interested in the extent to which you write about the lives of women.
Well, I am currently writing a life of Tom Stoppard, so that is a departure, and I have written critical books about male writers before. But, I am, of course, very interested in the lives of women, and of great women writers. Bowen, Cather, Wharton, Woolf, Fitzgerald are very different kinds of women, but they all have extremely idiosyncratic voices, very powerful personalities, very interesting lives and they are not all English. They inhabit the 1860s through to 2000, which has been my period, broadly speaking.

These subjects are all women whose work has influenced me tremendously and I wouldn't be writing about them if I was not interested in their work. That is where I start. I am a literary critic who turned into a biographer, and I teach literature, that is where I come from. I wouldn't want to write about someone whose work didn't interest me, just for the sake of the life-story.

They are all women who aren't easily categorised as feminists. Woolf is obviously a leading feminist writer, whatever she says about the word feminism! But Cather and Wharton and Bowen are ambivalent about belonging to any group or movement.[12]

How would you describe your relationship with your subjects? I am interested in the idea of the biographer and the biographee as having a conversation.
I am very attracted to them as minds, and as people. I am curious about them, I want to find out more about them. I want to write the book about them that I haven't read. So, with Edith Wharton I didn't feel that the European dimension had been satisfactorily dealt with, that she was always the grand American Gilded Age lady who happened to spend some time in France. I wanted to turn that version of her around and look at her life from a different point of view, which is why that biography starts in Paris.

With Woolf, I was reacting quite strongly against a phase in the late 1980s when she was being seen by some writers as a kind of victim or invalid. I wanted to write about the very active, politically conscious, professional side of her, and that approach is clearly of its time too. Someone would write a different book about Woolf now. With Bowen and Cather, I felt they were underread at that time, and I felt the same about Fitzgerald. My books were partly rescue operations. In a sense, I wanted to present them to the world. That is a very important motive for me. I want more people to know about these wonderful writers, and to fall in love with them, even though my own relationship is not necessarily that of someone who has fallen in love.

I don't believe in having to be completely adoring of your subjects. You have to be critical, you have to be objective. It's a job, it's not a marriage, and you have got to have a sense of perspective. And when they do and say horrible things, which all of them do, you have got to make this clear.

So, my relationship with my subjects is based on a mixture of attraction to the work, attraction to the idea of the person, curiosity about the person, a need to write something that I don't feel had been written about them before, and a desire to have an objective sense of what their life adds up to.

Do you think of yourself as a writer?
Yes, I am a writer, I am very interested in the writing process. I like my books to be well-written and if possible stylish, I like to write good sentences. I hope there are some bits that are moving, or funny. But I wouldn't be writing these books if it weren't for these great creative minds who have spun their work out of themselves like spiders' webs.

I can tell stories, and I can marshal the detail, evoke a person, structure an anecdote, but I can't make things up. And I don't think biographies *should* make things up, so I am clearly in the right business.

As a biographer, you are an amateur mixture of an anthropologist, a social historian, a psychoanalyst, a detective and a doctor. If biography is going to be good, you have probably got to have a set of adaptable skills, or be prepared to read up on certain ways of analysing a person.

To what extent have you tried to challenge the conventions of realist biography?
My writing is not intentionally unconventional. I have tried to think very hard about biographical form, and biographical structure. The essence of it for me is trying to make the form work for the subject. Although my books all look much the same—big, solid—I have tried to make the forms somehow suit the subjects, or evoke the subjects.

You have written that "biography for the moment will give the truest answer to the question, what was she or he like?" Could you explain what you mean by that?
You have got to feel that for this moment I possess this subject, and I am the person who is going to get this subject across in as true, authentic and vivid a way as possible. While you are writing, unless you have got this sense of ownership, it is not going to work. You must feel that you have something to say about this person that matters. Then you have to let go, because someone else will come along and write another biography about the same person, although possibly not about Penelope Fitzgerald for a while. But Wharton, Cather, Bowen and Virginia Woolf will be redone and redone. And that is the wonderful thing about them, they stay with us. The next biographer will write their version, and it will be a different version, and you will read it and you might not like it, but you must let go and not be possessive.

I am interested in the extent to which you take a thematic approach in your biographies, so could you say something about that?
I don't think I had a theory about this when I wrote a life of Virginia Woolf, I began to think very hard about the structure. She writes so much herself about her suspicion of, and resistance to, traditional biographical modes, which in her time were still somewhat hagiographical and bland. She had been brought up on the kind of three-volume Victorian biographies where not a word of criticism is uttered about

the subject. Though she does rather caricature Victorian biography! I wanted to reflect on her own thoughts about biography, and the first chapter in that book is about that. I wanted to imitate what she said she did with her characters in *Mrs. Dalloway*: "I dig out big caves behind my characters". I didn't want to keep just driving the action along a chronological line. I wanted to have moments of thematic stillness, where you think about her reading, or her friendship with Katherine Mansfield. Many is the time when I was writing that book that I thought, why did I set myself this difficult structure? The narrative also needed to move chronologically, because not everyone reading the book would have already read another book about Virginia Woolf. And you are always torn, as her biographer, between two kinds of readers, the ones who know all about her, and the ones who know nothing about her.

Then, with Edith Wharton, because she is such a material girl, I wanted the chapters to be like very thickly furnished rooms. The book is thick with stuff. You go into the Henry James room, or the Italian room, or the France-at-war room. It is more stately, it is more caparisoned than my book about Woolf. And with Fitzgerald I wanted to thin down and make it more spare, because her own writing is very, very spare. She buries a huge amount, and she would have buried more if she could. I wanted to make that book less freighted, less weighty. And with Stoppard, because he is alive, because he is a playwright, it needs to be more rapid, more immediate in tone, more provisional and dramatic.

One real issue for any biographer is what to do with all the other lives in the life of the person you are writing about? It is a big challenge with Tom Stoppard, and with Woolf and Wharton. They are surrounded by fascinating people. You have to say, 'Sorry, I can't tell your story, you are on the edge of this story'. But these are people who have got to be included, because they may be very important in the life of your subject.

You have written about biography as a type of makeover?
Not exactly. I am very interested in performativity. There is a chapter in my biography of Woolf called "Selves" where I try and get at all the different ways in which she is presenting herself both to herself and to other people. There are many different selves in her make-up. She herself says in *Orlando*, we don't have one self, we have thousands of selves. I was particularly interested in the different ways in which she presents herself in the diary, to other people, in her writing. Everybody is complex and contradictory, and, perhaps, particularly writers. You need to look at the clash between how they are presenting themselves and what they are

feeling. And sometimes you can't get at that, because it is hidden. But I like secrets, and I like things that I can't get at.

There is one specific example of 'making up' in one of my books. As a small child, before she could read, Wharton used to take books out of her father's bookcase and put them on her lap, usually upside down, and then she would make up a story which she would speak out loud. And she called this 'making up', she had a compulsion to do it. When her mother would say, 'Edith you have got to come and meet these nice little boys and girls who have come to tea', she would say, 'Mother, I would much rather stay indoors and make up'. This was obviously a natural writer in the making, and someone resisting her parents.

In biography, to what extent can we can understand the lives of writers through their reading, and can biography be understood as a form of reading a life that you then share with other readers?
One of my main motives for writing these books is that I want people to read the work of the writers I write about. I believe that many more readers in the United States and in the United Kingdom have been reading Fitzgerald because of my biography, and that was part of the motive for writing the biography in the first place.

As for the reading that my subjects do, any writer is partly what they read. What they read and how they read is an enormous part of their lives. I think this is true of all of my subjects. Very much so with Wharton. Wharton's library is an integral part of that whole story, which I physically lived with for quite a long time when I worked in a room that had all her remaining books in it.

Woolf's reading is a hugely significant and deep part of her life, and that is why I have a whole chapter on it. Hours and hours of time was spent just reading and reading and reading and often lots of things at once. And you can see it soaking into her work. It is a crucial part of the life-story, and I love writing about that.

NOTES

1. Lee defines them as: 'Making up' is "to compose or constitute a whole (of parts); to put together or prepare something (like mortar) from parts or ingredients; to arrange type and illustrations on a page; and to concoct and invent a story" (28), and 'Making over' can mean both "'to transfer

the possession of something to someone', and 'to completely transform or remodel something'" (2005, 28).

2. Other recent studies of biographical perspectives in science include Higgitt, Rebekah, *Recreating Newton: Newtonian Biography and the Making of Nineteenth Century History of Science* (2007) and Kafar, Marcin, ed., *Scientific Biographies: Between the 'Professional' and 'Non-Professional' Dimensions of Humanistic Experiences* (2014). Higgitt's study considers the extent to which Newton's biography was fashioned by others, and illustrates "the way in which the biography of an important figure is moulded through the interaction of a number of individuals" (2007, 194). This has meant that some aspects of his life have received different levels of attention.

3. In an essay, Lee discusses Michael Cunningham's different versions of Virginia Woolf in his novel *The Hours* (1998), which was used as the basis of a film of the same name in 2003. Cunningham's novel is concerned with "whether a single person has more than one self, one way of being. He is particularly interested in life as being, like writing, a kind of performance" (Lee 2005, 37), and he asks questions "about how we value our lives" (38). This notion of performance is a useful way of thinking about the way in which biographers fashion the lives of their subjects, re-creating a version of a life or lives.

4. Allen Hibbard proposes that

> The dynamic between biographer and subject resembles the hermeneutic process described by Paul Ricoeur, in which the configuration of the work is refigured in the act of reading. This collaboration is made possible by the writer's and reader's shared notions of language and time (represented through narrative). In a similar fashion, a subject's life is refigured and given definition by the biographer. Ricoeur argues that the meaning-making activity is characterized by interaction, not independent activity. (2006, 33)

This suggests that the process of biography is bound up with both reading and writing, as it is in the life of any writer.

5. At a couple of points in the biography, Lee writes about the ways in which Wharton tries to put together her version of her life for any future biography by pulling together specific pieces of evidence, "in an envelope labelled 'For my biographer'" (2008, 382), and in one of her notebooks "where she had been jotting personal thoughts since 1924" (653). Like other writers, Wharton was concerned about how her life would be represented after her death.

6. Lee suggests that, "Privacy is of great importance to her, and its violation is one of her subjects" (2008, 11).

7. Lee makes the point that Wharton uses her poems "in contrast to the novels, to sum up her life to herself" (2008, 638). In doing so, they become another way in which she tries to transform her life in her writing.
8. Lee makes a comparable point in her study of Willa Cather's writing: "although she draws intensely on her personal experience her fiction is not satisfactorily accounted for in biographical terms" (1997b, 3). Cather draws on her memories and memorialising "and stories she had been told" (19). Lee comments that this "is how stories are made, by the 'grafting' of some other 'outside' person onto the writer's own life. Her characters are 'composites', not individual portraits" (21). Life is transformed in fiction, but is not directly autobiographical.
9. Lee writes in more detail about Edith Wharton's passion for house and gardens in "A Great House Full of Rooms" in a collection edited by Mark Bostridge, *Lives for Sale* (2004).
10. Lee, "'From Memory': Literary Encounters and Life-Writing" (2015).
11. Richard Ellmann argued that "biography is essentially social. For the biographer, who himself represents the outside world, the social self is the real self, the self only comes to exist when juxtaposed with other people. The solitary self is a pressure upon the social self … it has no independent life" (1971, 4).
12. Lee, *Willa Cather: A Life Saved Up* (London: Virago, 1989). Also see, *Elizabeth Bowen* (1981) by Hermione Lee.

REFERENCES

Aubin, David, and Charlotte Bigg. 2007. Neither Genius Nor Context Incarnate: Norman Lockyer, Jules Janssen and the Astrophysical Self. In *The History and Poetics of Scientific Biography*, ed. Thomas Soderqvist, 51–70. Aldershot, Hampshire: Ashgate.

Bate, Jonathan. 2009. First published in 2008. *Soul of the Age: The Life, Mind and World of William Shakespeare*. London: Penguin.

Ellmann, Richard. 1971. *Literary Biography: An Inaugural Lecture*. Oxford: Clarendon Press.

Hibbard, Alan. 2006. Biographer and Subject: A Tale of Two Narratives. *South Central Review* 23 (3): 19–36.

Higgitt, Rebekah. 2007. *Recreating Newton: Newtonian Biography and the Making of Nineteenth Century History of Science*. London: Pickering & Chatto.

Lee, Hermione. 1997a. First published in 1996. *Virginia Woolf*. London: Vintage.

———. 1997b. First published in 1989. *Willa Cather: A Life Saved Up*. London: Virago.

————. 1998. Am I Afraid of Virginia Woolf? In *Writing the Lives of Writers*, ed. Warwick Gould and Thomas Staley, 224–237. London: Macmillan.

————. 2005. *Body Parts: Essays on Life-Writing*. London: Chatto & Windus.

————. 2008. First published in 2007. *Edith Wharton*. London: Vintage.

————. 2009. *Biography: A Very Short Introduction*. New York: Oxford University Press.

————. 2013. *Penelope Fitzgerald: A Life*. London: Chatto & Windus.

————. 2015. 'From Memory': Literary Encounters and Life-Writing. In *On Life-Writing*, ed. Zachary Leader, 124–141. Oxford: Oxford University Press.

MacCarthy, Desmond. 1953. Lytton Strachey and the Art of Biography, Circa 1934. In *Memories*, ed. Desmond MacCarthy, 31–49. London: MacGibbon & Kee.

Monk, Ray. 2004. Objectivity, Postmodernism and Biographical Understanding: Andrew Collier on R.D. Laing. In *Defending Objectivity: Essays in Honour of Andrew Collier*, ed. Margaret S. Archer, and William Outhwaite, 33–47. London: Routledge.

Wagner-Martin, Linda. 1994. *Telling Women's Lives: The New Biography*. New Brunswick, NJ: Rutgers University Press.

CHAPTER 6

R. Holmes Vibrating in Uncertainty

A discussion about the haunting by R. Holmes of recent British biography is just one way to approach a comparative reading of late twentieth- and early twenty-first century popular biography. There are three R. Holmes biographers from this period who are all based in Britain— military historian Edward Richard Holmes, known as Richard Holmes, Rachel Holmes, and the Romantic biographer Richard Holmes—and each of them has a distinctive approach to storytelling in biography. Unless one is writing a chronicle of all the facts about someone's life, narrative will inevitably intervene to create a story that is more than a chronicle, a list or a statement of events. In doing so, in the case of more personal, popular biography, a story is re-created that is a version of a life or lives. Each of these biographers offers a version of a life, or group of lives, based on the facts available, and an imaginative approach towards structure, language, style and tone in their narratives.

Our first R. Holmes, Edward Richard Holmes (1946–2011), a well-known British military historian and biographer, is fascinated by the life of Wellington (1769–1852). His subject is a member of the establishment, a representative of his class and a major heroic military figure. Towards the end of a dazzling military career, Wellington, who "never lost a major battle" (2003, xv), led the British army that defeated Napoleon at Waterloo in 1815 and went on to become prime minister. E.R. Holmes was drawn to this iconic figure:

© The Author(s) 2017
J. McVeigh, *In Collaboration with British Literary Biography*,
DOI 10.1007/978-3-319-58383-9_6

> I was the sort of boy who has heroes, and ... the Duke of Wellington was
> firmly enshrined in my personal pantheon. He seemed to have every virtue
> ... I admired the duke's iron sense of duty ... He was brave ... Like many
> young men, I saw bravery as the ultimate virtue. (xv)

However, as he grows older "and looked harder at the evidence" (xvi),
his biographer realises that, "there were an awful lot of cracks in the
ducal portrait. Wellington was not invincible" (xvi). Holmes tries to
find the "real Wellington" (xviii), and to get as close to him as he and
some of his biographers would let him. He is "determined to rub away
as much of the varnish as I could" (xviii). In doing so, he pursues his
subject to places that lay at the heart of his professional life by visiting
"as many Wellingtonian battlefields as I could" (xviii). E.R. Holmes
believes that, "travelling by road in India at the tail of the monsoon told
me just as much about the man as *The Maratha War Papers of Arthur
Wellesley*" (xviii). At times, he writes in the first person when describing
some aspect of these journeys: "I have long felt that there is a particular merit to viewing a battlefield from horseback: that extra few feet of
height improves the view, and the horses can go where most vehicles
cannot" (75).[1] As a result, the biographer could share Wellington's view
of the battlefield. When he crosses the Kaitna river on his horse, this
"emphasised the sheer difficult of Wellesley's plan" (77). He writes lyri-
cally about this experience: Rani, his horse,

> was not at her best after three hours in the back of a truck. As I nudged
> her down the muddy slope into the fast-flowing Kaitna, my spirits, cast
> down by the weather and worries about more floods, lifted. (77)

There are a few entertaining moments in the biography that almost lapse
into melodrama. Commander-in-Chief Arthur Wellesley, subsequently
appointed as the Duke of Wellington in 1814, is nearly caught by the
French in the battle of Talavera, on 27-28 July 1809:

> Wellesley pounded along the upstairs corridor from the tower and leapt
> down the stairs to escape. He jumped onto his horse and was away with
> the shots of the skirmishers popping away behind him. (135)

The biography paints a picture of a man who had the "lonely quality
of the outsider about him" (3), was prone to "sweeping judgements"

(15), with "utter confidence in himself" (42), and an "almost pathologi-
cal need to remain in control" (58). He believed that "things inevitably went wrong if he was not present" (151), and he became "what we
would now term a control freak" (169). Wellington had a difficult relationship with his wife Kitty and was very distant, both literally and metaphorically, from his sons. The biography comments that he feels more at
home in his professional life and "managed to create, in his busy head-
quarters, that happy family life that had eluded him elsewhere" (181).
The biography closes with Wellington's doubleness as a man "easy to
admire, harder, perhaps, to like" (303), and with his biographer's voice:

> Now that I have followed him from Ireland to India, from the Peninsula
> to Waterloo, and finally from Walmer Castle to St Paul's Cathedral, I
> admire him more than I ever have … he was indeed a great man. (303)[2]

Some biographies, given their interest in a particular field or profession,
promote versions of a life that may touch on the personal values and interests of the biographer. Edward Richard Holmes's biography of Wellington
is such a biography, in which his subject's flaws are presented but do not
dim his biographer's admiration for his professional achievements. He
may or may not have agreed with the British twentieth century historian
A.J.P. Taylor about the status of biographical narratives. Adam Sisman's
biography of Taylor notes that "One of Alan's favourite phrases was that
history is a version of events. 'The fact that there are other versions does
not make any one of them wrong. It is just like taking different views
about a human being'" (1994, 400). E.R. Holmes's biography has created his version of Wellington and been brave enough to make this overt
by writing about his connection with his subject. This suggests that the
Commander-in-Chief was a solitary man admired for his military achievements, whilst not, perhaps, being a great husband or father.

E.R. Holmes's other books include biographies of Winston Churchill
and John Churchill, 1st Duke of Marlborough, a commentary on his visits to battlefields and a social history about the life of ordinary soldiers.[3]
He commences his biography of Marlborough with questions about previous hagiographies of the general. His opening line is, "Some will tell
you that John Churchill … was Britain's greatest ever general" (2008, 1),
but this biography is keen to do more than just make this case. His biographer suggests that, "there is much more to the man than stout hagiography can possibly acknowledge" (5). Again, he wants to "get as close …

as I can to the man" (6), and, in doing so, to make "extensive use of the duke's own words" (6). The biographer is keen to present the voice of his subject, to set him talking.

In his biography of Winston Churchill, *In the Footsteps of Churchill* (2005), published to accompany a BBC television series, E.R. Holmes finds it much harder to maintain the distance from his subject that he hopes he has achieved in his other biographies: "the fact that I generally refer to him … as Winston is indicative, for I would no more have styled Wellington Arthur than I would have called French Johnny [Field Marshall Sir John French, commander of the British Expeditionary Force in 1914–1915]" (2005, 7). This is another biography in which the biographer finds it important to visit the places that played a part in Churchill's life and "coloured my view of the man" (8), but he is aware that, metaphorically speaking, "following in Winston's footsteps involves being wary of the false trails he laid, as well as of the places where his tracks have been deliberately obscured by the enraged trampling of those upon whose toes he trod" (9). The title of this biography echoes the perspective of his namesake, the Romantic biographer Richard Holmes, that he follows in his subjects' footsteps. Again, the main aim of his biography of Winston Churchill is to "illuminate the character of the man" (8), but there are dangers in doing so as his subject makes up and fashions a version of his life in his own writing.

E.R. Holmes writes about both the lives of 'great' generals of whom he is in awe, although they may not be particularly likeable men, and ordinary men and women who serve as soldiers. British journalist John Crace notes in an interview in 2004 that he is "not in the business of glorifying war" (2004, 20), and E.R. Holmes himself is quoted in the interview as believing that "the ordinary soldiers have been somewhat marginalised" (20) in military histories. Military historian Gary Sheffield, in a review of his history of British soldiering, suggests that E.R. Holmes "combined learning with a wonderfully entertaining writing style and formidable communication skills" (2011), and that he was "a fine scholar who was also, in the very best sense, a highly effective popular historian" (2011). Edward Richard Holmes writes popular biography, and is interested in both the lives of the 'great and the good' as well as 'the good but not famous'.

In an article about some of the problems of writing military biography, he suggests that a military biographer "must strive particularly hard to strike a fair balance and to remain objective" (61), and he understands the dangers of hagiography, given that "an author is presumably far more likely to embark upon a biography of somebody he is at least sympathetic with rather than of someone he detests" (61). In his view, "Few reputable biographers present their subjects as omniscient figures who invariably make the right decisions. They balance strengths against weaknesses" (61). E.R. Holmes considers the pros and cons of First World War generals who maintain a safe distance from the battlefield, or get too close in an effort to empathise with their troops, thereby putting their own objectivity at risk. Similarly, it is hard for a biographer to understand the personality of a general, a key figure in any conflict: "Step too close, and you risk being caught up in the surge of your subject's charisma: step too far, and his gestures and traits seem absurdly contrived and theatrical" (61). He is a biographer who empathises with his subjects but understands the dangers of getting too sympathetic and partisan, as he aims to remain objective. His narrative is full of anecdotes and lyrical passages that keeps his story moving. As a biographer, he makes a connection by visiting the places that were important to his subject and he is not afraid to use the first person or make his personal connection with his subject overt. He also tries to ensure that the reader can hear the voice of his subject in his writing as much as possible.

Our second R. Holmes, contemporary biographer and cultural historian Rachel Holmes, is interested in an iconic figure of quite a different nature in *The Hottentot Venus: The Life and Death of Saartjie Baartman Born 1789—Buried 2002* (2007). Feminism and a concern with the discrimination and racism experienced by black people in the nineteenth century lies at the heart of her writing. She notes that Saartjie Baartman is "South Africa's most famous and revered national icon of the colonial era" (2007, xiv). She was a black South African woman transported to experience appalling discriminatory treatment in nineteenth century London and Paris. She died unloved and dreadfully mistreated in Europe. But, in 2002, her remains were returned to a funeral in South Africa attended by thousands of people. Rachel Holmes suggests that Saartjie's tragic experience as a black woman translates her into

> a living ancestor. Nations, like individuals, need myths and icons to salve and heal the psychological and physical injury inflicted by oppressive systems ... Saartjie's homecoming was a tangible act to right a historical wrong. (177)

Moreover, Saartjie "became a representative historical figure in South Africa's struggle for gender equality" (177). This life matters because it is representative, illuminating larger themes and issues about the lives of women and colonial abuses of power and endemic discrimination.

The title of Rachel Holmes's biography is an important aspect of the story that it tells. It indicates that this is a life of someone who came from a place where the Greek image of a beautiful woman, like the goddess Venus, had an additional meaning. Hottentot was the name given by white Europeans to the tribe of Khoisan people that Saartjie belonged to and is now understood as an offensive label: "'Hottentot' and 'Bushman' are among the most pejorative and contested terms in the lexicon of South African history" (Holmes 2007, 11). The name Venus suggests a story about a woman who is known for her beauty, but it is in fact a story about the abuse of beauty and identity, as Saartjie Baartman was commodified as an exhibit. Her body was put on display to paying audiences in London and Paris. Her life literally embodies the discrimination that she and other black people experienced in nineteenth century Europe. Furthermore, the title draws attention to details about her death and after-life. This is reinforced by the date reflected in the title, when Saartjie was returned to, and buried in, South Africa in 2002, more than two hundred years after her birth. The use of time and chronology is important in this biography as the story becomes about more than the life of the woman herself. It is representative of the decades in which her body was further objectified after her death, as her body parts were kept for dissection and analysis. Her body was still on display until the 1970s; even in death, she remained an exhibit.

In the opening two sections of the biography, "A Note on Naming", and a first chapter, "Phoenomenon", Rachel Holmes draws further attention to the nature of her story and seems to play on the nature of a phenomenon by using an obsolete spelling of it as her title. The way in which Saartjie Baartman was treated should have been obsolete, but she is displayed as a 'phoenomenon' on the advertisement that promoted her appearance in London. In a short section on naming, the biography explains that the '–tjie' diminutive in Afrikaans ironically expresses endearment; however, "because using the diminutive form of a noun reduces the size of what it names, the '–tjie' suffix has also been used to subordinate and enforce servitude" (xiv). The '–tjie' suffix during the colonial eras and apartheid was used "to indicate contempt, belittlement and domination over black people" (xiv). Saartjie has also been known by the Anglophone Sarah, or Sara, and both names "share the recognition that naming is one of the profound forms of power" (xiv). The first chapter of the biography also opens with a focus on her name: "Saartjie Baartman, stage-name 'The Hottentot Venus', emerged from behind a crimson velvet curtain" (1), so the performative and commodified nature of her identity is reinforced straight away. A sense of her body on public display, as her privacy is stripped away, is emphasised by a copy of the advertisement that announces her appearance on stage at the start of this first chapter. A short anecdote about a visit to the theatre to see her by John Kemble, "the nation's most famous actor" (3), and the celebrated comedian Charles Mathews, illustrates the extent to which attending this kind of event was acceptable, as Saartjie becomes infamous rather than famous. It is recorded in Mathews's diary that Kemble feels very sorry for her.[4] Nevertheless, they did nothing to help her, as did nobody else. Saartjie becomes a hugely successful theatrical phenomenon and the biography goes on to tell the story about what happened to her, whilst much of her personal identity and experience remain hidden. Her life is representative of colonial repression and discrimination, as Rachel Holmes notes at the end of her book in a further allusion to her name: "Baartman is a very common South African surname; there are Baartmans among all races and religions" (177). Her first name, Saartjie, also becomes representative of the experience of black South African women abused by colonial and patriarchal forces beyond their control.

Dr James Barry served as a military doctor in South Africa and was a senior army officer by the time of his death. This is a figure whose footsteps Rachel Holmes, in *Scanty Particulars: The Mysterious, Astonishing and Remarkable Life of Victorian Surgeon James Barry* (2003), follows on "many unexpected journeys" (2003, 1) in the pursuit of evidence about his life. Her biography, taking a conventional biographical approach, begins at the beginning of his life, although the opening sentence highlights her difficulty with doing so: "It is a vexing prospect for any biographer to attempt to write about a subject who appears to have had no childhood" (1). In the preface, she discusses the extent to which most narratives about Barry start with discoveries made following his death. The very fact that this biography comes across as a conventional chronological tale and does not deal with, or discuss in any detail, Barry's death until the end of the book, is its main rhetorical characteristic: "James Barry's death in the hot summer of 1865 occasioned a revelation that sent shockwaves throughout the British medical and military establishment" (2). Rachel Holmes is concerned that if "we start at the end of Barry's story, we lose the sense of how the public life of one of the nineteenth century's most innovative and charismatic doctors was lived" (3). This biography is concerned with questions about gender equality and both the public and personal life of the subject. It is about an exemplary but unsung military and medical hero who

> campaigned tirelessly for the humanitarian rights of the patient ... [opened] up the vistas of modern medicine ... [and was a] champion of the socially marginalized and economically disposed ... On three continents, Barry implemented new methods of hygiene, sanitation, quarantine, diet, and effective treatment of some of the most virulent diseases known to the age. (4)

But the nature of what we mean by a hero is questioned in this biography. Like Saartjie Baartman, Barry "was much more than just the sum of his physical parts" (320) and his public-facing self comes to embody his professional identity, whilst his physical body and personal identity remains hidden: "His body conditioned his experiences, but it did not finally determine who he was or what he achieved. This is what makes James Barry a hero" (320). The biography identifies Barry as a man, but his death revealed that he had the body of a woman. The evidence to positively confirm why he adopted a male persona is not available, although his life as a doctor would have been impossible without it.

Rachel Holmes has written a coherent narrative based on uncertainty, given that we do not know what Barry himself thought. She is keen not to seek a simplistic resolution to questions about Barry's gender, and believes "his choice of identity should be respected" (323). What matters in this biography is to acknowledge the huge achievements in his professional life: "All great men are defined by the institutions they create, join or develop. James Barry was a great man in just this way" (322). This is an exemplary biography about a heroic figure who was very much part of the 'great and the good' but who subverted many of the conventions of his time. At the end of her biography, Rachel Holmes, using the first person, describes the end of her pursuit and journey with Barry:

> I sit writing the end of Barry's story at the southernmost tip of the world ... Barry never truly belonged anywhere, but it was in his progressive

desire to struggle against injustice and inequality that Barry finally can claim his belonging ... I bid adieu to James Barry. My journey is over.

Dr James Barry has haunted me, but will continue to wander the pathways of our imaginations, in search of the spirit of an age, now or in the future, that can accommodate his difference. The world will continue to disagree on the phenomenon of James Barry, but then as Barry observed, "in fact, the world in general disagrees". (2003, 326)

She makes connections between place and time; her own journey has been haunted by her conversation with Barry. He fashioned his life literally and metaphorically in a way that was a direct challenge to the world of the great and the good in which he moved. This is an innovative and alternative form of exemplary biography.[5]

Samuel Johnson famously stated that "more knowledge may be gained of a man's real character, by a short conversation with one of his servants, than from a formal and studied narrative" (1888, 83). There is one figure in this life-story about whom we know even less, the life of Barry's "constant companion, his nameless black servant ... [who] might have been able to tell us something more about the truth of Barry's identity" (Rachel Holmes 2003, 324), particularly as he accompanied him on his travels for three decades. We know less about him than the life of Frances Barber, Johnson's own servant, and both his relationship with Barry and his own life remain hidden from view.

Finally, Richard Holmes, the Romantic biographer, is fascinated by the life of his first biographical subject, Percy Bysshe Shelley (1792–1822), which also has historical resonance. Holmes argues that his biography was "part of a much larger and continuing biographic process of bringing the present to bear imaginatively on the past" (2005b, xii). Shelley had "an overwhelming consciousness of his duty as an *artist* in the immense and fiery process of social change of which he knew himself to be a part" (xiv). Out of his hatred of authority grew, according to Holmes, Shelley's passionate radical beliefs. The biography suggests that his poems and other writing were "responses to political and social crises in society" (569). He comments that Shelley "did not say that great literature actually produced great revolutions; or vice versa. He seemed rather to feel that the two ran a mysteriously parallel course" (584). Holmes draws on connections that he sees between the 1960s, when he was a student, and the Romantic period. He suggests that his Shelley biography, like all biography, "reflects often unconsciously the concerns and questions of its own age, and it passes on something hidden to the future" (x). As he puts it in *Footsteps* (1985), looking back on the 1960s, "what I was feeling, what my friends were feeling, seemed to be expressed perfectly by the Romantics … It was a replay, a rerun, a harmonic echo across nearly two centuries" (1995, 75). This is a journey that reflects the life of people who were young, like Holmes, in the 1960s. For Holmes, his connection with Shelley has a broader historical relevance as it informs the present of a generation through a greater understanding of the past. He also aims to bring new readers to Shelley's poetry, as an important aim of any literary biography is to highlight its subject's works.[6]

Holmes identifies himself as an experimental biographer; this is a reflection of his approach to hard and fast distinctions between nonfiction and fiction and re-creative ways of writing narrative nonfiction. By offering readers a new way to read the life of his subjects he pays homage to their memory and by indirection we find out something about the direction of their lives. Holmes understands his writing as part of a contemporary trend in which the work of "scholar-artists, [is] totally committed to both painstaking research and polished story-telling" (2005a, 373). In *Sidetracks* (2000), he describes his particular approach to this form of storytelling:

> much of modern biography has something of the inescapable tension, and steady unfolding, of the classical detective story: with the psychological promise of some sort of 'revelation' (not a crime solved, but of a human mystery—at least partially—resolved). The resolution often appears not in narrative, but in figurative form, which a skilled biographer can sometimes give almost poetic force. (373)[7]

Holmes also believes that, "Empathy is the most powerful, the most necessary, and the most deceptive, of all biographical emotions" (2005a, 4), which sits, at times uncomfortably, alongside the need for objectivity but nevertheless remains central to his approach and connects with his view of biography as a pursuit, a journey, to unravel human mysteries.[8] Nonfiction biography is a form that offers a structured and coherent narrative, yet what is distinctive about some biographies is that they do not offer a satisfactory ending, a resolution or revelation, but rather give one biographer's version of that life. This means that the person or people re-created in a biography are often not simplified or coherent, nor can their lives be understood in a neat linear progression, nor do we ever really come to know them. Holmes's allusion to a detective story implies a focus on plot, but his argument places a particular emphasis on figurative form, not content. This suggests that biography can reveal something of human mystery but any sense of resolution will inevitably be partial, fragmentary and incomplete. Holmes's writing is distinctive in part because of his writing about Romantic figures and his approach as a Romantic biographer. His style is one in which the balance between content and form, and connections between subject and biographical narrator, are absolutely central to the stories he wants to tell.

Holmes's biography of Shelley aims to be experimental in a number of ways.[9] He believes that the "open-ended nature of biography is one of its mysterious attractions ... Biography is only scientific in the sense that it is experimental: it tests one version of the facts" (2005b, x). This statement seems to lie at the heart of Holmes's approach and connects with Harold Nicolson's concerns about 'scientific' or applied biography, as discussed in Chap. 2. Holmes is turning the use of the term scientific on its head here. Scientific biography may need to focus exclusively on facts in Nicolson's view, but it is also experimental in its use of those facts. In his group biography, *The Age of Wonder* (2008b), Holmes celebrates the creative and Romantic force and wonder of scientists in the eighteenth century. His book reinforces an understanding of science as creative, imaginative and an epic journey. In his writing, the nature of the scientific is rewritten. Facts are challenged and understood from different and innovative perspectives in scientific experimentation, as they are in Holmes's writing. He discusses aspects of his biographical experimentation in the 1994 preface to his biography of Shelley:

> This is a young man's book ... It shares something of the recklessness of its subject, the pursuer and the pursued ... It is an attempt to write literary biography as a form of modern epic, in which speed of action, colour and movement, travel and the sense of poetic adventure, predominate over everything else. (ix)

Here, Holmes is rejecting Nicolson's early twentieth century concern that biography has to either be fiction or take a more 'scientific' approach, and he is aware that he is taking risks and being reckless in doing so. Holmes's writing is a form of re-creative nonfiction that uses literary techniques, such as the form of modern epic, to frame the life he wants to tell, in which the biographer and his subject are both in motion, in pursuit. Holmes is explicit about the pattern and form he wants to impose on his narrative. His focus remains on particular aspects of Shelley's influence whilst recognising the partisan nature of the version he has created and the different qualities of a more historical and scholarly form of biography.[10] In his metanarratives about the genre, Holmes remains alert to the tension between chronicle biographies and narrative or re-creative nonfiction rooted in storytelling:

> All good biographers struggle with a particular tension between the scholarly drive to assemble facts as dispassionately as possible and the novelistic urge to find shape and meaning within the apparently random circumstances of a life. (2004, 17)

He believes that both are important because, "We make sense of life by establishing 'significant' facts, and by telling 'revealing' stories with them" (17), although he acknowledges that it is "tricky terrain, the impossible meeting of what Woolf herself called 'granite and rainbow'" (17). Others may well not agree with Holmes's point of view, with his methodology, or his approach to storytelling, or with the connections he has made. But, if one accepts that a definitive biography of a life, or lives, is not possible, this explains one of the reasons why biographies of the same subject are needed. We often make up our minds about a lot of things in life by listening to the different views of other people about the same subjects.

If one reads Holmes's biography of Shelley as an epic narrative, several aspects of his approach become clearer. Extended similes in the biography reinforce an understanding of Shelley's life as an adventure, full of movement and travel, as he pursues his dreams for both his poetry and day-to-day life. In his metabiographies, Holmes discusses his belief that the biographical process becomes "a way of making sense of my own world" (1995, 83) and that is why the story of his subject, Shelley, is "a continuing one" (153). In doing so, he wants to go "most especially to the *places*" (136) that were important to him, although he knows that "I must maintain an objective and judicial stance" (143). He advocates a wider, Romantic role for biography, given that "All life could be seen as exploration, an endless search for cause, shape and meaning" (2005d, 367). In

Sidetracks (2000), Holmes reiterates that, for him, biography has always been a personal adventure of exploration and pursuit, a tracking (ix), although because "no biography is ever definitive … Sometimes all one achieves is another point of departure" (2005a, ix), "with one foot in the present and the other continually in the past" (4). The notion of a journey is thus central to Holmes's work.

The notion of a pursuit across internal and external landscapes becomes an important trope to describe Shelley's own self-reflexive journey:

> the notion of the mind as an unexplored cave, a bewildering labyrinth through which the explorer must risk his search for a personal identity, was to fill his poems, his notebooks and his prose speculations … The image of the journey, especially the subterranean journey, constantly recurs in this respect. (2005b, 65)

One way that Holmes understands this subterranean journey is to set it "as vividly as possible in its immediate physical setting" (xvii). Holmes writes about the constant restless movement in Shelley's life, as he lives in many different places in England, and then Italy, as he looks for places to write: "The idea of the search for a *place*, from which he could launch his ideas of changing society, was to become increasingly important for Shelley" (200). Holmes argues that, for Shelley, "'inquiry' came to mean in essence travelling, movement outwards or inwards, rather than analysis" (65). In 1811, Shelley stayed in the Elan Valley in Wales, and "this curiously symbolic geographical setting became the recurrent and dominant motif of the many different houses in which he chose to stay" (74). Holmes writes evocatively about the mood of some of these places:

> it was the climate and the countryside of the Italian Apennines that fascinated and attracted Shelley. He spent hours and hours simply gazing upwards at the changing skyscapes, and the shifting light values in the trees … Nearly every one of these details, the cloud growths, the storms, the sheet lightening, the planets, the fireflies, even the owl, were later to find their places in his poems. (428)

In Holmes's view, this "need to move is certainly one of the profoundest questions which can be asked about his life" (575). This trope, used throughout the biography, reiterates Shelley's importance not only as a poet who wrote epics but as an epic hero in his own right.[11]

The pursuit of the biography's title also becomes a tale about the pursuit of the subject by his biographer following in his footsteps, as Holmes visits the places and homes that mark important moments in Shelley's life. For Holmes,

> Biography ... was to become a kind of pursuit, a tracking of the physical trail of someone's path through the past, a following of footsteps. You would never catch them ... But maybe, if you were lucky, you might write about the pursuit of that fleeting figure in such a way as to bring it alive in the present. (1995, 27)

In the second volume of his biography of Coleridge, Holmes spells out his point of view that the "power of human association with physical places and objects was perhaps the foundation of biography" (1999, 7). In Holmes's case, this refers to both the life of the biographical subject and the biographer following in his footsteps, literally and metaphorically.

Holmes wants "to show what sort of visionary Coleridge really was, and why—among all the English Romantics—he is worth rediscovering today" (2005c, xiii). Rather than debunking his subject, like Strachey, he is explicit about his attempt to "examine his entire life in a broad and sympathetic manner" (xiii), and he argues that the "most radical thing" (xiii) about the biography is "simply that it is a defence of Coleridge in these terms" (xiii). Holmes's interest is in the man, his genius and his ability to understand his age. This is an unapologetic epic and heroic narrative in which its form has a particular importance and both the voice of the narrator and subject can be heard. It becomes a late twentieth century version of an exemplary biography that on the surface may seem like a traditional biography in praise of its subject but that has, as Holmes himself describes, several experimental features: "I have attempted, from the start, to set Coleridge *talking* ... to make his *voice* sound steadily through the narrative, and indeed in the end to dominate it" (2005c, xvi). In this biography, Holmes wants the voice of Coleridge, rather than his own, to dominate. He also introduces a third voice in the footnotes, what he describes as "a sort of downstage voice" (2005c, xvi).[12]

Holmes is very deliberately offering a passionate point of view that asks the reader to think about Coleridge not as a traditional exemplary hero but as a visionary, "though whether comedy, tragedy, or romance prevail, remains to be seen" (Holmes 2005c, xvi). This suggests that one reading of this biography is to understand it as a dramatic, performative piece about a tragic, even comic, hero of so much promise, who makes terrible mistakes that destroy not only his life but have bitter consequences for his immediate family. This is not a Greek drama, but one can almost feel Coleridge placed up on stage, coming to life in front of our eyes. The biography is certainly not suggesting that Coleridge is one of us—this is a man of huge proportions, of almost inhuman scope. The biography provides Coleridge with an opportunity to give one more lecture that lives on in the reader's imagination after we have finished reading. Of course, it may not be a lecture or performance with which all readers agree and it has stronger dramatic and performative qualities than some of the other biographies discussed in this book.

An inspiring man of great potential is set before us in the first volume of this biography, but in the second we watch his fall, as Coleridge treats his wife and children with neglect, is addicted to drugs, resorts to plagiarism and loses his friends as a result of what they see as his inappropriate behaviour. Some may understand this story as an illness narrative in which he becomes the unwitting victim of his addiction. Certainly, Coleridge's addiction becomes a central theme in the second volume of Holmes's biography, which is often a narrative about the consequences of a whole plethora of mistakes he has made that have been driven by his addiction. For example, on his way to live and work for the Governor of Malta in 1804,

> What Coleridge could not know was that by now complete withdrawal from the drug was physiologically a virtual impossibility without skilled medical aid. He could no longer do it alone, by a simple effort of will. So each time his will was broken, he suffered and lost confidence in his own powers. This terrible repetition of resolution and failure—like one of the endless, circular punishments of Dante's *Inferno*—shaped much of what happened in the second part of his life. (1999, 15)

One way to understand this biography's approach to Coleridge's addiction is to see his life as an epic fall from grace. So, this is not an illness narrative but a tragic tale of a man with so much potential brought down by addiction, the loss of the love of his friend, Wordsworth, a failed marriage and unrequited love for another woman, and by his own faults and weaknesses. He is lucky enough to find two families, first the Morgans and then the Gillmans, who care for him, although their patience is sorely tested due to his addiction and behaviour. At the time of one incident at the home of the Morgans in December 1813,

> he was suffering from the most acute opium overdose of his life ... the contradictions in his life were still largely unresolved, or at least unaccepted. Guilt for his many failings—opium, Asra [Sara Hutchinson, with whom he was in love], his unhappy marriage, his abandoned children— had put him in a condition of perpetual flight from inner realities. He was destroying himself, destroying his capacity for work, destroying the love of all those around him. (1999, 351)

Holmes suggests that there is a moment late in his life in 1814 when Coleridge realises some of the implications of his addiction in a series of confessional letters in which he admits that "he had been an opium addict for well over a decade. He had acknowledged this before, in 1808, but never with such a degree of self-exposure" (356). For some people experiencing substance misuse, this moment of recognition becomes a potential door to recovery, but for Coleridge it was already too late. This is a tragic hero who comes at last to achieve some sense of self-awareness but who, being no longer able to make any significant changes to his addiction, needs the help of others to help him manage his everyday life—after he has already lost favour with close friends and his wife.

In the afterword to the second volume of his biography, Holmes concludes that, "Coleridge's life continues in one's head, and mixes with the sounds of one's own existence" (1999, 561). This can also be said of Shakespeare's *Hamlet*, as each performance and reading of the play encourages us to reflect on what might have happened if Hamlet had been able to act more decisively following his father's murder. In a chapter with the title, "Hamlet in Fleet Street", Holmes draws attention to the connections between his hero and Shakespeare's own "study of moral paralysis. In doing so, he had created an archetypal Romantic hero—Hamlet as Everyman—who also seemed extraordinarily like Coleridge himself" (282). Coleridge's plagiarism is discussed in this chapter and Holmes argues that it "was a response to profound, almost disabling anxiety and intellectual self-doubt" (254). It is not perhaps that Hamlet or Coleridge did not know what action was needed, but that they lacked the ability to do the 'right' thing. This was their tragedy.

In this biography, the biographer explicitly states his relationship with, and empathy for, his subject. The literary qualities of this biography mean that we do not see this man as an actual person but rather as a character of Holmes's own making; Holmes has fashioned a version or makeover of Coleridge. This is a passionate, performative tale but the character of Coleridge is no less alive in our reading for all that. Holmes's relationship with his subjects becomes representative of a modern epic with a form and style that is central to the story that these single-life biographies tell.

In tune with recent experimentation, Holmes is interested in the nature of a particular friendship between Samuel Johnson and the Romantic poet, Richard Savage, in *Dr Johnson & Mr Savage* (1993). In doing so, he explores the nature of the relationship between a biographer—Boswell, Johnson and Holmes himself—and his subject, who is a biographer himself. This is a metabiography that, as Holroyd suggests, becomes a collaboration between these two biographers, Johnson and Holmes, as Holmes gives Johnson the chance to write one last book in collaboration with him, and in which Holmes also responds to James Boswell's version of Johnson.[13] In his writing about comparative biography, Holmes argues that in Boswell's biography perhaps "it is only the youthful Johnson … that somehow slips through his capacious net" (2005a, 368) and it is this period of Johnson's life that Holmes "tried to recapture" (368) in *Dr Johnson & Mr Savage*, which is "a further investigation of the strange byways of biography and friendship" (368). Holmes's study of Samuel Johnson's biography of the poet Richard Savage "is the biography of a biography. It concerns the kind of human truth, *poised between fact and fiction*, which a biographer can obtain as he tells a story of another's life" (1993, 5, my emphasis). Holmes sees in Johnson's writing a particular nonfiction form:

> It began to pose the largest, imaginative questions: how can we know our fellow human beings; how far can we learn from someone else's struggles about the conditions of our own; what do the intimate circumstances of one particular life tell us about human nature in general? This seems to me the historic significance of Johnson's *Life of Richard Savage*. (1993, 230)

These also become the questions that Holmes asks in his own biographies, in which he seeks a narrative that has the poetic force of an epic.

As Holmes notes, Johnson asks the reader to consider why Savage might occasionally be at fault as he journeys through life, rarely finding any one place to settle:

> if his Miferies were fometimes the Confequence of his Faults, he ought not yet to be wholly excluded from Compaffion, because his Faults were very often the Effects of his Misfortunes. (1971, 65)[14]

Savage is portrayed in Johnson's biography as a flawed figure who makes many mistakes, and who falls from grace as he makes them, almost against his will, or so Johnson suggests. Therefore, it is hard to see him as heroic, as a figure that comes to understand his shortcomings. The biography discusses one of these mistakes in Savage's break with Lord Tyrconnel, who had supported his release from prison after Savage's trial for murder, and arranges for him to receive an annual pension. This is an example of many similar instances in his life-story, as Savage walks away from those who try to help him. The image of walking is important throughout the book, literally and metaphorically, as Johnson and Savage come to know each other in their walks across London, often at night, and in his last days Savage takes long walks in the company of his gaoler.

Johnson comments wryly in his biography of Savage that "It is too common for thofe who have unjuftly fuffered Pain, to inflict it likewife in their Turn, with the fame Injuftice, and to imagine that they have a Right to treat others as they have themfelves been treated" (1971, 86). He sees this as one of the causes of Savage's inability to be contrite and accept some responsibility for his actions that embarrass or are offensive to his friends and supporters: "it was always dangerous to truft him" (182). However, Johnson believes that Savage is "a Man equally diftinguished by his Virtues and Vices, and at once remarkable for his Weakneffes and Abilities" (179), and asks that Savage be remembered for his writing, not the faults of his life. Whilst reflecting this empathetic view of Savage in his metabiography, Holmes takes a number of steps to transform Johnson's vision and to create an updated late twentieth century story that becomes a modern version of Savage's biography and a new collaboration with Johnson, Savage's erstwhile biographer. Holmes adds extensive new information about some of the key events in Savage's life, such as his trial for murder, his relationship with a woman who he alleged was his mother, and the extent to which he made up or fashioned his own version of events when he had a particular story about his life that he wanted to tell.

This metanarrative makes points about Johnson's biography of Savage that could also be said about Boswell's life of Johnson. Both men only knew their subjects for a short time when they were much younger and their subject was older. Both Boswell and Johnson try to set their subjects talking. Some of the material they use is incomplete at best, or, at worst, some events are omitted or used sparingly to support a particular biographical point of view. Johnson based the first section of his biography on "a partial and secondary source" (1993, 56), called the 'Newgate' booklet. Holmes suggests that he does so because Johnson "responded overwhelmingly to the picture it presented of Savage as a ... victim of society, and particularly as a victim of one woman's cruelty" (57), Mrs Brett, who refuses to confirm that she is Savage's mother. However, Holmes argues that "if we consider what Johnson omitted, or never discovered, or left without comment or challenge, and what we now know ... then an entirely different figure begins to emerge" (65). He suggests that Savage's attack on Mrs Brett at one point is comparable to blackmail and that Johnson's portrayal omits key events that "comes close to a whitewashing of Savage" (93). Holmes takes one of his other namesakes to heart, in this case Sherlock Holmes, in a careful and detailed discussion about the events that led up to Savage's trial and conviction for murder: "The process of a trial, with its conflict of evidence and various possible interpretations of the truth, is to some extent a paradigm of the whole biographical enterprise" (115).[15] Johnson quotes extensively from Savage's poetry to give an impression "of Savage actually talking to the reader" (47). In Johnson's case, it becomes hard to determine when the biographer or subject are speaking, when the evidence under the microscope is not authentic but rewritten by the biographer, who is clearly an advocate for the defence.

On the other hand, Holmes argues that Johnson "is not taken in by Savage, but still extends sympathy and insight" (192):

What Johnson finally saw as the moral meaning of Savage's existence— the discovery of which he enshrined as the central purpose of biography—lay in the capacity of even a flawed man to struggle nobly against the misfortunes of life. (1993, 194)

Holmes extends a hand of friendship across time, what he calls "a handshake", to write a new, revised version of Johnson's book. It adds new material and information about Savage's life and it questions some of Johnson's analysis, but in offering a revised version it nevertheless pays homage to Johnson and to the flawed character he has created. It is faithful to Johnson's purpose, whilst saying something different.[16]

In his final chapter, Holmes describes himself as a biographer, a character within his own book, writing an experimental biography about the friendship between Johnson and Savage over the two years when they actually saw each other. He wants to study the retellings of Savage's life, to give an account of the quality of their friendship, and in doing so he writes a different version of Johnson's character from the one portrayed in Boswell's biography, influenced by his early life and his friendship with Savage. This book has an overarching serious purpose for Holmes:

> I believe in fact that biography itself, with its central tenet of empathy, is essentially a Romantic form; and that Johnson's friendship with Savage first crystallised its perils and its possibilities. (230)

Thus, he is placing Johnson's biography of Richard Savage centre stage as the archetypal form for biography, which becomes a study of friendship and collaboration between biographers. He makes a case for Johnson's biography from the eighteenth century to be understood as "a new hybrid, nonfiction form" (230), in which "biography became a rival to the novel" (230), that can help us to understand ourselves by looking through the lives of others.

Holmes's study offers one version of comparative biography as he writes this book in collaboration with Johnson. If no single biography can be definitive, and the genre is understood as generating an inherently dialogic, discursive, collaborative and conversational form, vibrating with uncertainty, in which nonfiction narratives need to be written by artists on oath who write one version of events, then comparative studies—as Holmes himself suggests—of life-writing, including fiction, nonfiction, and the growing hybrid forms available, offers huge scope for future books about life-writing.[17] Holmes argues that "the close textual study of biography could throw much more light on the unsuspected role of rhetorical devices ... in the apparently transparent narrative forms of life-writing" (2004, 17). It would also inform understanding about "the values and the limitations of accuracy and historical understanding ... [and] something of the complications of human truth-telling" (17), and would enable readers and students to enter "imaginatively into another place, another time, another life" (17). This is not to say that facts cannot be wrong or misrepresented in biographies but that the way stories about them are told really matters.

The approaches of the three biographers discussed in this chapter are very different and each has his or her own preoccupations. However, they share a commitment to understand aspects of the present of the biographer in the context of historical events and the lives of other people. These biographers are not invisible as narrators, given the way they tell and interpret their stories. In their approach to their subjects as representative figures for themselves as biographers, and for the readers they are trying to reach—representatives of either heroic, noncanonical, feminist, postcolonial or Romantic icons and myths—they re-create their version of their subjects' lives. They do not write scholarly biography that provides a chronicle of the facts. We know that no one version can be definitive and that a range of biographical narratives offering different, and experimental, perspectives about other people's lives have much to offer. All three of these biographers show empathy towards the people they write about. However, they may not agree with everything they do. Having said that, it probably does mean that their subjects are people whose lives they are interested in and who represent moments in history that are important to them. They are also biographers who make up their portrayals based on anecdotes and narrative styles and structures that inform the story they want to tell. R. Holmes pursues a journey in his or her writing, bringing people to life through his or her narrative. Some critics may conflate the voice of the narrator with the voice of the actual biographer, and link this to identification issues on the basis that the narrator reflects the views of the actual biographer. Perhaps there is a need to distinguish the narrator, the voice telling a subject's story, from the actual biographer who is external to the written text. In other words, assuming that we cannot know the intentions of the actual biographer, the narrator in these biographies is a construction created in the writing of the biography, which offers versions, with which not every reader will agree, of both the biographical narrator and subject.

The biographical writing of R. Holmes raises questions about the traditional and conventional notion of exemplary biography, highlighting the heroic and both the representative and unique significance of their biographical subjects. However, the approach of each biographer to the notion of what we mean by exemplary is very different. The military historian, Richard Holmes, writes about traditional canonical exemplary heroes, as well as other unknown military heroes. The Romantic biographer, Richard Holmes, writes about epic heroes, who may fall from grace, as well as exceptional figures from the arts and sciences who forged new ways of thinking about the world. Rachel Holmes's feminist perspective suggests that the notion of what we mean by heroic and exemplary has to be reframed, as hidden, undervalued and forgotten lives receive the recognition they are due.

A conversation conducted over email with the Romantic biographer Richard Holmes in 2016 gave me another reading of some aspects of his approach to biography.

In Conversation with Richard Holmes

How do you decide what details to include about both the lives of your single subjects, or subjects in group biography, and of other people who knew them in their intimate, personal and professional lives?

"How you decide upon the details?" is an impossibly general question. A frank answer might be "by instinct". You are listening for the notes that make up the tune, or looking for what Henry James called the pattern or the figure in the carpet. As well as scholarly research, you live and travel and dream constantly with your subject until you know them intimately (and, I would almost say, until they know you intimately).

To what extent do gender issues inform your approach to biography?

I don't recognise "gender issues" as such, but it is clear that before say 1970 very little good biography had been written about women subjects, and it was feminism that changed all that. I certainly don't think male biographers have to stick to male subjects, or female biographers to female subjects (e.g. Strachey on Florence Nightingale, Holroyd on Dora Carrington, Glendinning on Anthony Trollope or Spurling on Henri Matisse.) In my own case, I have come to enjoy more and more writing about women subjects—starting with Mary Wollstonecraft and Mary Shelley, and going on with Zelide, Caroline Herschel, Sophie Blanchard (balloonist), and most recently with Margaret Cavendish, Madame de Stael, and especially Mary Somerville. I also feel that women's role in early science has been particularly neglected, and they have suffered from "the condescension of history". I have tried to repair some of this in my books and essays, from *The Age of Wonder* onwards.

In the preface to the first volume of your biography about Coleridge, you mention that "on the surface at least, I hope this book will read like the most traditional form of popular narrative biography" (xv); so, could you describe some of the main characteristics of 'popular narrative biography' (the focus of my book), and why you have added the caveat, "on the surface at least".

"Shelley" was my most conventional narrative biography, perhaps because he was my most radically *unconventional* character (and also because it was my first big biography, and I was learning the metier). In all my biographies from "Coleridge" onwards, I have tried to make special use of sliding narrative panels, dropped in backstories, "vertical" footnotes (see *Age of Wonder*), cinematic shifts from the close-up to the panoramic shot, detailed locations (see *Footsteps*), ventriloquism and the subject's own voice, plus interjections of the first-person aside, the "downstage" or "I" voice (see *Coleridge 1* and *2*). I am also interested in using shifts of biographical tone—for example between comedy and tragedy, or even black farce. The biographer has many voices (see *Sidetracks*).

On the basis that one of the purposes of literary biography is to encourage the reader back to the works of the author, to what extent can the work of the author turn the reader back to biography, autobiography and history?

Yes, ideally the life and the work always form a constant loop. The third volume of my two-volume biography of Coleridge was in fact *Coleridge: Selected Poems*, with sections of purely critical notes about the work, which amounted to another short book. Surprisingly, the same can be true of scientific biography.

In the context of recent experimentation within the genre, could you describe what might be included in the study of comparative biography today?

While "comparative biography" can mean many things, one specific example would be the study of a series of biographies about the *same* subject, but written over an extended time period, and preferably over more than a century (c.g. of Mary Wollstonecraft, or Isaac Newton, or Oliver Cromwell, or Charles Dickens; but also, of course, Sylvia Plath). This throws into perspective a whole series of questions about the changing nature of evidence; historical shifts in moral judgement; and the social and psychological assumptions implicit in every biography which always belongs to, and unconsciously reflects, its own period and hence can never be "definitive". This also applies to the biographer. Indeed, Holmes's Law states that biographies steadily become more autobiographical the more they age. Hence Boswell's *Life of Samuel Johnson* (1791) is now read two hundred years later as essentially *James Boswell: My Life*.

How do you think that the online presence of people's lives, and social media more generally, will influence biography in future?
I'm afraid I don't follow social media: a case of old dog, new tricks. But it is clear that blogs, of which there are several million online, have utterly transformed the concept of "privacy". However, in the end I suspect the blog is as much a form of literary "mask", with its own conventions, as the "intimate" diary used to be.

Who are the implied and actual readers of popular biography and what are they looking for in a biography?
One of the fascinations of going to Literary Festivals is actually seeing who your readers are. For example, literary biography seems to attract older readers, science biography younger ones. When I taught an MA in biography for five years at university, I was astonished at the range of people it attracted, both in age (21–67) and background. Quote from my latest book, *This Long Pursuit*: "My Notebooks record an Irish poet, an American Mormon, a general physician from Oxford, a Pakistani air force pilot, a Japanese business woman, a TV researcher, the ex-headmistress of an English girl's school (not Greta Hall), a human rights barrister from London, a Vassar literature graduate, a Canadian TV executive, a financial journalist from the City, a Norfolk asparagus farmer, a Birmingham social worker, and a mother of three from Sussex, whose sailor husband (I eventually discovered) was dying of cancer."

NOTES

1. For example, E.R. Holmes mentions a number of his visits to the battlefields where Wellington fought: "One of my abiding memories of the battlefield of Assaye is the sheer prevalence of canister shot" (2003, 15); "I first saw Seringapatam ..." (54); "I visited the battlefield [of Assaye] in September 2001" (75); "I finished my day on the battlefield near Assaye itself, surrounded by eager children selling canister shot" (81); and "I was glad to get away from Badajoz" (161).
2. Walmer Castle was Wellington's official residence as Lord Warden of the Cinque Ports (E.R. Holmes 2003, 279).
3. Other books by the military historian Edward Richard Holmes include *In the Footsteps of Churchill* (2005), *Marlborough: England's Fragile Genius* (2008), *The Complete War Walks: From Hastings to Normandy* (2003) and *Soldiers: Army Lives and Loyalties from Redcoats to Dusty Warriors* (2011).

4. Holmes, Rachel, *The Hottentot Venus*, 4.

5. Rachel Holmes has published a biography of Eleanor Marx, *Eleanor Marx: A Life* (2014). She is also an undervalued but important exemplary figure as a woman who "changed the world" (xi).

6. *Shelley: The Pursuit*, ix. This is also a very important aim for his biography of Coleridge: "I believe passionately that one of the main purposes of a literary Life is to renew the appreciation of—no, the *love* of—a neglected body of literary Work, and to make it alive for a new generation. My first and last loyalty has been to Coleridge the poet" (1999, 563).

7. In 2008, Holmes also describes his approach to nonfiction storytelling in biography and he understands some of the tensions within it: "It has a protagonist, a time-sequence, a plot, and a dramatic pattern of human cause and effect. Its essential discipline is secular, it does not accept supernatural explanations ... The basic unit is the anecdote, strung along the narrative like beads on a string. But there are also numerous epistemological problems in storytelling. How reliable or selective are our sources? What are the vagaries of human memory? In what sense can one write he or she "thought" or "felt" something? How far can we "know the other", philosophically speaking?" (2008a, 134). In this essay, Holmes acknowledges that new experimental forms of biography are being sought: "There is widespread questioning of the traditional forms and chronology. There is a fascination with briefer and more experimental work. There is renewed interest in marginal and subversive subject-matter. The 'monolithic' single Life is giving way to biographies of groups, of friendships, of love-affairs. The smooth, confident third-person narrative of the traditional biographer is sprouting dangerous, first-person pronouns" (140).

8. Holmes understands the essential process of biography to include, firstly, the gathering of facts and "the assembling in chronological order of a man's "journey" through the world" (1995, 66), and secondly, "the creation of a fictional or imaginary relationship between the biographer and his subject" (66), in which empathy between them is an essential component of the biographer's approach.

9. Holmes states in *Sidetracks*, in a chapter about the relationship between Mary Wollstonecraft and William Godwin, "Writing as an experimental biographer myself" (2005a, 199). His work subverts conventional ways of writing biography. Holmes argues that Godwin's memoir about his wife "is the most significant and revolutionary short biography since Johnson's *Life of Savage* (1744). Both mark the shift, as well as anything can, from eighteenth century to a modern world of feeling. Both bring the inner life of a human being significantly closer to our own experience

of it" (2005a, 266). This is more akin to the literary form of biography important to MacCarthy.

10. Holmes, Richard, *Shelley: The Pursuit*, ix.

11. Coleridge's relationship to places and landscapes are also important in Holmes's two-volume biography that explore the nature of his journey, and that of his biographer; for example:

> The imaginative connection between his solitary study, and the solitary fell-tops, was to become a vital metaphor in his writing about the Lakes. And such wild "wanderings" were to become a physical resort, almost as powerful as the inner one of opium. (2005c, 292)

12. In *The Age of Wonder* (2008b), a group biography about eighteenth century scientists, Holmes also applies this third voice. In one footnote, he comments on the impact of venereal disease in eighteenth century Tahiti, noting that "It was soon accepted that the Europeans in general were responsible" for a disease "which devastated the Pacific populations over the next two generations" (2008b, 18). Tahiti was, he comments in the footnotes, "Literally a Paradise Lost" (59). In *This Long Pursuit* (2016), Holmes describes his use of footnotes in this group biography as "the 'vertical footnote'. This worked as follows. While my main narrative moved forward in a largely conventional chronological form, a 'horizontal' progress as it were, the footnotes provide sudden 'vertical' or vertiginous plunges *down* into past history, or *back up* into contemporary science" (2016, 34).

13. Holroyd believes that the literary biographer "can stretch out a hand to his subject and invite him, invite her, to write one more work, posthumously and in collaboration" (2003, 19).

14. Holmes, Richard, *Dr Johnson & Mr Savage*, 153.

15. In an essay with the title, "Le Grand Sherlock", published in *Works on Paper* (2003), Holroyd discusses Holmes's metanarrative, *Footsteps* (1985).

16. Holmes notes that Sir John Hawkins, Johnson's earliest biographer, "thought the friendship [between Savage and Johnson] was the single most inexplicable fact about Johnson's entire career" (1993, 1), but then he had a dismissive view about the importance of Johnson's friendship with Frances Barber.

17. Holmes argues that "One can say that *vibrating in uncertainty* is part of the human power of biography" (2008a, 135).

References

Crace, John. 2004. Richard Holmes: officer and gentleman. *The Guardian*, 18 May: 20–21.

Holmes, Edward Richard. 1981. War and the Past: The Problems of Military Biography. *History Today* 31, 10 (OCT): 61.

Holmes, Edward Richard. 2003. *Wellington: The Iron Duke*. London: Harper Collins.

Holmes, Edward Richard. 2005. *In the Footsteps of Churchill*. London: BBC Books.

Holmes, Edward Richard. 2008. *Marlborough: England's Fragile Genius*. London: Harper Collins.

Holmes, Richard. 1993. *Dr Johnson & Mr Savage*. London: Hodder and Stoughton.

———. 1995. First published in 1985. *Footsteps: Adventure of a Romantic Biographer*. London: Flamingo.

———. 1999. First published in 1998. *Coleridge: Darker Visions*. London: Flamingo.

———. 2003. Inventing the Truth. In *The Art of Literary Biography*, ed. John Batchelor, 15–25. Oxford: Oxford University Press.

———. 2004. The Proper Study. In *Mapping Lives: The Uses of Biography*, ed. Peter France and William St Clair, 7–18. Oxford: Oxford University Press.

———. 2005b. First published in 1974. *Shelley: The Pursuit*. London: Harper Perennial.

———. 2005c. First published in 1989. *Coleridge: Early Visions*. London: Harper Perennial.

———. 2005a. First published in 2000. *Sidetracks: Explorations of a Romantic Biographer*. London: Harper Perennial.

———. 2008a. 'Whatever is Happening in Biography?'. In *The Protean Forms of Life Writing: Auto/Biography in English, 1680–2000*, ed. Righetti Angelo, 129–142. Napoli: Liguori.

———. 2008b. *The Age of Wonder: How the Romantic Generations Discovered the Beauty and Terror of Science*. London: Harper Press.

———. 2016. *This Long Pursuit: Reflections of a Romantic Biographer*. London: William Collins.

Holmes, Rachel. 2003. First published in 2002. *Scanty Particulars: The Mysterious, Astonishing Life of Victorian Surgeon James Barry*. London: Penguin.

———. 2007. *The Hottentot Venus: The Life and Death of Saarjie Baartman: Born 1789–Buried 2002*. London: Bloomsbury.

———. 2014. *Eleanor Marx: A Life*. London: Bloomsbury.

Holroyd, Michael 2003. First published in 2002. *Works on Paper: The Craft of Biography and Autobiography*. London: Abacus.

Johnson, Samuel. 1888. The Dignity and Usefulness of Biography, The Rambler Saturday October 13, 1750. In *The Essays of Samuel Johnson: Selected From The Rambler 1750–1752, The Adventurer 1753 and The Idler 1758–1760*, ed. Stuart Reid, 79–84. London: Walter Scott.

———. 1971. *The Life of Richard Savage 1728*, Yorkshire: Scholar Press.

Sheffield, Gary. 2011. Soldiers: Army lives and Loyalties from Redcoats to Dusty Warriors. *History Extra*, November 3 : http://www.historyextra.com/book-review/soldiers-army-lives-and-loyalties-redcoats-dusty-warriors.

Sisman, Adam. 1994. *A.J.P. Taylor: A Biography*. London: Sinclair-Stevenson.

CHAPTER 7

Claire Tomalin and Several Strangers

Claire Tomalin's biographies are popular. One reason for this is her ability to write compelling stories. The quality of her writing bears out Michael Benton's distinction between "the *histoire*, the chain of events, the people and their settings, and the *recit*, the discourse that gives them expression" (2015, 19). Tomalin believes that the biographer's imagination is important in evoking dramatic scenes, perhaps a cornerstone of both creative and re-creative writing:

> Biography has become my province, and I have never attempted fiction, although I have come to think the gap between biography and fiction is not so great. Novelists and biographers are both excited and inspired by the patterns of human activity. They are both story tellers. Both use the basic raw materials of life, birth and childhood, work and love, family structures, betrayal, woe and death. You need imagination even if you don't invent, and writers who invent very often depend on research too, their own or someone else's. (1999, 131)

Tomalin unravels the multiplicity and contradictions in the lives of her subjects. She speculates when facts are missing whilst approaching the use of autobiographical evidence with caution. This chapter is interested in how she applies literary strategies to represent aspects of her subjects' characters—including her approach to the embodiment of her subjects and the performativity inherent in their lives, how she creates dramatic scenes that often represent a key moment or turning point in

© The Author(s) 2017   147
J. McVeigh, *In Collaboration with British Literary Biography*,
DOI 10.1007/978-3-319-58383-9_7

her subjects' lives, and how she subverts the use of chronological time in biography. Her subjects are understood in the context of their relationships with other people, and in terms of the historical and cultural contexts in which their life-stories are framed, to enhance our understanding of the past and inform our present. Finally, her work is rooted in her commitment to feminism and the lives of her women subjects.

Tomalin understands that the nature of truth in biography is always mediated and provisional; nevertheless, a biographer can make meaningful connections between different aspects of someone's life and produce authentic portraits.[1] Tomalin upholds the biographer's mantra that she is 'an artist on oath' and does not invent evidence, although some might question her use of this material. She reserves the right to speculate when hard evidence is not available and is aware that autobiographical evidence may be unreliable. Her writing does more than offer a form of biography based on conventional, chronological realist narrative.

The biographers discussed in this book often recognise that the person they are writing about is struggling with a multifaceted character, and that the portrayal of a unified and fixed identity would be impossible. Tomalin positively seeks out the conflicts and complexities that give rise to divided understandings of her subjects' lives. At the beginning of *Katherine Mansfield: A Secret Life* (1987), she comments that, seen "through different eyes, her image trembles and blurs ... she transformed into multiple alternative versions to suit different moods, different friends, different facets of her personality" (1988, 5). Mansfield is a complex character, capable of sophisticated, empathetic writing whilst at the same time taking up "sentimental postures" (243) and committing acts of "treacherous malice" (243) in her relationships. At the end of *Jane Austen: A Life* (1997), Tomalin decides to spell out and celebrate the different versions of the Jane Austen she has explored. These are just a few of them:

> on the last page I must return to Jane Austen herself. To the child, for whom books were a refuge ... To the girl whose imagination took off in startling directions as she began to see the possibilities of telling stories of her own. To the energetic young woman who loved dancing and jokes, and dreamt of a husband even as she apprenticed herself to novel writing ... To the person who on occasion preferred to remain silent rather than cut across the views and habits of those she loved; and who kept notes of what people said about her work, to read over to herself. This is my

favourite image of Jane Austen, laughing at the opinions of the world. (2000, 288)

Benton suggests that this ending creates "a summative picture" (2015, 27) and "a cameo portrait" (27). It is a picture that emphasises her complexity, not a fixed portrayal. A passage in her biography *Samuel Pepys: The Unequalled Self* (2002), reflects an important component of Tomalin's vision for biography as a whole. She believes that his diary is "a demonstration of how impossible it is to make a tidy account of any one life" (2003, 88). Tomalin considers that one "of the principal themes of the Diary is the classic conflict between his practical, sensible self and his romantic and erotic impulses" (205). This doubleness is reflected in both the public and private lives of Pepys, who "lets us know that each of us inhabits a perpetually fluctuating environment, and that we are changed, moved, and sometimes controlled by our inner tides and weather fronts even when we are most engaged in official functions" (xxxvii). Moreover, Tomalin emphasises two motivating factors, or what she calls "grit", for Pepys's diary: "One was his determination to prove himself ... The other grit was [his wife] Elizabeth, to whom he was bound emotionally and imaginatively" (xxxviii). In this biography, we have a complex story of a man and his personal relationships, particularly with women, someone who lived with pain, often severe, for much of his life, a writer and his diary, and an ambitious professional administrator.

Tomalin also detects doubleness and division throughout Hardy's life in *Thomas Hardy: The Time-Torn Man* (2006). At sixteen, his "life was dividing into three quite separate strands. There was the office, where he was entering the professional world ... There was, mostly inside his head, the world of books and scholarship ... Then there was home and family" (2007, 47). Hardy soon moves to London but if "he had come to London to escape from a divided life, he soon saw that he had failed" (74), because the rural background of his childhood felt at odds with his expectations as a gentleman. This aspect of his life is explored in part in Tomalin's study of his relationship with his first wife, Emma, who was middle class: "This was the first time he had met one of her class and age on equal terms. Class mattered to them both" (100). Later, after they marry and Hardy begins publishing his novels, the tensions in their relationship and the pull of his past start to appear: "Hardy was achieving the sort of success he wanted ... At the same time he was feeling the pull of his old home" (183) and the pressure of his marriage was taking its toll (183). The paradox of Hardy's life, as a seemingly successful public man and husband who is deeply ill at ease, is an important theme in this biography. Tomalin emphasises that he "remained hard to know. The poet in him was developing; the man avoided intimacy" (282). Tomalin believes that his dark view of life had something to do with his constitution that "made him extraordinarily sensitive to humiliations, griefs and disappointments" (223). He only seemed to be able to pursue the dream of love that he wanted in his writing and "his inner life took precedence over everything else" (378). Hardy's performance as a professional writer creates a drama which fulfils him in a way that his life cannot. Similarly, in Tomalin's *Charles Dickens: A Life* (2011), we are given a version of a hugely complex man who Tomalin describes as having several new lives at the age of forty-seven, in 1859—as a public reader, journalist, country squire and magazine proprietor—when he was already a family man, successful novelist and philanthropist (2011, 305). Tomalin suggests that "everyone finds their own version of Charles Dickens" (416), the man and the writer, and her biography of Dickens ends with another list of the roles Dickens took on in life.

The composite and multiple versions of Tomalin's subjects are not only understood through their relationships and caught up with their public and private roles, they can also be found in the very performance of their lives. In his diary, Pepys writes about events that actually happened, but he does so on his own terms as he fashions the life that he describes within it. Tomalin argues that this self was "created daily in his narrative, a creature more complete that he could ever allow himself to be again, complete as no fictional, dramatic or historical portrait had ever been" (2003, 279). But it is only complete in the sense that it is performed within this diary. In describing a row with his wife, Tomalin suggests, that "he detached himself from the self who acted out the scene" (xxxiv) in his diary, as he becomes the narrator of his own life. Tomalin argues that the official life and intimate experience in the diary "demonstrates precisely how close and interdependent they are" (xxxvii); it is this interdependence between his narrated identity in his diary and his material life that her biography seeks to explore. The biography is a study of authorship, and of Pepys's self and his experiences that he fashions in his writing.

Dickens loved the theatre and often 'performed' off the stage throughout his life—in his role as a public and professional man, as a father and husband, as a philanthropist and social reformer; it was hard to know who Dickens really was. He was also passionate about more obvious or literal forms of performance and, as well as being a frequent theatregoer, he produced and directed many plays at home and amongst friends. He had thought about becoming a professional actor. Later in life, he met a young woman with whom he had a close relationship over many years, Ellen Ternan—usually known as Nelly: "he was now confronted with a real girl who could be seen as the embodiment of two of his themes. Nelly, her sisters and mother were all actresses; they inhabited the world of art and imagination" (1991, 94). Tomalin's biography of Nelly Ternan, *The Invisible Woman* (1990), is concerned with the impact of Dickens's love for her and of the theatre, on Nelly, his wife, family and, indeed, Nelly's children, given that "it was no accident that Dickens fell in love with an actress, since the stage and performance were from his earliest days the other life, the other love, the other ambition" (1991, 262). Ternan learns to act on and off the stage in her life with Dickens. She has to hide who she really is and rewrites her life following his death. Similarly, Dickens acts different roles off stage throughout his life. Tomalin comments in her biography of Dickens that "being himself was more exhausting than impersonating a stage actor, who would run on predictable tracks, whereas Dickens did not always know where he was going next" (2011, 171). Performance on stage and in fiction is under the control of the author, whilst life is not. Tomalin remarks that Ternan does not have control of her life as she waits at home, cut off from society, for Dickens's visits: "However cultivated she might have become, there was not much to do with her cultivation if she was destined for a life of nervous isolation" (1991, 171).

The experience of actresses is also pursued in Tomalin's biography of Dora Jordan, whose life, like Ternan's, becomes a performance on and off the stage, although, as a hugely successful actress living openly and unmarried with a member of the royal family, William, the Duke of Clarence, her performance was far more in the public eye than Nelly Ternan's, and she was caricatured by the press as a result. Tomalin does not believe that "justice has been done" (1995, xvii) to Jordan's story or to her personality: "There is a special tone that creeps into eulogies of actresses, presenting them as lovable, wayward creatures and striking them stone dead in the process" (xvii). Tomalin wants to bring her to life in her domestic setting and challenge the condescension of previous scholars and writers: "To those who knew her story she became a symbol of the strength a stage career could confer on a woman, and a warning of its dangers" (7). In her biography of Jane Austen, Tomalin shows that Austen is subject to the whims of patriarchal society, she learns to perform in amateur dramatics in her childhood (2000, 32), and she then "found the power to entertain her family with her writing" (175). Tomalin argues that, like Dickens, "through her writing, she was developing a world of imagination in which she controlled everything that happened" (175), something unattainable in her day-to-day existence. Fiction may be able to offer a world controlled by the author, but biography has to illuminate the intangibility of the everyday in life itself, a different kind of performance.

An interesting detail about the actress Dora Jordan's story is that she was never 'Dora Jordan', her name was merely a construction and tied up with her life as a performer, and she was certainly never legally Mrs Jordan. Her name was Dorothy Bland, although her mother was never legally married to her father. As Tomalin comments, "Grace Phillips was not really entitled to be set down as Mrs Bland, and Dorothy should perhaps have been given Phillips as her family name" (1995, 10). Jordan used her theatrical name, Dora Jordan, on the stage of life as well, performing under it both professionally and personally. In these biographies, Tomalin illustrates that it was so difficult to know what her subjects were really like, as they paraded different aspects of their character depending on who they were with or in the different settings in which they lived and worked.

Tomalin argues that "What you look for when you are thinking about a biography are the stories in somebody's life" (2004, 92). In her view, "the impulse behind writing biography is the same as the impulse that lies behind most writing. It's the ability to see stories, to tell stories" (94).[2] The form and style of narrative that underpins these stories influences the nature of the story being told. But Tomalin is cautious about making connections where facts are not available and she approaches autobiographical evidence with care, speculating when she has a particular point of view to offer. In her biography of Nelly Ternan, little evidence is available about the period 1862–1865 when Ternan possibly lived in France and may have had a child who subsequently died. In this period, "Nelly now disappears from view completely" (1991, 135) and Tomalin is clear that at this point in her biography she is writing "a chapter of guesses and conjectures, and those who don't like them are warned" (135). She supports her case for a close intimate relationship between Nelly and Dickens in a chapter about Dickens's lost diary for the year 1867, in which 'N' features frequently.

In her biography of Katherine Mansfield, Tomalin considers that she has a different perspective in relation to Mansfield's medical history and she offers a "reinterpretation of certain key questions in her life" (1988, 1). A description rooted in speculation takes place when Tomalin describes why in her view Mansfield's miscarriage and love affair with Floryan Sobieniowski changed her life: "without an understanding of what happened to her in 1909, the rest of her life simply does not make sense" (70). Tomalin is alert to accusations of invention: "In a biography, the problem is one of documentation; it is not possible to prove every detail of the story I propose to trace, but it does fit all the facts we know" (71). Following an early love affair and pregnancy and a rushed, disastrous marriage to another man, her mother whisks her off to Europe and then abandons her to have her baby alone. She has a miscarriage and goes on to meet Sobieniowski, who, Tomalin suggests, infects her with gonorrhoea, a disease which, the biography speculates, contributed to her early death:

> It could even be said that her story hinges on a single physical fact. By becoming pregnant during the first months of her passionately sought freedom in London, she set in motion a sequence of events which ran to her death fourteen years later, events which darkened her relations with her family most unfortunately; which profoundly affected both her marriages; which involved her reputation as a writer; and which destroyed the foundations of her bodily health. (1988, 7)

The crucial speculation concerns not only the diagnosis of the disease itself, but whether Mansfield knew that she had gonorrhea. Tomalin uses a simple direct statement to make her position clear: "My own view is that she must have suspected something" (78). At the time, the illness could successfully be treated in men but was far more serious for women, particularly if the infection entered the bloodstream. This happened, in Mansfield's case, following poor medical advice, a feature of her treatment for both gonorrhoea and the tuberculosis that eventually killed her.

Sobieniowski introduces Mansfield to Chekhov; another key moment in her life follows. When Mansfield subsequently meets a publisher to discuss the publication of her first story, he picked out ... "The Child-Who-Was-Tired". The dilemma for Mansfield was acute. When he singled it out, she should obviously have said at once, "That one is actually a version of the work of another writer—the Russian writer, Chekhov." ... She said nothing. (1988, 80).

Here, Tomalin is interested in both the act of plagiarism by Mansfield and how she handles the publication of this story, both of which question her integrity as an author but also her state of mind at the time these events took place. Her ex-lover subsequently goes on to elicit money from Mansfield.

In teasing out the different 'visions' of each subject, Tomalin speculates but, as already noted, she is not looking for a one-size-fits-all representation of her subjects, and at times she does rely on probably and maybe. Tomalin comments that when Wollstonecraft went to live with her publisher Joseph Johnson, "probably she was awkward about how their association might be interpreted and he may have wanted to reassure her that his intentions were businesslike" (1992, 93). When Austen was sent away to school with Cassandra at seven years old, it "was Jane's second banishment from home" (2000, 35). This assertion is followed by speculation that the "very wretchedness may also have done something for her" (38), as reading and writing became a retreat given that "Other people's worlds offer an escape ... her own imagination may have offered her another escape route" (38). The fact that she attended the school is a fact, but what Austen thought about it and the extent to which it transformed her writing is speculative. It becomes part of the story about what may have been on Austen's mind when she came to write about a school in one of her famous novels.

Tomalin draws extensively on letters written by her subjects. Jordan's story is rich in letters which form the heart of the biography's evidence: "Dora Jordan produced no autobiography, but we have something almost as good, at least for twenty-five years of her life, and that is her letters" (1995, xviii). Tomalin is aware that the narrative in letters, and other autobiographical material, is mediated, as her subjects fashion an image for themselves that they want others to believe, or when they know that their letters could become public documents; she speculates about why this may have been the case. Tomalin responds directly to one of Dora Jordan's letters when she writes of her desertion by the Duke of Clarence, who had been her lover for many years. As an heir to the throne, he was under pressure to leave her. In the letter, Jordan writes that he "'has done no *wrong*, and he is *suffering* for it. But as far as he has left it in his own *power*, he is doing everything *kind* and *noble*, even to distressing himself'" (247). Tomalin then comments, "whose power was he in, if the royal family was so much engaged on her behalf?" (247), when Jordan is faced with being cut off without adequate support because her lover, as a future king, needed to find a wife and greater respectability. Of the letter as a whole, Tomalin comments:

> Dora was reluctant to find a villain, and unable to suspect she was being lied to by the highest in the land in order to keep her quiet.
>
> Was there no one to tell the Duke to his face that his behaviour was that of a monster? Not a single adviser? ... Apparently not. (1995, 247)

At the end of her life, an outcast living in France where she had fled from her debts, Jordan tries to make the best of her situation in her letters to her children. For Tomalin, these letters were a lifeline, and less a record of reality than a means of coping with it. In her last surviving letter, she expresses confidence that "'We shall all meet again, and I trust be very happy'" (296), although since her separation from their father, Jordan had rarely seen her children and must have known that she was unlikely to do so again. By drawing attention to this letter, Tomalin makes the reader aware of Jordan's role as a mother, keen to reassure her children, whilst at the same time highlighting the tragic irony of the loneliness, poverty and sadness at the end of her life.

Tomalin has on occasions drawn our attention to one particular autobiographical document that seems pivotal in the life of her subject. One letter gives expression to the core division in Jordan's life:

> her pride in what she had achieved in her profession and her acknowledgement of the price she and her family had to pay for it ... It is a statement that sounds like the exact truth: she is equally distressed at her separation from her family and proud of her achievement in the theatre. (1995, 229)

In another letter to her son George, written two years before her death, Jordan wrote: "'I begin to feel that acting keeps me alive ... in fact it keeps me from thinking'" (294). Tomalin's use of words is interesting as she draws our attention to the nature of autobiographical evidence here. A "statement" implies something that is fixed and closed, rather than open-ended, and "sounds like the exact truth" draws our attention to Tomalin's rare suggestion that this letter gives an authentic, albeit mediated, picture of what Jordan thought.

When the direct voices of her subjects are not available, Tomalin turns to autobiographical evidence written by those who were close to them. In the case of Dora Jordan, Tomalin describes those written by her sons. Henry writes to his sibling George about their father's desertion of their mother, which he learns about from a newspaper story shown to him by a friend. Tomalin is moved by his anger on his mother's behalf:

> When I opened the double sheet with its crumbled edges and began to read, the clear, true voice of Henry's outraged grief brought him to life before me with all the force he put into the writing, and I found I had tears in my eyes as I read. (1995, 251)

Then, Tomalin describes that on the day of Jordan's funeral, 13 July 1816,

> the Duke wrote to Henry [stationed thousands of miles away in India] from Bushy as though nothing had happened ... Henry must have received his father's letter round about Christmas 1816, along with the one from Barton [John Barton, an advisor to the Duke] informing him of his mother's death. We don't know what he thought. (305)

Tomalin does not make any specific suggestions about what Henry may actually have been thinking. But she immediately goes on to discuss Henry's health, drawing the reader's attention to the sudden deterioration in his physical state, which led quickly to his death. It is not possible to know if Henry died of a broken heart as his health may well have been compromised already. Tomalin is describing one version of what may have happened so soon after Henry hears about the death of his mother and his father's casual denial:

> There was not much joy in Henry's life. After the news of his mother's death reached him, his health began to give cause for alarm; and before he was due to start the long journey home from Madras, before he could even visit George [his brother], he became ill. For four days the fever raged in him; and after four days he died. (307)

Here we do not know what Henry thought but Tomalin's view is clear. We, as readers, can make up our own minds about whether we agree. At the end of the biography, Tomalin is explicit in her point of view:

> A woman who should have been honoured and supported, surrounded by family, comforted in her illness, was instead first driven out of her home, then separated from the sons who were her natural protectors, and divided from her young daughters, who were encouraged to forget about her while she lived ... No one lifted a finger to help her in practical matters; no one spoke for her in her isolation and illness. (304)

This is a poignant, moving and partisan passage where Tomalin's sympathy with her subject is out in the open as she highlights the patriarchal denials that resulted in Jordan's lonely death. Jordan fashions one version of her long-term partner's rejection, and Tomalin offers another. We, as readers, can decide for ourselves what we believe.

Mansfield's autobiographical material, plus published and unpublished autobiographical documents from or sent to her husband, John Middleton Murry, as well as first-person narratives written by others who knew her, Virginia Woolf and D.H. Lawrence in particular, are key sources for this biography. Tomalin's biographies resound with the voices of her subjects. However, Tomalin reflects on the reliability of the correspondence between Mansfield and her husband when she was in Europe because of ill health: "Sad as it is to read their plans for an impossible future, it is worse to eavesdrop on their mutual flattery, which becomes part of the fantasy" (1988, 167) that they create in these letters about their future life together. The letters show how they tried to bolster each other's confidence and to delude each other about the seriousness of her illness.[3] The biography highlights the extent to which her correspondence, unpublished during her lifetime, became an essential part of Mansfield's writing life and the version of it that she creates in her letters. At one point, she wrote ninety-eight letters to her future husband Murry, along with many to her friends, over a three-month period.[4] The biography comments that, in her letters to other women, "they do suggest she was adopting poses to impress" (182). Although she encouraged Murry to destroy many of her letters and manuscripts before her death, the biography adds wryly that "she could have destroyed her papers herself and insisted on Murry returning her letters, had she really been set on their destruction" (227), suggesting that she thought they might have an extended life after her death. Commenting on Mansfield's journal and notebook entries, Tomalin notes "that she made up wild stories to impress" (24). This is a key theme of Tomalin's biography: she was "a liar all her life—there is no getting around this—and her lies went quite beyond conventional social lying … lies became not lies but fiction, a perfectly respectable thing" (57). Murry was also a flawed character, and at times Tomalin is particularly ironic in tone when Murry is being weak and self-centred: "For Murry, everything in life had to be turned into literature … Clearly, he had no inkling that he was saying something that makes one quiver with embarrassment on his behalf" (141). Lies, or the distortion of facts, may be appropriate for fiction, but Tomalin is alert to their use in the autobiographical material of her subjects and to the way that they fashion their lives by telling them.

In *The Life and Death of Mary Wollstonecraft* (1974), Tomalin tells the story of Wollstonecraft's courtship with William Godwin, who became her husband and the father of Mary Shelley, the future wife of the poet Shelley, by using autobiographical material, in particular their letters. Yet again she is careful to draw our attention to their potential duplicity given that "Neither of them was entirely reliable as a witness about the sequence of events in their wooing" (1992, 258). Tomalin offers evidence from a letter by Wollstonecraft to a friend to highlight one version of her feelings for Godwin:

> The wound my unsuspecting heart formerly received is not healed. I found my evenings solitary, and I wished, while fulfilling the duty of a mother, to have some person with similar pursuits, bound to me by affection; and besides, I earnestly desired to resign a name which seemed to disgrace me. (1992, 269)

For Wollstonecraft, becoming a married woman would relieve her loneliness and help remove the social stigma of using her ex-lover Gilbert Imlay's surname. Tomalin then goes on to comment on Wollstonecraft's behaviour:

> Godwin was clever and famous and sought after; she was fond of him, wanted a companion and bedmate, a father for Fanny; she had become pregnant by him; he was willing; it was enough. (270)

In this passage, we hear how the biographer has assessed Wollstonecraft's aims, suggesting that "her cool account of her motives in marrying represents the truth of one of her moods if not the whole truth" (270).

Tomalin draws out the many complexities of her subject throughout her biography, and she reflects on other aspects of autobiographical evidence, as we come to know something about the different sides of Wollstonecraft's personality. In her youth, Wollstonecraft ran a school with her two sisters and during this period she wrote a manual on education, *Thoughts on the Education of Daughters* (1786): "A striking omission from her book, as from her letters, was any mention of her own pupils ... She never could write without inserting more or less veiled remarks about her own emotional state" (58). Tomalin argues that during the closing stages of her affair with Imlay, Wollstonecraft's letters show that she "could not bear to acknowledge that she had been wrong about him. It was impossible for her to accept that he was simply not interested in her sorrows" (222). Tomalin does not say that she is confident about what Wollstonecraft actually thought and felt, but by looking closely at autobiographical evidence and making connections between what happened in her life and what she reveals in her letters, we read a portrayal of a flawed, at times self-centred and complex character which seems authentic and reflects the highly emotional tone in her letters throughout her life.[5] The letters are not read naively, or at face value, and Tomalin's tone is a reflection of her point of view.

The biography also highlights the importance of Wollstonecraft as a politically active writer who sought to transform the lives of women—her *Vindication of the Rights of Women* (1792) remains in print today—despite her antipathy towards some women, including her sisters who she patronised and were, in her view, "always her albatrosses, burdensome, irritating and inescapable" (1992, 21). She was incredibly brave, or some might say foolhardy, as she experienced living in Paris at the height of the revolution. The tone of this biography is as important as the tenor of Wollstonecraft's letters. When describing her attempts to support Ann, a small orphan girl, Tomalin comments wryly that the girl "was a victim of Mary's egocentric imagination. Those who came into her power and could not play the roles she had planned for them were not let off lightly" (108). We should not miss the irony in her tone here, as Tomalin seems perhaps less than sympathetic both to Wollstonecraft's desperation and her anger when she has not been able to get someone to do what she wants. So, on the one hand we have a courageous and feminist political campaigner who wrote the *Historical and Moral View of the French Revolution* (1795) whilst pregnant with her first child and having been all but abandoned by her lover. On the other, we have a woman whose political sympathies seem at odds with her personal life and who is unable to face up to the contradictory and conflicting aspects of her life and writing. It is the doubleness in her life that makes her story so fascinating and brings her to life in the biography. This seems to be informed in part by a form of vulnerability that continues to make her a victim of patriarchal forces. In her romantic notion of her relationship with Imlay, Tomalin reads Wollstonecraft as a victim of the hope that men who seem to share common values of equity and freedom with their lovers will treat women well and believe that "they will be loved the more ardently and faithfully for their pains" (187).[6] Sadly, in Wollstonecraft's story this was not the case—an experience she shares with Dora Jordan.

In her biography of Austen, Tomalin dedicates a chapter to the earliest of Austen's letters to survive, to her sister Cassandra, wishing her happy birthday. At this point in her life, Austen dreams of love and marriage. As Tomalin makes us aware, it is

> the only surviving letter in which Jane is clearly writing as the heroine of her own youthful story, living for herself the short period of power, excitement and adventure that might come to a young woman when she is thinking of choosing a husband; just for a short time she is enacting instead of imagining. (2000, 119)

This letter was written in the mid-1790s when Austen was writing the reworked drafts of novels that went on to become *Pride and Prejudice* (1813), *Sense and Sensibility* (1811) and *Northanger Abbey* (1818). It was a pivotal period in her career as a novelist. But the letter is important for another reason. Very few of her letters survive, only one hundred and sixty for her whole life and twenty-eight for a prolific period in her writing career, 1796–1801. As a result, says Tomalin, her biography is "not an easy story to investigate. She herself wrote no autobiographical notes, and if she kept any diaries they did not survive her" (2000, 4). Many of her letters were destroyed by Cassandra and the problem for a biographer is that this "leaves the impression that her sister was dedicated to trivia ... She leaves out the empty spaces, the moments of solitude and imagination, the time spent thinking, dreaming and writing" (124). Tomalin is aware that what "you do pick up from the letters of the 1790s is the sisters' great reliance on one another for information and understanding that could not be expected from anyone else" (124). The nature of the autobiographical evidence discussed here draws attention to the extent to which our lives may be fashioned by others creating myths that are at the very least partial and fragmented.

Literary biographers leave themselves open to criticism when they ascribe direct connections between the life and work of their subjects. Tomalin is careful how she approaches this. She believes that we can make a few guesses about connections between Austen's life and writing, but she cautions that, "What Jane Austen wanted from the life around her, she took and used, finely and tangentially ... Austen took precisely the elements she wanted from her neighbours and no more" (2000, 102). This biography makes the case that "her books are never transcripts of what she saw going on around her" (169), and in particular that Austen's "work was done in her head" (169). In other words, her experiences, reading, views and feelings were transformed in her writing and it is as a story about this process of authorship that we can, in part, understand this biography. Similarly, Tomalin argues that Hardy was able "to store up experiences and draw on them imaginatively in his writing years later" (2007, 19), and that he "wasted no scrap of experience" (60) in his writing. Sadly, many of these seem to have reinforced his anger and sense of rejection and "the wounds inflicted by life never quite healed over in Hardy" (83). The world he creates in his fiction is almost more real to him than his own life. Tomalin notes that "Emma [his first wife] complained that he cared more for the women he imagined than for any real woman" (197), and the biography goes on to argue that Emma becomes such a woman after her death as she is brought to life again, or at least through Hardy's creative memorial to her, in his poetry.

Tomalin is interested in the representative nature of her subjects' appearance. In the case of Austen, she notes that "Biographers soon learn that there is no such thing as a reliable description or portrait" (2000, 110), just as there is no one way to describe who Austen was as a person. Tomalin observes that Austen was not really interested in how she looked: "the impression we get is that, had she lived two hundred years later, she would have rejoiced in the freedom of a pair of old trousers, with a tweed skirt for church, and one decent dress kept for evening" (113). Tomalin concludes, as much from what has not been said about her appearance as what has, that Austen was "Not a beauty, but attractive to those who knew her best and responded to the animation, responsiveness and intelligence of her expression" (113). Tomalin offers us a version of a rather frumpy Austen, attractive because of her nature, but at other times rather alarming. In her biography of Dora

Jordan, most certainly a beautiful woman, Tomalin begins and ends the story with the statue that her lover, the future king, commissioned following her death. This encourages a reading of Jordan as a possession, an iconic image to be observed, lusted after—not a fellow human being, to love and care for: "her pose, in its simplicity and tenderness, makes one think less of an actress or muse than of a Renaissance madonna" (1995, 3). The fate of the statue, hidden away from public and even private viewings, embodies the way that the royal family sought to hide the truth about Jordan's life away from public gaze. Tomalin emphasises that the statue, referred to as a woman rather than an object, "made her first public appearance, more than one hundred and twenty years after she was sculpted, in 1956" (320). As a writer interested in feminist issues, Tomalin uses embodiment as a narrative tool. Austen's physical image and body are as elusive as her true self, and Jordan is on a pedestal, an angelic, asexual being (a Madonna) for the Duke of Clarence after her death, although he was not able to care for her as a woman at the end of her life.

At times, Tomalin interjects a more lyrical passage in particular scenes, shifting the tone and pace of her story. Lee suggests that anecdotal sharpness is "one of the vital qualities of biography" (2009, 55), and the detail and tone of a particular scene becomes representative of one aspect of a biographical subject's life or character. Benton argues that Tomalin is good at scene setting: "it is the emotional colouring and vivid recreation that they bring which lifts the life off the page and into the reader's imagination" (2015, 24). In the following example, which reflects interesting features of the economic and social conventions of the period, Tomalin conjures up Austen's happy and idyllic childhood with her parents and with the fee-paying school boys who shared her home and were taught by her father:

> Bread was baked, and beer was brewed at home and stored down in the cellars; the parsonage had its own cows to be milked, and the cream churned by the diary maid for their butter ... In June there was haymaking, when the children were supplied with small hayrakes; in July there was boiling of jams and jellies; in August the harvest; in September you heard shooting. (2000, 31)

On the day that baby Jane Austen left the house with her mother and family to be christened at the local church, Tomalin writes that "after a harsh, dark morning, the sun came out. Little Jane was well wrapped in shawls ... and the family processed up the lane to the church" (4). On her entry into the world comes the sun—a lyrical moment. As her life draws to a close, Tomalin comments that 15 July "was very rainy" (271). Austen rallied round and on 17 July "the sun shone all day until the evening, when rain again set in for the night" (272), and Austen died. Cassandra wrote of her sorrow because Austen "'was the sun of my life'" (274). In both of these examples, Tomalin draws in the reader—we almost smell the baking bread, hear the distant shooting, and feel the warmth of the sun. She is offering evocative storytelling and it is up to the reader to decide if this seems authentic. They will more than likely know that they are reading a story about this life and that the way the story is told is part of their experience as a reader.

In another example, Tomalin opens her biography of Wollstonecraft by describing an area of London representative of her family heritage:

> At the ragged eastern edge of the City of London is a district known as Spitalfields ... By the middle of the eighteenth century the streets were dark, dirty and crammed ... for the most part it was a place of stench, din and ruthless competition. (1992, 12)

Her grandfather was an ambitious and hardworking entrepreneur in this environment and this setting places Wollstonecraft firmly within the confines of a ruthless city where she did not have the support of an intellectually stimulating family. She felt rootless and had to fight for herself from her early childhood, "If we are to trust Marty's own account" (14), and she "observed early that people rose by their wits and fell for lack of them" (14). Tomalin fashions her subject as a woman who shared "the creed of all her contemporaries who, like her, became revolutionaries in the [Seventeen] Nineties" (14). Although Wollstonecraft does live for a time outside the city, London and Paris are the places where she seems most at home. The opening of the biography roots her early life in a harsh urban environment, one very different from the internal, domestic setting in which many middle-class women's lives might be placed. Wollstonecraft's death is even more bleak and violent. The opening of the biography emphasises the brutal nature of life on the streets of London with "dog fights, duck hunts ... the baiting of an ox" (12). Her life ends in London as the physician struggles to remove with his hands all the placenta from Wollstonecraft's womb, without anaesthetic, while puppies suckle at her breasts and the bed shakes violently due to feverish shivers as she fights for her life. This is a violent and brutish battle that she loses.

In her later biographies of male writers, Tomalin is more circumspect in her writing style; lyrical, somewhat romanticised passages are avoided. She does include strong opening anecdotes in the prologue of all three of these biographies; each of them is concerned with her subjects' relationship with women. Hermione Lee emphasises the importance of openings in biographies, as does Benton. Lee suggests that "Beginnings want to catch the reader's interest ... they also set up the biographer's tone" (2009, 124). Both Tomalin's biographies of Pepys and Hardy open with anecdotes about her subjects' relationship with their wives and these relationships are a crucial part of the story Tomalin wants to tell. In the prologue to *Samuel Pepys: The Unequalled Self* (2002), Tomalin describes a scene between Pepys and his wife, Elizabeth: "At seven o'clock on a January morning, as the sky over London was growing light, a row broke out in a bedroom between a husband and wife" (2003, xxxiii). Elizabeth has written a letter to explain how lonely she is, but they argue and Pepys destroys some of their personal papers, including letters: "To both husband and wife the written word was of great importance. Both were readers, and destruction of written evidence of their love and its history was a symbolic act" (xxxv), and this was "a painful landmark in the marriage" (xxxv). It also draws attention, at the very start of the biography, to documents that chart their life but have been destroyed by Pepys, whilst he was careful throughout his life to protect his diaries. His writing life is placed at the centre of this biography from the opening pages, as they are in Tomalin's biography of Hardy. In the case of Hardy, the prologue starts as follows:

> In November of 1912 an ageing writer lost his wife. He was not expecting her to die, but then he had not been taking much notice of her for some time ... This is the moment when Thomas Hardy became a great poet ... it was the death of Emma that proved to be his best inspiration. (2007, xvii)

The first chapters of both these biographies start far more traditionally. Pepys "was born in London, above the shop, just off Fleet Street, in Salisbury Court, where his father John Pepys ran a tailoring business"

(2003, 3), although a moment of drama is created in Tomalin's Hardy biography:

> Hardy's life began like this. His mother went into labour on 1 June 1840. She sent for the midwife, a neighbour. The short hours of darkness passed, the sun rose and filled the bedroom with its light, she had a bad time, and at eight o'clock the child was born, apparently lifeless … Then the midwife … exclaimed, "Dead! Stop a minute, he's alive enough, sure!" And so he was … not dead yet. (2007, 3)

The irony was, of course, that Hardy went on to live a long and successful life. Tomalin's Dickens biography opens with a woman, but, in this case, it is a young servant who Dickens supports during a criminal trial. It serves to highlight two of the key themes in Dickens's life— the extent to which he was upset by "the poverty, the hunger, the ignorance and squalor he saw in London" (2011, xlii), and the role that young impoverished women played in both his life and his fiction.

Tomalin at times takes a thematic approach to her subjects' lives, whilst retaining chronology. A look at her chapter headings often makes this clear, as they relate to a particular story or anecdote. Among the chapter headings in her biography of Mary Wollstonecraft are "Fuseli", "Imlay", both of whom she loved, and "Godwin". They also mark keys moments in her life, such as "London 1792", "Paris: Expatriates and Politicians", "A Vindication" and "Putney Bridge", where she tries to commit suicide. This approach is particularly important in the second part of her biography of Pepys. It covers the period in which Pepys was writing his diary and makes up approximately half of the book. The biography does not move chronologically through the diary, discussing key moments or events, but takes a thematic approach as indicated in the chapter headings, including "Families", "Work" "Jealousy" (within his marriage), "Death and Plague", "War", "Marriage", "The King", "The Fire" (about the Fire of London in 1666) and "The Secret Scientist", regarding his membership of The Royal Society. This section invites us as readers back to the diary itself—a primary purpose of literary biography.

In Tomalin's biography of Hardy, the chronology of his life is partly marked out as key moments or phases in his life are identified. As a boy, "a new phase of his life started when … he set off alone on the three-mile walk to school in Greyhound Yard in the centre of Dorchester"

(2007, 31). As a young man, Hardy moves to London: "Now he was shaking off mother, home, all the web of experiences and associations that had formed him but also cramped him in the country. It was a brave move" (62). In March 1870, Hardy "set off on what proved to be the most momentous journey of his life" (98), when he met Emma. In 1871 Hardy became a full-time writer: "This was the turning point in his professional life. He had made the leap into being a full-time writer … it was a great moment" (121). This biography moves through these turning points, but in Tomalin's biographies chronology is often less straightforward than it might seem in a cursory reading.

It is very difficult to write about all the different strands of a life that run alongside each other, particularly as they will move at different paces and have their own key moments. Benton suggests that biography may

> capture the way time is experienced by the subject and everyone else—that odd mixture of continuity and stillness, anticipation and memory, routine and surprise, a mixture that is likely to be particularly significant in the biography of a poet or novelist. (2015, 29)

He argues that "The 'life narrative' covers a longer period and flows at a different pace from the 'literary narrative'" (29), the life of writing. Richard Ellmann comments that:

> It may well be that biographers are wrong to assume, as they generally do, that their subjects have essences or characters that flow liquidly in childhood and jell in youth, and perhaps petrify in old age. There may be almost as much discontinuity as continuity. (1988, 204)

Whilst Tomalin does use a broadly chronological approach to her subjects' lives, she is certainly interested in the relationship between a 'life narrative' and a 'literary narrative' and one of the themes in her work as a whole is the relationship between her subjects' professional and personal lives, particularly when the chronology of different strands of a life can be difficult to unravel. The 'life narrative' flows at a different pace to the 'literary narrative' and they are integrally intertwined, even if this process is somewhat hidden from view. Benton argues that continuity in biography "is subverted by the inevitable gaps in the *histoire*" (2015, 24) and, as a result, "biographical narrative demands selection from a range of possibilities to lend continuity to the life story" (24). As MacCarthy notes, a pattern has to be created, but it is interesting to consider what a biography does when there are gaps in the facts about a life. There may still be a compelling story to tell, albeit that some of the key facts are missing.

Tomalin structures her biography of Austen chronologically for the most part but the existing evidence, or lack of it, does not encourage a steady chronological approach. The biography draws together available evidence from Austen's life, but it also places her life within the context of the lives of her family and friends and within the political and social culture of the time. For example, the life of her cousin, Eliza Hancock, is brought to life and is a fascinating contrast to Austen's own. Hancock may have been the illegitimate daughter of Warren Hastings; she was widely travelled and married a landowning Frenchman caught up with the French Revolution. She supports her disabled son at home and moves in the best social circles, going on to a second marriage with Henry, one of Austen's brothers.

Chapter headings also indicate the wider context within which Austen's life is being understood: "The French Connection", "Weddings and Funerals", "Neighbours", including the local gentry and villagers, and "Dancing". The French Revolution in the late eighteenth century and the military service and conflicts that rule the lives of her brothers are other key themes in this biography. Two chapters consider her appearance and one particular letter written in her youth to her sister, Cassandra. This chapter marks the end of Austen's life before she began a significant period of writing, and the next four chapters, chapters twelve to fifteen, focus on her life and writing over four important years, 1795–99, during which she wrote the first drafts of three novels which would either not be published until many years later, or until after her death. Chapter twelve opens with a turning point, her brief love affair in 1795 with Tom Lefroy who was sent away by his family as soon as his entanglement with a penniless girl became clear:

> A small experience, perhaps, but a painful one for Jane Austen, this brush with young Tom Lefroy. What she distilled from it was something else again. From now on she carried in her own flesh and blood … the knowledge of sexual vulnerability … Her writing becomes informed by this knowledge, running like a dark undercurrent beneath the comedy.

> Writing is what she increasingly turned to now. (2000, 122)

Tomalin's use of her subject's name is interesting here, as she emphasises the life of the writer, Jane Austen, rather than a young woman
called Jane, and the extent to which this experience may have been transformed in her life of writing. So, "in four years three major novels were
under way; and she was not yet twenty-four" (123). Chapter sixteen is
called "Twenty Five", noting her age, when Austen, with three unpublished manuscripts under her belt, stops writing and "she fell silent.
For ten years she produced almost nothing" (169). In this period, she
moves away from her beloved childhood home, Steventon, to Bath,
where she is unhappy. The next ten years of her life are covered in three
chapters in Tomalin's biography amounting to only thirty-three pages.
Then, in 1809, Austen, her mother and sister move to Chawton and she
takes up her pen again to write *Mansfield Park* (1814), *Emma* (1816)
and *Persuasion* (1818); her life as a published author then begins in
1811. Austen died only six years later in 1817. In Tomalin's biography,
Austen's 'life narrative' and 'literary narrative' interweave in a complex
pattern.

For Tomalin, the points of direct connection between these two lives
relate to Austen's need for a particular writing environment and to have
some control over her life:

> What she did depend on was particular working conditions which allowed
> her to abstract herself from the daily life going on around her; and these
> she lost just after her twenty-fifth birthday. What made her fall silent was
> another huge event in her 'life of no event': another exile. (2000, 170)

Tomalin thus appears to follow what Claire Harman calls the "most
persistent theory about Austen's creative life ... that she had two
'phases' of composition, in the 1790s and after 1809, which were
divided by eight years of dearth; that the family's move to Bath in 1801
silenced her and that her muse returned only when she settled back in
Hampshire" (2009, 42). Harman repudiates this theory, providing evidence that whilst in Bath Austen sold her manuscript for *Susan* in 1803,
and that she started work on a new novel, *The Watsons*. Harman suggests that whilst Bath clearly was a "time of retrenchment and change,
Austen is unlikely to have given up her habit of writing in these years"
(Harman 2009, 45). In her view, in relation to the manuscripts of
two of Austen's early novels written before the move to Bath, "First
Impressions" and "Elinor and Marianne", she "must have been working

on both of them in the years 1805–1810" (49), after which she moved to Chawton. Tomalin acknowledges that Austen sold her manuscript of *Susan* and that she began to write a new novel during these years in Bath. But she understands both of these experiences as difficult for Austen. *Susan* was an earlier title for what become *Northanger Abbey* (1817), and this novel was not published until after her death, although an early manuscript was sold to a publisher in 1803 but remained published. Tomalin comments that this sale was worse than an earlier refusal of the novel, because "this time Jane's hopes had been raised by an acceptance" (2000, 185). Later in the biography, Tomalin makes it clear that Austen tried to chase the publisher, but to no avail. Her new novel, *The Watsons*, was started during the Bath period, but Austen abandoned it after the death of her father in 1805. Tomalin also notes how much care Austen must have taken with the manuscripts of her other completed but unpublished novels: "Keeping them under her eye must have been one of the unmentioned but essential disciplines of her life" (185). By noting her care of her manuscripts and the events in her life which prevented the publication or completion of other novels, Tomalin's biography suggests that a 'literary narrative' needs to acknowledge that a writer will have periods when they write pages of text, and times when they do not, but they nevertheless live their lives very conscious of themselves as writers, the act of writing itself ebbing and flowing through their everyday existence and caught up with plans for publication, as well as actual writing.

To varying degrees, in her biographies, Tomalin places the lives of her subjects within the historical context of their time, and in doing so she immerses herself in these periods. She is "very interested in context" (2004, 95). For instance, when writing about her biography of Pepys, she describes "stepping into a new century and trying to inhabit it" (90). In the biography itself she notes "my virtual disappearance into the seventeenth century for several years" (2003, xiv). Furthermore, the biography understands Pepys's life in the context of the huge political events of which he was part, including the lead up to the civil war, Cromwell's leadership and the return of Charles II. Tomalin also describes aspects of Pepys's role in developing the navy, in the mid-1660s, which was "the biggest industrial concern and the biggest employer in the country" (139). It is extraordinary to think that he "was the first to keep written records of both officers and ships" (148). The diary also records the plague in 1665 and the Great Fire of London in 1666, in which Pepys played a pivotal role by advising the king on how to handle the fire and recording the progress and impact of the fire in his diary. In her biography of Dickens, Tomalin emphasises, as noted earlier, the extent to which he was concerned with the social condition of the poor and vulnerable throughout his life, despite his harshness towards members of his own family. He gave direct help in terms of money for specific people or causes and developed Urania Cottage to support prostitutes and women who had been in prison, although he believed that "working through his writing was more effective than any political action" (2011, 376), and Tomalin makes clear how much of his social welfare work is transformed in his writing, including *Bleak House* (1853), *Hard Times* (1854) and *Little Dorrit* (1857), all of "which addressed themselves to the condition of England" (239).

Tomalin places her subjects centre stage, but they also tend to be understood in the context of one key relationship, as in her biographies of Dora Jordan and Nelly Ternan, or of a wider group of family, friends and professional peers. Writing about the preparations for her biography of Thomas Hardy, Tomalin notes that, when planning, she prepares a "cast list" (2004, 95). His life is understood in the context of his relationships with his wives, other women he was attracted to, his mother and sisters, and professional men such as Leslie Stephen, although Hardy seems "hard to know" (2007, 282) and detached for much of his life. The lives of others are even more significant in Tomalin's biography of Pepys, "an intensely sociable being" (2003, 290), which opens with a lengthy "List of Principal Figures" (xxi). Pepys is clearly the main figure, but others are crucially important in this biography, including his wife, Elizabeth, Jane Birch, his maid, Mary Skinner, his partner following the death of his wife, William Hewer, his closest associate, and professional colleagues, including Edward Montagu and William Coventry. Mrs Montagu was also a close friend for many years. A similarly long list is called a "Cast List" in Tomalin's biography of Dickens. Like Pepys, Dickens was a social and performative being. Tomalin's biography covers a huge number of relationships, including the ones with the women in his life, particularly his wife, Catherine, Nelly Ternan, his alleged mistress, and his wife's sister, Georgina, who supported his household and family for many years after he separated from his wife. Dickens's close friendship with John Forster is an important theme in this book, as are his friendships with other writers such as Wilkie Collins, and professional relationships with men like William Wills, central to his life as a journalist and journal editor, and George Dolby who ran his reading tours. His relationship with Forster, his first biographer, seems central to an understanding of his life. Forster read and advised on his writing and personal affairs throughout his life and "he was the only man to whom he confided his most private experiences and feelings" (2011, 80). This biography also emphasises Dickens's need for his public. The thousands of people who attended his reading tours later in his life "gave him reassurance that he was loved" (290), and "he saw readings as a way of strengthening what he felt to be almost a personal friendship with his readers" (295). There is another group of people towards whom Dickens could be extremely harsh: his "unwanted sons" (108), although he dealt with Charley and Henry less harshly than the others. Sidney had wanted to go to sea, and Dickens took trouble to help him do so. Alfred and Plorn were sent to Australia, Walter and Frank to India. Once Dickens had decided not to pay off any more of his sons' debts, "he was pitiless" (388) towards them, as he was towards Catherine when he evicted her from the family home.

Claire Tomalin is explicit in the introduction to her biography of Katherine Mansfield that she empathises with her subject as a woman writer:

> I am of the same sex as my subject. It may be nonsense to believe that this gives me any advantage over a male biographer. Yet I can't help feeling that any woman who fights her way through life on two fronts—taking a traditional female role, but also seeking male privileges—may have a special sympathy for such a pioneer as Katherine, and find some of her actions and attitudes less baffling than even the most understanding of men. (1988, 2)

In her other biographies, those about Jane Austen, Mary Wollstonecraft, Nelly Ternan and Mrs Jordan, Tomalin explores women's experience in a patriarchal world. In Tomalin's writing, an underlying gendered focus emphasises the relationship between the public and private in people's lives. Austen as a woman is subject to the whims of her relatives and has to mediate between a range of different expectations about how she should behave and live her life. Austen's life is understood in Tomalin's biography in the context of the lives of married women who die in childbirth, including her sister-in-law, and whose lives are determined by money and marriage.[7] Tomalin comments that, in her writing, Austen "went on to create young women somewhat like herself, but whose perceptions and judgements where shown to matter; who were able to influence their own fates significantly" (2000, 175). As a woman writer, she could have some control in her fiction, if not in her own life.

Tomalin's biography of Nelly Ternan is "of someone who—almost—wasn't there; who vanished into thin air" (1991, 3); not only was her life and those of other members of her family "blotted out" but she was a "blot on the good name of Dickens" (4). At the end of her life, Nelly has to reinvent herself and is given a "second chance to blot out the shadowy shames and miseries of the past" (220), as Dickens had tried to blot her out of his public and professional life by hiding their relationship from view. This blotting is a wonderful image, which links the whole idea of writing, with ink, and the way that a life can be written out of a relationship and history. Tomalin is concerned about more than one victim in Ternan's story: "If she was Dickens's victim, her husband and children were her victims" (255):

> Geoffrey became a casualty of his mother's history because he had so faithfully absorbed and accepted the view of women generally put about in his youth and wholly subscribed to—as far as he could tell—in his family. It was also a view deeply embedded in the works of Dickens. (1991, 259)

Ternan's son, from her marriage after Dickens's death, was devastated when he learnt about her past life after she had died.

One of the ways that feminist biography rewrites the history of women in biography is described as a process of rewriting or revisioning their lives. Linda Wagner-Martin suggests that Tomalin's biography of Ternan, is a "fascinating re-visioning" (1994, 162) written from Ternan's point of view, rather than Dickens's, who sought to hide his relationship with her. This biography points "to the difficulty of writing about subjects forced to be voiceless" (163), particularly when so little evidence about their lives is available. We know little about what Nelly Ternan thought and felt, but we know a lot about Dickens. Tomalin notes that how "the balance of power was held between him and … [Nelly] (and her family) … must be mostly guesswork" (124), but she credits Ternan with some of the strength of will and "boldness she had observed in Dickens and learnt from him" (220). By seeing his life as part of hers in Tomalin's biography, we come to see Ternan herself, or something of her. For Tomalin, this relationship represents far more than just the lives of two specific people:

> Sometimes ... the telling of one particular story ... will resonate in a larger
> area. When I explored the relationship between Ellen Ternan and Charles
> Dickens, it seemed to me I had stumbled on a story, fascinating in itself,
> that also illuminated a whole era and the assumptions made about relations
> between men and women of that era. (1999, 132)

Tomalin writes about the experiences of other actresses at the start of this biography, because "it is necessary to the story of the Ternans if we are able to see them in context and understand something of the world into which Nelly was born" (1991, 23). The rags-to-riches tale of a younger woman loved by a rich and successful older man is hardly new, even for a canonical figure such as Dickens.

Tomalin's later biography of Dickens tells the story of Nelly and Catherine, his wife. It says little about what his wife said or thought, but the repetition of her pregnancies is a constant reminder that she was his sexual partner and had little or no control over her own life—something which the tone of the biography highlights: "Marriage was for him at least a solution to the problem of sex" (2011, 66). When he chooses to sleep apart from her at the end of their marriage, commenting in a derogatory way about his wife's body to his friends and having met a younger woman, the tone is again important:[8] "It was his way of breaking a sexual habit that had been reduced to a humiliating form of relief, with no residue of tenderness" (292). In her biography of Thomas Hardy, Tomalin is interested in the balances between Hardy's public and personal life and draws attention to the separation between his writing and his married life. Both Hardy's first wife, Emma, and his second, Florence, initially believed that they contributed to his work, only to be severely rebuffed when they strayed into his professional territory:

> as Emma had once resented Hardy's failure to acknowledge her help and
> dedicate books to her, so Florence resented still more furiously his writ-
> ing about Emma ... Having married the world-famous writer, the least she
> expected was to be celebrated as his muse. Instead she felt a humiliation
> from which she seems never to have recovered. (2007, 320)

Hardy published work that neither of his wives had ever seen. The narrative voice in this biography is not uncritical and in one comment, when Hardy chose not to acknowledge the role that Emma played in the writing of *The Woodlanders*, the biography notes that "A dedication would have cost Hardy nothing and meant a great deal to her" (239). Again, tone is important in both these biographies.

Tomalin clearly understands that the nature of narrative in biography is always mediated and provisional but argues that this does not mean that an attempt to make connections is invalid and cannot produce authentic portraits. Tomalin upholds Desmond MacCarthy's mantra that she is "an artist on oath", but reserves the right to speculate when hard evidence is not available. Tomalin's analysis invites an alteration to MacCarthy's rule: a biographer is an artist on oath who re-creates a story based on the facts of a life or lives. Lyndall Gordon puts this in a comparable way in her biography of Charlotte Brontë by suggesting that Elizabeth Gaskell's biography "tells a coherent story" (Gordon 1994, 329) that conveys "a lasting imaginative truth based on a selection of facts" (329). However, biography leaves itself open to criticism if key facts about a life are not selected; as Johnson suggests, fidelity to the available facts is important in a narrative that is not fiction. It is important that the facts are not misrepresented, although perspectives about when this has occurred will inevitably vary. It is also helpful to readers if it is clear if any aspect of a story is based on speculation and readers are alert to the anecdotes where this takes place in biography. Tomalin is aware that autobiographical evidence may be unreliable and that biography can do more than offer conventional, chronological realist narrative. She also acknowledges the potential for biography to illuminate wider social, cultural and political discourses as her work is intimately connected with the lives of women and the concerns of feminism.

An interview with Claire Tomalin in 2016 explored some of these aspects of her writing. I wanted to find out how much of what her biographies had meant to me would be reflected in our conversation. I was also keen to ask her some wider questions about the genre as a whole and to ask in particular about her writing on women, an aspect which seems so central to her work.

IN CONVERSATION WITH CLAIRE TOMALIN

Why do you think biography is so popular?

I think people have always been interested in other people's lives. It is part of the human condition. If you go right back to Plutarch and the Bible, there is an absolutely constant curiosity about other people. You want to imagine what it's like to be another; to have a sort of adventure. If you think of reading about David in the Bible, whether he was a real figure or not is open to dispute, but it's just the extraordinary adventurousness of his life and all the things that happened to him: the friendship with Jonathan, the killing of Goliath, the marriage, the adultery, the loss of his son, one incident after another in his life, which people respond to with very strong emotions and perhaps compare with their own lives, perhaps not.

I, myself, think more and more as I get older that I learn from my subjects. I've particularly learned about the courage of people and the way people face death. One thing that becomes very obvious is that working to the end is very important, work keeps people alive. Jane Austen, as long as she could write with a pen, she did. When she could no longer write with a pen, she wrote with a pencil. It always brings tears to my eyes. Dickens was working on a novel. Pepys was very active to the end of his life. Mrs Jordan went on acting and once she couldn't act anymore, really she couldn't *be* anymore, because work and her children were her life. Mary Wollstonecraft alas died in childbirth, leaving unfinished novels.

The old idea that a biography could be exemplary, that you can find from it examples of the good life (or the bad!) is absolutely true. I think you can. Perhaps the author of the book feels this more strongly than the reader. When you're writing the book, you live with your character. You live in the world they lived in and you feel that you're alongside them.

That is one thing I wanted to ask you about; How would you describe your relationship with your subjects?
Well, it has to be close I would say. Some of your subjects will keep you more at a distance. Jane Austen doesn't invite intimacy, although it is possible, through what we know from her and the few letters there are, to feel a connection. For instance, towards the end of her life when she's trying to get on with rewriting the end of *Persuasion* and her sister Cassandra is away, she writes this little note in a letter where she says, "thoughts of mutton and doses of rhubarb make it very difficult to get on with composition". It was a tiny, tiny remark about having to run the house while she had her brother's children staying, but my God it carries weight for any woman writer, doesn't it?

*Is it difficult to leave your subjects behind when you finish writing a
biography?*
It is. In one sense when you get towards the end of the book, you're
feeling rather cheerful because you've nearly finished but, in another
sense, grieve at parting company. Pepys, for instance, was a marvellous person to live with and one of the reasons for that is that he had
such a strong sense of the shape of his own life—it makes him a gift
to a biographer. If you think of the very end of his life, of the way he
organised his funeral, he was bringing everything together. He had his
body taken from Will Hewer's house in Clapham, across London to St
Olave. St Olave was the church where he and Elizabeth worshipped and
Elizabeth was buried in the church. Elizabeth's bust is up on the wall of
the church and Pepys is having his body taken right across London to be
buried there with Elizabeth looking down on him. Pepys also organised
carefully how the great achievement of his life, his diaries, would be pro-
tected by Magdalene College, Cambridge, his old college.

And Pepys thought about the shape of people's lives. When he went
to the funeral of Admiral Myngs in 1666, he actually says in his diary
that he thought about how Myngs may be forgotten and how he would
leave no record. Obviously, he's thinking about himself. He's thinking
about fame. He's thinking about whether you're remembered or not,
whether you've done anything which will ensure that your name will live
on. Pepys, of course, did ensure that his own name would live on. I find
all that interesting, and moving too.

To what extent has writing about the lives of women been important to you?
I began specifically and deliberately as a feminist biographer. I felt that
women mentioned in history were either royal women or saints, or great
eccentrics or famous whores. From very early days, you get collections of
biographies and it's the men who are famous achievers and the women
tend to be whores. I thought people had no very clear idea of what Jane
Austen's daily life would have been like and I wanted to say so. I began
with Mary Wollstonecraft, who was a wonderful subject and an extraordinary revelation to me, because here was a woman I could instantly
relate to. She was living and writing two hundred years ago, living in
the same part of London I was living in, working for a magazine like the
New Statesman, having difficult relationships with men, trying to organ-
ise childcare and work, going over to Paris. The circumstances of her life
seemed so curiously close to my own that it was an extraordinary bridge

over those two hundred years, suggesting that perhaps working women's lives have always had many things in common.

I also found that some women had been entirely excluded from history. My book about Ellen Ternan was called *The Invisible Woman* because she was effectively made non-existent. When the biography of William IV was written in the 1880s Mrs Jordan was entirely excluded although she had borne him ten children. This seemed ridiculous as well as sinister.

People ask, "Why did you change from writing about women to writing about men?" Well, I didn't actually, because you write about both in any biography. Pepys gives a record of the women of the 1660s, which is absolutely marvellous. From the serving maids, the shop girls, right up to the Countess of Sandwich, Jemima. He is completely fascinating about women, because he's very interested in them and very informative about them.

Richard Ellmann thought of biography as a social genre as the lives of others are inevitably caught up with the lives of friends, family, peers, and the period in which the biographical subject lived. Do you think he is right?
I think he's right. I think context is as important as establishment of character. Biography is a branch of history and one of the things you can do in a biography is illuminate a moment in history, illuminate a period, a movement. In my biography of Mary Wollstonecraft, you see her friendship with the dissenters, like the wonderful publisher Joseph Johnson and William Godwin, of course. Her experience in Paris during the Revolution and what was going on among the French feminists was a great revelation. Context is always extremely important.

One of the pleasures of being a biographer is that you have to be a sort of jackdaw. You have to draw on so many different aspects of history: the history of psychology, of politics, of art, and the history of medicine. I think with practically all my subjects I've had to do some medical research. I could have written a short book on what was happening in the medical treatment of gonorrhoea in the early twentieth century after my research on my biography of Katherine Mansfield.

Well, again, a lesson from Pepys. In the first page of the diary, he puts together in adjacent paragraphs what is happening in the outside world, which was, of course, huge political upheaval, and the fact that his wife hasn't had her period. At that moment Pepys is telling us, and throughout the diary he keeps telling us, that the private and the public life are inextricably connected with one another. That seems to be an absolutely fundamental lesson about life, which, perhaps, English professional men have not always wished to acknowledge. This has probably been more of a female point of view.

What kind of imagination do you need to write biography?
You need imagination, not in the sense that you invent things, but you need to have your mind open to thinking about how other people might be.

When I wrote my first book my editor said, "Couldn't you actually fictionalise it a bit?"; and when I was working on Ternan it was suggested to me that I should make it into a novel. But I like the challenge of making a narrative out of the material you've got. It *is* a challenge and it is demanding and it requires ingenuity and sometimes it's very difficult. That's what I want to do. If I could write fiction, I'd write fiction, but that's not what I do.

When you think about how you are going to approach a subject, do you have an idea of the sort of form and style that it is going to take and does that change?
I don't to begin with, no, but I always keep files in which I jot down various ideas. I like to introduce my subject in some really telling and characteristic moment in their life. In Pepys, I thought the really important thing to do was to talk about how the diary was a picture of the truth. As he writes it down it becomes art. The point of the introduction to that biography was to show life turning into art in front of you, which is really extraordinary. Another thing I tried to do in that book was to have thematic chapters using the diary and at the same time move his life through time.

With Dickens, an important point I wanted to stress was his goodness, and his desire to do good things. What he did for a totally unknown, feeble girl was so extraordinary. I think you can see how that balances against what happened, in a way, with his relationship with Nelly. I also wanted to see him at his most glorious at the start of the book, when everything was going well for him.

In the Hardy, I chose to start at the moment of Emma's death because I thought that really was when he became a great poet, very, very late in his life. That was something really unprecedented in English poetry. What I most wanted to do in my book was make his poetry the centre, because that's what he really thought he was, a poet. He had the inspiring event of the death of a wife, so long neglected, so long unloved, and she suddenly becomes his muse. It's so weird, so strange and so beautiful. The poems are so marvellous. It's Hardy the poet who means the most to me.

I remember struggling and struggling with Katherine Mansfield. It was the book I found most difficult to write. It was a nightmare, for all sorts of reasons, but I sensed fairly late in the narrative that I just could not go on chronologically. So, I devoted a chapter to her relationship with Lawrence and a chapter to her relationship with Virginia Woolf, a chapter to her relationship with Ida, and then one to Murry—because each was crucial to her life in quite a different way. Deciding to do that liberated me from the stranglehold of chronology.

For Mrs Jordan, I started the book with the story of the statue which makes a wonderful parallel commentary on her life experience.

I have always written about people who've had a struggle. I don't write about people who were born into privilege. I am much, much more interested in people who make it by their hard work and skill. Although, you don't always have all that many details about someone's life.

I do try to make my books accessible to the general reader. You want them to feel they're getting somewhere on every page and want to turn to the next page.

I don't think biography can be fictional. If it's fictionalised, it's not biography. I feel very strongly about that. Biography is not fiction, it is historical narrative.

In your biography of Jane Austen, there is a chapter in the middle of the book about her appearance and I wondered why you decided to do that?
I thought that was the moment to do that, to talk about how people saw her and what we know about what she looked like physically, or the different versions of what she looked like. In fact, the chapter about the earliest of her letters to survive, addressed to her sister Cassandra, is my favourite chapter in the book.

I was visiting a family descended from Mrs Jordan and William IV and asked about any letters. They brought out a cardboard box and let me look through them. I found letters from Dora Jordan's second son Henry to his brother. He had heard that his father was going to leave his mother. I drew attention to this letter because it was such a powerful statement and felt quite modern.

What you have to do with letters is to squeeze them, read, re-read, think, read again. You have to go on looking at them and the more you look at them, the more you find out, the more you see the implications of every sentence. If you really, really pore over it, you can get so much from it.

NOTES

1. In the context of a discussion about the use of sources and evidence in biography in the twentieth century, Lee suggests a range of reasons why authenticity may be difficult, in *Biography: A Short Introduction* (2009): a biographer may not be at liberty to identify sources if secrecy was agreed with interviewees; it may not be possible to identify statements by living witnesses; questions of copyright and permission may arise, to name but a few (11). She notes that extensive footnoting "seems to be on its way out. Trade publishers dislike footnotes: too academic, too space-consuming. Some historical biographers are solving this problem by putting their footnotes online, some popular biographers are minimizing their notes" (2009, 11).
2. The collection in which Tomalin's essay appears, *Lives for Sale: Biographers' Tales* (2004), is a useful resource that includes interviews with a number of British biographers.
3. *Katherine Mansfield*, 167.
4. Ibid., 164.
5. Tomalin, *The Life and Death of Mary Wollstonecraft*, 19.
6. Rachel Holmes's biography, *Eleanor Marx* (2014), about Karl Marx's daughter, a nineteenth century political campaigner for the right of workers and women, tells another similar story.
7. Tomalin, *Jane Austen: A Life*, 81.
8. Tomalin, *Charles Dickens: A Life*, 274.

REFERENCES

Benton, Michael. 2015. First published in 2009. *Literary Biography: An Introduction*. Chichester, West Sussex: Wiley Blackwell.
Ellmann, Richard. 1988. *A Long the Riverrun*. London: Hamilton.
Gordon, Lyndall. 1994. *Charlotte Brontë: A Passionate Life*. London: Chatto & Windus.
Harman, Claire. 2009. *Jane's Fame: How Jane Austen Conquered the World*. Edinburgh: Canongate.
Lee, Hermione. 2009. *Biography: A Very Short Introduction*. New York: Oxford University Press.

Tomalin, Claire. 2011. *Charles Dickens: A Life*. London: Viking.

———. 2000. First published in 1997. *Jane Austen: A Life*. London: Penguin.

———. 1988. First published in 1987. *Katherine Mansfield: A Secret Life*. London: Viking.

———. 1995. First published in 1994. *Mrs Jordan's Profession: The Story of a Great Actress and a Future King*. London: Penguin.

———. 2003. First published in 2002. *Samuel Pepys: The Unequalled Self*. London: Penguin.

———. 1999. *Several Strangers: Writing from Three Decades*. London: Viking.

———. 2004. "Starting Over." In *Lives for Sale: Biographer's Tales*, ed. Mark Bostridge, 90–95. London: Continuum.

———. 1991. First published in 1990. *The Invisible Woman: The Story of Nelly Ternan and Charles Dickens*. London: Penguin.

———. 1992. First published in 1974. *The Life and Death of Mary Wollstonecraft*. London: Penguin.

———. 2007. First published in 2006. *Thomas Hardy: The Time-Torn Man*. London: Penguin.

Wagner-Martin, Linda. 1994. *Telling Women's Lives: The New Biography*. New Brunswick, NJ: Rutgers University Press.

CHAPTER 8

Michael Holroyd Re-creating Lives

Michael Holroyd's writing spans more than fifty years, since the publication of his first book, *Hugh Kingsmill: A Critical Biography* (1964). He is perhaps best known as a biographer, but his writing also encompasses fiction, memoir, and metanarratives about writing and the lives of objects. There are a number of reasons why Hugh Kingsmill was important to Holroyd.[1] He was indebted to Kingsmill for making "literature real for me: who made the connection factually and imaginatively between what we read and how we live" (1981, 12). This seems to be one of the values that underpins his re-creative writing as it becomes a discourse about the nature of humanity. Kingsmill set him on the road to be a writer about other people's lives "where there appeared to be more going on" (1981, 13) than in his own life. He suggests that "I have not chosen subjects who resembled me—that would defeat the purpose. I set out to escape into my subjects' lives rather than identify myself with them" (1988, 97). So, in reading about others' lives, we reflect not only on our own day-to-day experience, but supplement it with something extra, that not only helps us to understand what makes us human, flaws and all, but also makes us feel part of something outside and beyond ourselves. Finally, in his Kingsmill biography, Holroyd suggests that, "Where economy and selection are absent, where information replaces insight, writing ceases to be an art and becomes an accumulation" (1964, 105). This chapter is one reader's attempt to understand how Holroyd's re-creative writing, as well as his fiction, can be understood. His writing is in tune with a form of life-writing

© The Author(s) 2017   183
J. McVeigh, *In Collaboration with British Literary Biography*,
DOI 10.1007/978-3-319-58383-9_8

that seeks a pattern, in conversation with his subjects, based on rigorous research and compelling storytelling. In his biographical writing, Holroyd is an artist on oath who re-creates a story based on the facts of a life or lives.

Holroyd, like Johnson, is fascinated by the detail of the everyday through which we can understand more about people and their make-up, fashioned both by themselves and others. This chapter explores the extent to which, in his writing, Holroyd shows how both biography and memoir, in common with other forms of life-writing, are essentially discourses in which both the subject, or subjects, and the narrator are in conversation, and through which we learn as readers, as in all storytelling, about the lives of others and ourselves. In his memoirs, Holroyd is not only interested in the lives of the people he is writing about, many of whom are from his own family; he may also be in an exchange with his narrator, his writing self and his own autobiographical voice. He asks himself in his memoir *Mosaic* (2004), "Can I bring these two selves, the writer and the subject, together on the page? Can I write about myself not passively as a listener or reader, an echo of others?" (2010b, 388). In some ways, his memoirs and biographies ask, how much can our public identity—how other people see us and how we see them—inform our understanding of private and domestic realms, including our own?

In his writing, Holroyd's conversations cross the boundaries of genre. He does not seem to draw a rigid line marking the differences between biography, autobiography or memoir, and he constantly plays with the boundaries between them, as well as between the text and the reader, applying the techniques of biography to his own life. He is attracted to "an 'intimacy between strangers', a closeness growing up during the acts of writing and reading between an author, the reader and their subject" (2010a, 13). In writing his first memoir, *Basil Street Blues* (1999), Holroyd comments that his "identity was shaped by what I wrote, though this identity was concealed behind the people I wrote about" (2010a, 8), and, in doing so, his memoir becomes "a vicarious autobiography" (8). Each act of writing, and one could say the same for each act of reading, creates a change in one's self. Holroyd describes this as a process of being "reborn the child of my writings" (2010a, 14). This reading of his work makes the case that his approach is social and constantly interrogates the ways in which each life interweaves with those of others, whilst at the same time recognising that each of us is often alone, bound within our selves, and lonely. He watches other people, strangers in the street, the lives of his family and those connected with them, and follows them in his imagination: "I never tire of watching. I watch, therefore I am; I am what I watch; and what I watch entrances me. This has been my exit from myself" (2010a, 278). I, too, never tire of watching, often through reading, and what I read entrances me and is an exit from myself. Reading and writing become both social and solitary, dialogic and yet unique. Holroyd is interested in the different selves that each of us inhabit and sees himself as a writer intimately caught up with his life running alongside his writing, although it can be difficult to distinguish the two as writing becomes the man. In his writing, he is interested in how people fashion themselves and the lives of others, rewriting different stories about the same anecdotes or people and reinforcing the view that any life has value, whether the individual is perceived as a publicly successful figure or not. People who transgress and challenge cultural conventions and expectations, or whose lives seem like failures because they do not meet these expectations, are often his subjects. Finally, Holroyd explores the nature of memory and the extent to which forgetting and hiding aspects of ourselves from view are part of the lives we live.

Holroyd is an advocate for the art of re-creative writing, believing that "a cross-fertilization of ideas between fiction and nonfiction is vital for literature" (1981, 22). Perhaps both creative and re-creative writing are part of the literature that supplements our lives, whatever form that literature might take. Literature is increasingly coming to be understood as encompassing digital and non-written forms of text, and not only about canonical or exemplary subjects. This reader tends to see issues about literary style and form on the back of cereal packets, in every text and email, and is a firm believer that re-creative writing informs all aspects of our lives, particularly in forms that are not invented like fiction but could be understood as art—to the extent that the way that a story is told becomes an important part of the narrative, whatever form it takes. Holroyd seems to find literature in both creative and re-creative writing, in reading the lives of others, in reading and writing about his family, other people connected with them, in objects associated with their lives, and in writing about his own life. As Ben Okri puts it:

Great literature is rarely about one thing. It transcends subject. Sometimes an important work has a significant subject, but it is usually its art, rather than its subject, that makes it constantly relevant to us. If the subject were the most important thing we would not need art, we would not need literature. History would be sufficient. We go to literature for that which speaks to us in time and outside time. (2014, 43)

The subject may be ourselves, another person, people or a people, or a culture, along with a historically relevant theme and time, perhaps relevant to our own time as readers, or at least to that of the writer. This is the kind of literature that Holroyd writes, as he reaches out to his readers and by learning about the lives of other people we, as readers, also learn something about ourselves. This is is relevant to all of his writing, including his memoirs and his writing about his aunt Yolande.

Holroyd's *Lytton Stratchey* (1967) is considered a turning point, one which highlighted a dramatic move from public to private concerns in biography. According to Anthony Curtis, "It was then that the Age of Reticence was succeeded by the Age of Candor" (1996, 127). Mark Bostridge has suggested that:

In our own time, modern biography is often said to date from 1967, and the publication of the first volume of Michael Holroyd's life of Lytton Strachey which broke through the barriers of biographical discretion. (2004, xii)

Holroyd's biography achieves the fidelity to the facts of a life, which is important to Samuel Johnson, and it does more than address Strachey's sexuality. As critic Nicholas Wroe comments in a 2008 interview with Holroyd:

Before Holroyd's ground-breaking biography of the Bloomsbury writer Lytton Strachey in 1967, the default form was still based on the stately and portentous Victorian model ... it was Holroyd who first successfully combined rigorous scholarship, wide-ranging research and astute interpretation while also humanising the form through elegant narrative and emotional cognisance. (12)

Holroyd's approach to narrative is elegant; it becomes very much part of the story and, in some of his writing, provides a discourse about the nature of genre itself. Holroyd suggests that if we have secret lives, "the biographer, like an archaeologist, attempts to bring this hidden life into view" (2003, 30). It is this hidden life that Holroyd digs out, although inevitably the picture will be partial and his version of what he has found.

In his preface to *Eminent Victorians* (1918), Strachey argues that "the explorer of the past" (1986, 9) should adopt "a subtler strategy" (9), finding his subject "in unexpected places" (9). He believes that from a "great ocean of material" the biographer should bring "up to the light of day some characteristic specimen ... to be examined with a careful curiosity" (9). He is keen to "present some Victorian visions to the modern eye" (9) and "to illustrate rather than to explain" (9), thereby elucidating "certain fragments of the truth" (9). He makes a plea to deal with biography as part of history, but with a particular part to play given that people "have a value which is independent of any temporal processes" (10). The rigours and length of chronicle biography are to be avoided in favour of a form that offers information and examples: "How many lessons are to be learnt from them!" (10). Strachey suggests that the first duty of the biographer is to exclude "everything that is redundant and nothing that is significant" (10). The second is for a biographer "to maintain his own freedom of spirit ... to lay bare the facts of the case, as he understands them ... dispassionately, impartially, and without ulterior intentions" (10). In full-length biographies, Strachey's approach might encourage overworked caricature. Holroyd creates a pattern with his material in which, as in Strachey, tone and style are influential and he does look for details about his subjects' lives in unexpected places. But his full-length biographies do more than merely seek out people who are characteristic of a particular time or representative of exemplary, influential public figures. It is not a case of excluding everything that is redundant but rather of looking for the details of a life, or lives, that may be hidden from public view yet are significant to describing their story. In a 1986 introduction to Strachey's book, Holroyd comments that what Strachey offers is not dispassionate, nor impartial; rather, Strachey creates portraits that are "a circus spectacle, half amusing, half grotesque" (1986, x). He also notes that objections to Strachey's book reflect concerns about the balance between form and content in biography:

> Objections to *Eminent Victorians* centred on its alleged inexactness of fact and language, and on the false moral basis from which this inexactness arose. Strachey had taken liberties. (1986, x)

Holroyd's biographies are based on all the significant facts, or at least on a less partisan selection than in *Eminent Victorians*, on rigorous research and on re-creative storytelling; they seek a balanced landscape of both granite and rainbow, and his lens is much wider than Strachey's—although his writing at times can adopt a debunking tone.

There is one aspect of storytelling that Strachey and Holroyd have in common, although their approaches to it are very different. Holroyd suggests that Strachey sees the ridiculous and that "laughter was his weapon" (xii). There is a sense of comedy in much of Holroyd's writing; it is important in his biographies of Strachey and Augustus John. We can see the tragic fallibility of Strachey, who struggled with his health and his relationships, and never seemed to quite fit in with his world. In his life of Strachey, this reader finds a busy but lonely, comic figure. John becomes a man who falls from grace and the comedy in Holroyd's biography is significantly darker and more uncomfortable. It shares some of the debunking features preferred by Strachey. Holroyd's writing as a whole is often full of pathos—laughing with Strachey rather than at him.

Holroyd offers his own version of a tragicomedy as he describes specific moments in Strachey's life. A constant moaner, Strachey visits his brother, James, living in his old room in Cambridge. Strachey,

> left unaided to put the coals on the fire, he was unable to find a shovel, the tongs broke, and he was finally obliged to bend down and prise out each black lump with his long, trembling fingers. It was a nightmare. (1967, I: 303)

This portrait is affectionate, whilst not denying some of Strachey's rather eccentric behaviour. Strachey's appearance is an extended trope in the biography that helps to frame his character and presents him as an unconventional and boffin-like figure. He struggled with his gangly appearance when young and, at Liverpool University, before he went on to Cambridge, "he felt he was a freak" (Holroyd 1967, I: 86). He refashions himself and becomes a distinctive figure with a long brown beard and a trademark long dark cloak, and this marks him out as different. Holroyd argues that his beard and cloak "were worn partly as a token of his new liberation, partly for the joy of provoking the too hidebound and conformable" (1968, II: 45). His appearance at times lies at the heart of Holroyd's comic portrayal:

On hot days in the summer, he would arm himself with a green and white parasol or an enormous wopsical sun-hat, and descend from the safety of the veranda, manipulating his elongated joints as he stepped across the lawn with the slow, calculated elegance of some spectacular and precise secretary bird. Then he would subside into a deck-chair, a crumpled, age-less figure, his long, lanky legs tightly pressed together, his knees on a level with his head, his diaphanous hands resting on his baggy trousers; and he would begin to talk. (1968, II: 485)

We cannot help but be drawn to this eccentric and diffident figure.

Strachey also struggled with chronic ill health that meant he had many periods when he had to rest and take life more quietly. This is a theme in the biography that helps in some way to explain why "Lytton was not wholly an observer, nor a participant, but a sufferer of life" (1968, II: 631). As well as physical ill health, he suffered with anxiety and he seems vulnerable to hurt when others reject or upset him. At times, Holroyd's description is not only funny but emphasises his naivety and this lack of toughness. Maynard Keynes is a close friend and Strachey loves Duncan Grant with whom he hopes to have a relationship. When he learns to his distress about an affair between Grant and Keynes, Lytton travels to the Isle of Skye with his brother James:

From the absence of all herded jostling humanity he derived a wonderful solace … Occasional blazing sunbursts would light up within him unsus-pected reservoirs of hope and anticipation; and even the perpetual rain was soothing and merciful, like a gentle antiseptic washing away the stench and stagnation of human intercourse. (1967, I: 343)

Holroyd could have said, 'and the trip made Strachey feel a lot better'. It is unclear to what extent here Holroyd has drawn from Strachey's diaries and letters to compose this passage, but the tone and the overworked symbolism and language are melodramatic and funny. A distinct ironic touch of 'he doth protest too much' is implicit here, but it is kind, rather than like the harsh tones of Strachey's own vignettes. We can almost hear Strachey's voice, as both biographer and subject write one last book in collaboration.

Comedy takes a more satirical and harsher tone in Holroyd's biogra-phy of Augustus John, which is a critique of a rather unsympathetic man. The biography becomes Holroyd's own version of a debunking. His one-volume biography about John "is cast as comedy: romantic comedy, domestic comedy, the comedy of morals and of manners, absurdist comedy, black comedy, tragi-comedy" (2011, xxxii). At times, his life is comic as he falls into larger-than-life roles and his domestic arrangements become more and more unconventional. But what seems Bohemian and avant-garde in his early life becomes more jaded and seedy as he grows older, particularly as we learn about the consequences that his behaviour has on others, women in particular. This fall seems to mirror his decline as an artist. Shortly before he marries Ida, the biography notes that John came to realise that other people seemed better at managing their lives and he "was growing increasingly dissatisfied by the series of pursuing landladies and girlfriends in retreat. Perhaps, after all, there was something to be said for 'moral living'. At any rate the novelty was appealing" (2011, 88). The tone is light here and we have a sense of a romantic comedy as John stumbles into marriage. During her first pregnancy, Ida is advised to rest and "Augustus felt he had been let out from a narrow place. He could go where he wanted, be what he liked" (105). So, he goes for a short walk and ends up in Bruges to see some paintings. This again comes across as comical and, on his return, their marriage takes up where it had left off. John's behaviour becomes even more unconventional when he brings his mistress, Dorelia, to live with Ida and his children; at times, Dorelia and Ida even live together without him. It is hard to keep up with their movements and sexual relations as they rebel "against the late nineteenth century culture of suppression, driven to act spontaneously" (192). But it is of course the women who have to cope with their children and whose lives are socially far more difficult, as John travels wherever he pleases, often without them. After complications following childbirth, Ida dies. She seems perhaps to have lost the will to live—her life with John, his behaviour, the inevitable tensions of Dorelia's presence in their marriage, his other affairs, and the burden of caring for a number of children may have become too much for her, although it did not occur to her mother "that Ida might not want to live, that she could consent to die" (232). The biographical narrator comments that, "It was, to a degree, for the sake of his work that Ida had died and Dorelia risked her life: for his work and himself and themselves altogether" (414). Immediately after her death, for John,

> The relief was extraordinary. As he ran out of the hospital on to the boulevard Arago, Augustus was seized with uncontrollable elation. 'I could have embraced any passer-by,' he confessed. He had had enough of despair. (233)

This is not funny. This passage has a sardonic comic tone; John seems a thoughtless, egocentric buffoon at a moment of great tragedy in his life.[2] The egocentric nature of John's life continues, but as he grows older his youthful bohemian flair gives way to a more unattractive figure. John becomes a war artist at the beginning of the First World War:

> His translation into a Canadian major appeared to offer him a new life, a fresh stimulus for his painting ... To be caught up by events, to be on the go again was exhilarating. The blood began to move more swiftly through his body. Cheerfulness broke through. (432)

As usual, John's view of experience is all about his own position, rather than the huge suffering all around him, and his lack of humanity and wider awareness creates the image of an unappealing and egocentric character.

In addition to candour and comedy, there are other aspects of Holroyd's approach to biography that were part of a move in the late twentieth century to create a more flexible and reflexive genre, which draws on some aspects of Strachey's approach but has more in common with Desmond MacCarthy, in whose view biography "is undoubtedly an art" (1953, 32). First of all, Holroyd's subjects in his single life biographies—Lytton Strachey, Augustus John, Bernard Shaw—are all men who could be described as examples but, unlike the lives chosen by Strachey as "characteristic specimens", they are not primarily representative of the 'great and the good', albeit that they were famous in their own lifetimes. Rather, they embody significant change in art, literature, theatre, and political campaigning and culture. We come to know Holroyd's version of John as a dazzling portrait artist who influences a whole generation of his peers, while Shaw is a polymath whose commitment to particular political values underpinned his professional and writing life as a campaigner and dramatist.

Secondly, in his single-life biographies, Holroyd places his subjects both within a network of family, friends and professional peers and in the wider political, cultural and social context of their time. Holroyd suggests that Strachey can only be understood in the context of his family and their roots in the past, as is the case for many of his friends. The biography argues that most of the Bloomsbury writers, such as Virginia Woolf, and artists, were "unable finally to sever the umbilical cord joining them to the inherited traditions of the past" (1967, I: 423), indeed they were "'the last of the Victorians'" (424). Specific people are central to these biographies but at times they stand to one side as the lives of others are briefly important. As noted in Chap. 1, Strachey does draw attention to the role of other people in the lives of his subjects but this is of far more importance in a full-length biography. Holroyd argues in an interview about his group biography *A Strange Eventful History* (2008), concerning the lives of actors Henry Irving, Ellen Terry and their families, that:

> When writing a big book it's no good standing back and presenting an uninterrupted panorama. You have to come in quite close every now and again. I like to insert these portraits in miniature of minor characters. The best way to introduce them and make them live is through comedy ... And they must tell you something quickly about one of the leading characters ... So you come in, get this intense close-up, and then you can go back out and return to the main story. (Wroe 2008, 13)[3]

This is the case for both his single-life and group biographies, in which the lives of his main characters are abutted against others who have a smaller part to play, although a minor character in one biography may become a major one in another. Thirdly, Holroyd offers us the different selves of his subjects who they 'perform' in front of different audiences and at different times in their lives. Finally, Holroyd writes his biographies in collaboration with his subjects, and sometimes with their relatives and friends.

Holroyd's two-volume biography of Strachey is full of the people who were important in Strachey's life, those whom he cared for and worked with, including figures such as Dora Carrington, Duncan Grant, Maynard Keynes, Ralph Partridge and his brother, James, and Virginia and Leonard Woolf. Strachey met a number of his lifelong friends when he was a student at Cambridge and the biography argues that "for this reason, part at least of his career at Trinity is best seen in relation to those who were closest to him" (1967, I: 102). Then, much later, in 1915, Lytton visited Duncan and his lover, Vanessa, Virginia Woolf's sister, for "a certain week-end which set in motion seismic repercussions that were to reshape the entire story of the last sixteen years of his life" (1968, II: 182). Here he meets the painter Dora Carrington. She falls completely in love with him and devotes her life to him, albeit that Strachey can never love her as a partner or husband. At times, Holroyd adopts a comedic approach towards his portrayal of Carrington. After her marriage to Ralph Partridge, a close friend of both Carrington and Strachey, she falls in love with someone else, Gerald Brenan, during a visit to his house in Spain. But, when Brenan arrives back in England to see her, she realises that he "had belonged to her daydream world, and now, rather inconveniently, he had materialized as a living entity" (1968, II: 493). This comment emphasises Carrington's emotional frailty and sets the tone for the death of this relationship and its impact on Partridge and Strachey. At the end of the biography, Carrington cannot cope with Strachey's death and her fumbled suicide is rendered in a tone both comic and tragic:

> First she removed her favourite rug so that it should not be spoilt by the blood, and laid down another inferior rug in its place … Finally she pulled the trigger.
>
> Nothing happened.
>
> She had forgotten to release the safety catch. Now she did so. (1968, II: 718)

Carrington is portrayed as a complex and sad character wrapped up in her love of Strachey and her inability to see a life ahead without him. She is not the central figure in this biography, but we feel that we have come to know something about her, as well as the impact she had on Strachey's life.

Strachey's very close relationships were often based on a form of ménage à trois, including his friendship with Ottoline Morrel and a man they were both attracted to, Henry Lamb; Strachey was also in love with Duncan Grant, and his close friend Maynard Keynes fell in love and had an affair with Grant too; Strachey set up house with Dora Carrington, who passionately, but platonically, loved him and together they set up house with Ralph Partridge, who loved and married Carrington, although she was never in love with him, while Strachey was. It was complicated. These tangled trios Holroyd calls the "basic triangular pattern of Lytton's emotional life" (1968, II: 196). They suggest that Strachey desperately wanted to be part of a close and loving partnership but, almost in spite of himself, ended up on the fringes of other partnerships, separate and alone, never giving of himself totally to anyone.

Holroyd's biography of Bernard Shaw is full of snapshots of the lives of different people, including the women he loved, such as an early lover, Florence Farr, and his wife, Charlotte; other women he revered, such as Ellen Terry and Beatrice Webb; and men with whom he worked in the theatre, including Granville Barker, and in politics, in particular Sidney Webb and William Morris: "Morris and Webb were more than friends to Shaw: they were his political mentors" (I: 189). However, in the Shaw biography, we do not get to know these other people well and their lives are primarily described as abutting onto Shaw's own. They are primarily important as people with whom Shaw had a relationship, whether personal or professional, that tells us something about him. On the other hand, the lives of a number of key figures, particularly Ida and Dorelia, are central to the life of Augustus John, and we do come to know something of them in this biography.

John had to have people around him: "He did not know why he needed this entourage, only that he must have it" (2011, 124), and "He liked to keep an army of acquaintances in reserve, upon any number of which he could call when the mood was on him" (201). There were two motives behind his friendships, "inspiration and entertainment" (201), and "Without an audience he disappeared" (203). When he was younger and became famous, John's lifestyle was seen as "representing the principle of living through your ideas, not merely conveying them to canvas or on paper" (369); life became art. This life involved multiple affairs and, for a time when he was married, he lived with both his wife, Ida, and mistress, Dorelia. Then his casual affairs were apparently needed to help him avoid an "awful sense of deadness" (414). Concerning one mistress from later in his life, the biography notes that John asks her to avoid journalists, "especially on those occasions when she happens to be missing a tooth or is unable to conceal a black eye" (457). He had the same attitude of fickleness towards his friendships: "What he needed in the way of friends was variety, from which, like notes on a piano, he could select any tune of his choice" (453). As he grows older, the tune jars and sounds off key.

Holroyd suggests that, "To know Augustus John was to know not a single man, but a crowd of people, none of them quite convincing" (2011, 26). He "needed to move from one self to another, to play many parts" (262) in different settings, such as the rich salon of Lady Ottoline Morrell, in which he found "an attractive theatre where he could assume a different role" (262).

In his life of Bernard Shaw, the man, Shaw, seems aloof, and we learn more about the successful character of a political campaigner, writer and lecturer than a man who can empathise with others. Holroyd suggests that Shaw, or his professional identity as G.B.S., a "bearded literary superman" (IV: 81), "covered up his vulnerability with dazzling panache" (81) and we learn about different aspects of his personality in this biography. In his writing about Shaw, Holroyd is concerned in part with the life of Sonny, his version of Shaw as a young innocent, aspirational man; Shaw the adult man; and also with G.B.S., the dedicated and hardworking professional: "a writer, the magnificently impersonal G.B.S." (II: 35). Holroyd comments that, "'G.B.S.' was a manufactured identity: not a victim of capitalist society—a weapon to be used against it" (I: 76), and many people came to think of him "as having only ink in his veins and having been born with a long white beard" (IV: 81). Throughout the biography, Holroyd refers to this complex make-up that Shaw fashions in his life: "Sonny had yearned for love; G.B.S. soared wittily above it; and Shaw was pulled between the two" (I: 109). At one point, Shaw was in love with an actress, Janet Achurch, who makes a trip to Australia in 1891: "once or twice Sonny took advantage of Shaw's 'intoxicated, enamoured will', and G.B.S. would find himself wasting his time with a long letter to Janet" (I: 256). Shaw went on to write for another actress, Ellen Terry, who he came to know through their regular correspondence:

> As Sonny, he had lived in Shakespeare's world more vividly than his own … But when Sonny had turned to Dickens, he had taken his first step into the protective sphere of the stage where G.B.S. now enshrined Ellen Terry. (I: 359)

Shaw literally performs these different selves. In the theatre, Shaw struggled to establish himself as a dramatist, although he is eventually very successful, but "there was another theatre where he could perform; the theatre of politics" (II: 36), in which he performed thousands of lectures: "Many who heard him were convinced that here was the finest public speaker in England" (II: 217). Shaw created performances on and off the stage often as his different selves tussled on the 'stage' of the theatre or the lecture hall.

Holroyd wrote his biography of Lytton Strachey in collaboration with Strachey's brother, James. In his one-volume version of this biography, Holroyd notes that James Strachey went through the biography "syllable by syllable" (1973, 22) and requested that both volumes were published at the same time. Over two and a half years, James commented on both volumes, and "Sometimes, of course, we could not agree. In these cases I stuck to my guns and put James's dashing comments in the footnotes" (22); their conversation and collaboration ended in some kind of compromise, although the writer held sway.

In his biography of Bernard Shaw, Holroyd suggests that biographies are written in collaboration with the biographical subject, searching out for what has been overlooked or forgotten: "It is, like the process of reading itself, 'an intimacy between strangers'" (I: 4). In doing so, the biographer offers his or her subject "the chance of what amounts to a posthumous work written in collaboration" (1981, 16). Holroyd notes towards the end of this biography that, "As subjects of literary biographies will collaborate with their unknown biographers in the future writing of their lives, so our general history may be considered as part of an unfinished narrative that did not cater for our self-interest, but would be influenced by our acts and thoughts" (III: 37). However, like Thomas Hardy, Shaw preferred to have control over his biography whilst he was still alive. He worked alongside a biographer, Archibald Henderson, during his lifetime. He wanted Henderson "to recreate the life of G.B.S., replacing the isolated person who had presided over the death of Sonny and felt out of touch with the world he wished to influence, by a representative figure 'who is up to the chin in the life of his own times'" (1968, II: 212). Shaw wanted his ideas to have "the endorsement of biographical authority" (II: 212) and he was closely involved in editing and writing Henderson's biography himself. In comparing this with another biography of Shaw by G.K. Chesterton, also written during Shaw's lifetime, Holroyd notes that "Henderson had the information; Chesterton was the literary artist: one book complemented the other—though neither book intensified its perception of truth through a fusion of form and content" (II: 213). Here we have an early twentieth century example of both chronicle and personal biography, each offering different versions of a life. Perhaps Shaw understood that he needed both and that no one version of a life can reach every reader, or be definitive, although some will be viewed as more authentic than others by different readers.

One of the most notable aspects of Holroyd's writing is the extent to which he has created work in other genres. In addition to both group and single-life biography, he has written fiction, a book about cars, and memoirs, and these all share some of the qualities found in his biographical writing, reflecting what he describes as "a never-ending love-affair with human nature" (IV: 83). His early fiction, *A Dog's Life* (2014), first published in the United States in 1969, is a funny and affectionate novel which draws on his childhood experience when he was brought up by his grandparents following his parents' divorce. The novel is full of anecdotes about the chaos that ensued in many aspects of this fictional family's daily life. For instance, rather than open the front door to a stranger, who is in fact the local vet, the elderly grandparents panic in the hallway. Anne, the grandmother, decides to try to peer at this potential intruder, but can only reach a window by getting on to a table with the help of her husband:

> Anne had somehow attained a position on all fours on top of the table and, by leaning gently forward, could at last draw back the net curtains and peer out. Eustace hovered uncertainly in the background. For nearly half a minute Anne stared intently, then, letting go of the curtains, she turned her head and muttered: "Eustace! It's a MAN!" (2014, 108)

This domestic comedy is an example of the way in which this novel is, according to Holroyd, "a study of ageing with the accent on old age, not a photograph of my family" (203). His father disagreed and only saw it as a fictional autobiography. He fiercely opposed its publication, and the novel did not appear at all in the United Kingdom until 2014. The autobiographical sources for this novel and his father's reaction turned Holroyd away from fiction: "the troubles I had over my novel-writing … reinforced my desire to tell nonfiction stories by adapting some legitimate fiction devices" (2010a, 114). Holroyd's style in this novel is indicative of aspects of his biographical writing: "It is a matter of tone, as I see it, rather than of facts" (2014, 203), and this is a tone in which comedy, with a sardonic and tragic twist, is often important. Another key figure in this novel is Anne and Eustace's middle-aged and single daughter, Mathilda. It is her dog who needs the vet:

> Mathilda skidded to a halt, dropped to her knees, and began barking. Her sharp staccato yelps, released from the front of her lips, were addressed to

the prostrate Smith in his bed in the corner of the room. With a dog's sigh, he looked up at her and, gathering strength to reply, gave a feeble thump of his tail. It was enough. Mathilda rose ... "Smith was very ill again last night. He needs a vet." She spoke with quick formality. (2014, 47)

Despite the amusing arrival of the vet, he is too late and the dog dies. We may have laughed in earlier scenes but this only increases the sense of tragedy as Mathilda is bereft:

> None of her family, though they knew her so well, had lived with her so closely most of her life, and for whom she had renounced what had been the best in that life, could now, in her moment of distress, reach out and touch her ... Mathilda saw them round her, heard their voices, but was alone. (171)

This sense of pathos is important at moments throughout the novel as the grandparents squabble about the everyday activities of life, and the divorced parents of the young man struggle to build new lives, whilst Mathilda struggles on alone.

Holroyd has written three volumes of memoirs: *Basil Street Blues* (1999), which he calls "the prequel to my biographies" (2010a, 303), in which he applies his skills as a biographer to a narrative about his own life and family; *Mosaic* (2004), which he describes as experimental (2010b, 315); and *The Book of Secrets: Illegitimate Daughters, Absent Fathers* (2010).[4] Holroyd comments that Basil Street Blues and Mosaic, published as one volume in 2010, "mix biography with autobiography as I seek invisibility behind the subjects I am trying to bring alive on the page. They are the confessions of an elusive biographer" (2010c, 3). The titles of both these memoirs draw on the dialogic and conversational nature of these books, as Holroyd explores aspects of his own life in relation to those of different members of his family. This reflects G. Thomas Couser's perspective that "it is generally admitted that one cannot write about oneself without representing others as well; hence the contemporary interest in relational narrative" (2012, 34). Holroyd's memoirs certainly have the dual focus that Couser sees in these types of auto/ biography. Holroyd's parents had their honeymoon in the Basil Street Hotel and much of this memoir charts the misery of married life, with each other and other people, for both his parents.[5] He notes that his first memoir landed in the music department of some bookshops, although Holroyd does not feel that this is inappropriate:

> I had dreamt of creating something comparable to the music of the blues, the sadness sung out loud and long until the note of love breaks through. Could this word-music call up spirits from the deep? That is what I wished. For if they could reappear between the covers of my book and somehow touch other people's lives, then death itself perhaps might be less final. (2010b, 367)

Mosaic is a book written in collaboration with both his family and his readers, and *Basil Street Blues* "is not simply a search for facts, but for echoes and associations, signs and images, the recovery of a lost narrative and a sense of continuity" (2010a, 7). In doing so, Holroyd is writing about middle-class people, often short of money and living in distressed circumstances, they are "ordinary people" (2010b, 316), "humdrum people" (2010b, 361), including his aunt Yolande: "their exploits and adventures reveal how compelling fantasies, as well as mundane facts, guide our lives. It is how a writer mixes these facts and fantasies that divides the historian from the novelist, and determines whether a book is classified as fiction or (that most mysterious category) nonfiction" (2010b, 316), and in which Holroyd re-creates his family's lives and those of his biographical subjects, challenging the boundaries of both. *Mosaic* is a book about the echoes and connections that he can see between the lives of his family, and between them and his readers. The book arose because of the letters he received from readers of *Basil Street Blues*.[6] He believes that "we are, all of us, approximately related one to another—which is why other people's stories, however puzzling or extreme, contain so many echoes of our own dreams and experiences" (2010b, 315). In *Mosaic*—which is a discourse about the nature of memory, what we can and cannot know about others' lives and about the very nature of life-writing itself—Holroyd rewrites memories about his family and tries to unravel the extent to which his recollections are based on fantasies, or whether new facts may emerge between the cracks in the stories he told in *Basil Street Blues*. Not unlike biography, *Mosaic* is a rewriting and a reimagining of his first volume of memoirs:

> Gradually an alternative family history began to emerge, a sadder one than I had known ... I hold the view that the lies we tell ourselves and others, the half-truths that through repetition we almost come to believe, the very fantasies that follow us like our own shadows, become part of our actual lives. (2010b, 322)

In rewriting his family and those connected with them, Holroyd comes to tell a different version of their lives and the half-truths and fantasies embedded within them. His aunt Yolande is one of the key figures in this history.

Holroyd, part relative, part detective, part social commentator, writes about his close involvement with Yolande's life. The significance of his writing seems to lie in the ordinary details and, in this case, he writes about why every life has value, particularly when so little seems to have happened to her. Holroyd comments that he writes about other people in his biographies because so little happens in his own life and, of course, what his writing about his aunt proves is that this is an inherently ironic position because a great deal happens in any life. There is no such thing as a life of no importance, as his memoirs make clear. However, Yolande's is a life of disappointment after an engagement ends when her fiancé marries someone else and she becomes imprisoned in spinsterhood, looking after her parents.

In *Basil Street Blues*, Holroyd writes about her day-to-day adult life when he lived with her and his grandparents as a child. She is the one who looks after him: "Whatever was to be done with 'the boy', it was usually left to my aunt to do" (2010a, 136), and he owes much of his interest in books to his aunt. It does not seem an exaggeration to describe her life in this household as a tragicomedy, as she fights with his grandmother over the washing up:

> Sometimes my grandmother, taking advantage of my aunt's absence as she ran out to feed the birds, would put some knife or fork under the tap, and my aunt would snatch it from her as she raced back in and put it under the tap again. It was all done with extraordinary anguish and venom. (2010a, 138)

His aunt, like Holroyd, joins the local public library and, following her experience of borrowing books from the local Boots private lending library, it seems "she never lost the habit of lightly roasting the books she borrowed in a medium oven for the sake of the germs" (102). As a younger woman, Yolande becomes engaged to Captain Hazelhurst, the love of her life.[7] Holroyd reads about this engagement in Hazelhurst's letters to her, as it progresses over many years and seems to slip into friendship rather than a love affair. He is cautious about reading them and wonders, as he has in his role as a biographer, about the ethics of reading private correspondence, particularly as his aunt, although hardly able to speak or hear, is still alive when he does so. Nevertheless, these letters are evidence that "here, in its muted form, lie moments, private moments, from what is perhaps the most vital part of her life" (144). The letters help Holroyd and us as readers to understand something very important about Yolande's life, but they also have a wider significance, as does all life-writing, because "whenever the chorus of conventional family sentiment bursts forth, she should be able to step forward with others ... to remind us of what families may inflict on themselves" (144). In the end, Hazelhurst gets married at fifty to a twenty-year-old Italian woman, and Holroyd writes about his life as one in which a duplicitous and fickle character emerges. The consequence of Hazelhurst's rejection, the great tragedy of Yolande's life, results in a life of frantic dog walking, bird feeding and washing up, although Yolande could never bear to eat with the family and spent hours hidden away and isolated in her bedroom. Her tragic flaw or mistake, "whether from excessive loyalty or failure of nerve, was to have gone on living with her family ... And the consequences were awful" (2010a, 154).

Holroyd takes up her story again in *Mosaic*, when she dies in a nursing home. He feels saddened by the "contemplation of her life" (2010b, 331). On her death certificate, Holroyd and the registrar both agree to put a dash against her marital status and her occupation, avoiding in the process labelling her as an unemployed spinster, which perhaps would have seemed patronising and inaccurate—something like carer (of her parents) might have been more appropriate. He writes about the details of arranging her funeral, which he expects no one else to attend. His aunt's nursing home had sent their condolences to Mark Holroyd and regretted not being able to send anyone to attend. So, he is surprised when

> the door of the Chapel of Rest bursts open and a rather plump young woman in black, whom I have never seen before, runs in out of the wet ... She has that very week joined the staff at the nursing home and, though

she has not "had the pleasure and privilege" of meeting my aunt until now, wanted to come to her funeral in order to gain work experience. (2010b, 340)

It is hard not to chortle with dismay at this, particularly as this young woman then proceeds to cry volubly at the funeral itself. However, other care staff have touched his aunt's life in a more meaningful way. Jean and Rita looked after her at home for ten years, before Yolande moved to the nursing home, and in their letters to him with news about how she is getting on his aunt is "alive again" (346) and suddenly less of a victim. They write about one instance when a man "was very rude to her so she put her walking stick round his leg & down he came. She said he won't be rude to me again. Well, she laughed so much she cryed" (347). This is a tiny detail from his aunt's later years, but it provides a rare moment when her life seems light hearted and we laugh with her, not at her.

One of the other "secret episodes and half-suspected dramas" (2010a, 304) that Holroyd finds in his own family are stories about books that say something about their lives. One book was originally owned by his great-grandmother, "who ended her life at the age of thirty by swallowing carbolic acid" (2010a, 305), and is embossed with the word FERNS. Fern leaves are pressed into some pages and the book then passes, through the hands of her daughter, to Yolande. She pastes illustrations of actors and actresses into its pages. At the end of *Basil Street Blues*, he is aware how it is significant as an object so closely connected with three women from his family and with his own book about some of their lives. Another book that he cares about contains drawings for light fittings designed by his father, who became an agent in the 1930s for the Lalique company, which sold comparable objects. Holroyd opens *Mosaic* with this book, a Book of Lights, "that had lain many years with the Book of Ferns behind a curtain in that attic of my grandparents' house" (2010b, 323). The book reveals someone Holroyd barely recognises, "someone with an optimism and confidence that were fading when I got to know him, and which were altogether extinguished at the end" (328). His father struggled to find satisfying jobs after the war and ended his life with little money, sad and bitter. He comes alive in another book by Holroyd, *On Wheels* (2012), "a retrospective journey and an example … of nostalgic intertexuality" (2012, xi), in which his father's, his own, and his biographical subjects' connection with cars and other forms of transport is playfully explored. As his father is getting older, Holroyd drives behind his father and "saw him wandering crazily all over the road with his dog apparently at the wheel. Then it was I realised that in the future I would have to drive him where he wished to go" (2012, 61). Holroyd drives to places that were important in the lives of his biographical subjects. This comes to symbolise his connection with them and he believes that he "could very easily point to sentences or paragraphs I would have written differently had I not been to special places" (50) that were significant in their lives:

> This sense of intimacy with a landscape or architecture might not add to the factual evidence of my research, but I believe it changes the tone and validity of what appears on the page. It also brings the scene closer to the reader. (51)

This sense of place is important in his own memoirs and autobiography. Norhurst is the place where he lived with his aunt and grandparents. After their death, Yolande does not want to leave the home where she had spent much of her life, albeit that there was "no room that had not absorbed years of reverberating anger and the awful atmosphere of our unhappiness" (2010a, 284). She does move into a flat and then a nursing home, where she dies.

Holroyd believes that as he makes discoveries about his biographical subjects, "the biographer makes discoveries about himself" (1988, 97), although it is important to recognise the performative autobiographical self in his writing and not confuse this with the intentions of the actual man. In doing so, Holroyd seems to be in conversation with his subjects, actual conversations in some cases, seeking them out in the gaps and crevices of what they do and do not say. Like Johnson, he is fascinated by the details of private and domestic life that can reveal so much about anybody and through which we learn about ourselves and others. He argues that:

> Biographies create, or re-create, a world that the reader may enter, where his or her imagination may be stimulated, and some of the emotions, thoughts and laughter experienced in reading—as well as the information—may remain with the reader after the book is finished. (1988, 103)

Much of what remains arises as a result of the comedy and pathos in Holroyd's writing. One is also left with a feeling that we may never find

Michael Holroyd, and certainly not Michael, even in the hidden cracks between the lines of his text.

This chapter is written in collaboration with Michael Holroyd based on my reading of his work and an interview from 2016. Again, I had written the chapter before we met and hoped that our conversation would develop some of the themes that had arisen in my reading of his work. I also hoped that there would be echoes between my conversation with him and the other conversations that I have had with biographers, friends, colleagues and others during the writing of this book.

IN CONVERSATION WITH MICHAEL HOLROYD

It seems to me that in your single-life biographies the lives of other people are central to the story, and to the life of your main subject? A single-life biography can be understood as about more than one life perhaps?

That's absolutely true. Few people live wholly solitary lives, though solitude I think may be part of writing and of all the arts—you've got to shut a door on social life to work.

Minor characters sometimes take over a narrative. I have a masculine subject on the title pages of my books, but in fact the narrative is often taken over, I notice, by a woman. And I've written more about women than people realise. I don't know at the beginning of a book how it will develop. I find out as I go on. But I often have more to learn from women than from men.

Writing about Carrington in my life of Strachey was a surprise, and I greatly enjoyed doing it, as well as writing about Ida and Dorelia in the life of Augustus John. In fact, at present, I am coediting the letters of Ida John, covering some of the same story but from the women's position.

Technically I've only written two group biographies, *A Book of Secrets* and *A Strange Eventful History*, which covers over a hundred years and focuses on two generations of two families.

Of course, what you do is to some extent controlled by what letters exist, what diaries there are, what material you can find. Sometimes a biographer has to focus on a single person, and solitude becomes the theme of the book—the reasons for it and the effect it has on his or her work.

What happens to biography when the biographer does not like his subject?
I was quite astonished when I did my research about Gordon Craig in France, America and Britain. I knew he had a difficult childhood. His mother, Ellen Terry, was the most talented actress and an altogether charming woman, but she was certainly not a good mother. Craig was illegitimate and he didn't like the stepfather Ellen eventually presented him with. Craig was not his real name, he selected it for himself. His name came from an island rock off the coast of Scotland—rather apt I think.

I found his treatment of women quite awful. Over thirty years, scattered over five countries, he had thirteen children by eight women and managed to treat all of them badly, quite an achievement. I realised that I had before me what in a novel would have been called a villain. I had never before written about someone like that. I admired some of his theatre work and I used them as illustrations in my book, but I did not hide what he did to some of those women.

I did not want to introduce him to readers as a villain. I wanted to use his own words, what he said about people, and to describe what he did, rather than stating my own view. I decided to let him speak directly to the reader and see what they made of him. And they felt roughly the same as I did I think: some enjoying this, others decidedly not.

To what extent is comedy important in your writing?
Comedy is very important to me, but I do not mean cracking jokes or anything like that. I agree with Thomas Hardy who wrote all comedy is tragedy if only you look deep enough into it.

There are some passages in my biographies now that I find difficult to read, or at least I can't read out loud without having tears in my eyes. And one of those was the death of Henry Irving. People knew he was dying for almost a year, and they rose at one theatre then another to give him their applause for a lifetime of acting. Audiences were saying their final farewell, standing up and cheering him. He pretty well died on stage. A perfect death, you might say, for an actor. I found this surprisingly moving.

You have written both longer and then shorter, revised editions of some of your biographies?
Initially, I worked in private archives and explored letters and diaries which no one had seen. So initially I had to write quite long biographies because nobody knew the facts about my subjects. I had to show exactly

how I had come to my conclusions from letters, from diaries, which were unpublished and unknown. But twenty years later readers had got to know much more which enabled me to make the narrative more succinct. I also came across new material that I wanted to include. I think the shorter editions are better. The narrative is quicker and has more vitality; and the surprises are more surprising. I want the reader to be held by the open page but at the same time longing to see what happens next.

You have written fiction, single-life biography, group biography, a book about objects (On Wheels), metanarratives about biography and autobiography and memoir. What have been the challenges in crossing the boundaries between these different genres in your writing?
I learnt from biography how to experiment with autobiography. All my books are written by trial and error which is one reason why I write so many versions. And while I'm writing alone in a room I never think about readers, and I never think about publishers. I am the only reader there, and indeed I am the most difficult of all readers to please.

In your Shaw, you talk about two of the men who were writing his biography during his lifetime: Henderson has the information, so let us say he writes the scholarly chronicle, and Chesterton was the literary artist.
Yes. There are some books that are full of facts and not very readable. They are excellent for the shelf given over to research. You go to that book not for reading but for dates and facts. On the other hand, Chesterton's book is full of life though not always accurate. His Shaw is alive still, but it won't help you with your research. So, the two books are on different shelves in my library.

In your biography of Shaw, we share the different selves of Sonny, the young man, Bernard Shaw the front man as it were and George Bernard Shaw the hardnosed professional writer, and the biography comments on their relationship at various points. To what extent is biography a search for these different selves?
I think we all have different selves, I mean we all have different selves as we grow up. There's a wonderful series of drawings done by Max Beerbohm with the older man and the younger man meeting each other. Our older selves really would astonish our younger

selves and our older selves try to forget our younger selves—or reinvent them. As for me, I never thought I would be here now talking
about biographies.

*You have written about the problem of securing a publisher for your
biography of Hugh Kingsmill. Do you think this remains an issue for
publishers today?*
Yes, I think it does. To sell biographies about people who are unknown
is very difficult for publishers. We live in a culture of celebrities, and
publishers are really obliged to acknowledge that. Unknown subjects
get very small advances if they're published at all, and that's why I have
helped to create something called the Authors' Foundation, which pays
writers while they're writing their books in order that they can buy more
time for their research rather than prizes which come to them a year or
more after they finish their book.

*You decided to publish your footnotes for your biography of Bernard Shaw
separately. What do you think are publishers' and your readers' views about
footnotes in biography?*
It must have seemed very eccentric. I believe that biographies have two
main categories of readers, a general reader and the academic reader.
And reference notes are more useful to the latter. So, I tried with my life
of Bernard Shaw to offer more than 8000 reference notes, plus copies of
his wife's and his own wills as well as the story of his literary estate. In
future, maybe that sort of thing can be done online, or perhaps at public
libraries, if there are any.

*You have written about your experience of dealing with relatives and
literary estates, so what has this taught you about how biographers can best
deal with the pressures and tensions that arise?*
I offer living people who appear in my biographies the chance, before
publication, to see those pages on which their names appear. I don't
promise to change anything, but if I come across something that I didn't
know and think is significant yes, of course, I can change it then and
that's fine.

I've sometimes offered to change the men or women's names if
they're minor characters, or even to take them out of the book. But
they never want that. What I have found is that what they're really

questioning is the tone of a passage in which they appear, and I can usually alter that.

Could you describe aspects of your approach to writing?
I write by instinct. And my best days of writing are those in which I come to know something at the end of a day that I didn't know at the beginning of it. That is a good day's work. Sometimes I'm left at the end of the day with unsolved problems. I can occasionally come up with a solution after a good night's sleep.

My introductions to biographies are almost always written after I've finished the book. I'm not really telling the reader what I intend to do but what I have discovered I have done. And I rewrite my texts seven or eight times as I work on the subjects until at last I get the tone right. I'm like a piano tuner.

I think when I started out in my teens I thought I would write novels. But all the novels that I wrote were forms of autobiography about my family, about myself. I put my wish to be a novelist into what's called nonfiction.

I dislike very much hearing history or biography being called nonfiction. To begin it is so negative, so unattractive and also not completely true. Do we call poetry non-prose, or novels non-factual literature? We do not.

I suggest that we call novels creative writing, which I believe them to be, and biography and history as re-creative writing, because they re-created the past. That seems to me much more accurate. We investigate the past and perhaps alter our understanding of the present. I would describe several recent British biographies as re-creative literature. Novels and biographies are both branches of literature. They are not enemies— indeed they stimulate one another. Critics of fiction argue that it is a sort of lying which eventually makes a hole in the heart in a world of lies. Critics of biography accuse it of reducing everything including creative writing into nothing more than hidden autobiography.

I used a piece of fiction in a story I told in my Life of Bernard Shaw. Shaw sent Churchill tickets for two seats for the first night of one of his plays and invited him "to bring a friend if you have one". And then Churchill replied, sending back the tickets, and saying that that evening was impossible for him, but "he would like to come to the second night of the play if there is one". The story came from a newspaper and was wholly invented. I used it to show what the public thought of these two famous public figures and how wrong they were.

The writer is two people. There is the person who writes and then there is the person that does the research—the same person with a different job. While I'm doing research I long to be the writer, to get a move on and actually write. Occasionally, the researcher, who is going abroad, meeting people, travelling all over the place in the steps of his subject, will turn and ask the writer who's fast asleep and doing nothing and ask him if he needs something about bicycles and Shaw. The writer wakes up and replies for goodness sake don't ask me, I'm just the writer.

And then I come back and close the door and write—thinking of those wonderful days when I was a researcher. Then I suddenly get angry, why didn't that chap get that material on bicycles and Shaw, but the researcher is half asleep now and says well, you never asked for it before. And I have to go back, or send a letter asking for the bicycle pages: hence my biographies take a long long time to write.

Each of my biographical subjects I have got to know through my previous book. Strachey was a significant minor character in my Kingsmill, I got to know him and then wrote about him. Augustus John was in my Strachey biography, a minor character. I got to know him and much to my surprise he became my next subject. Shaw was painted by Augustus John, and he himself had a long correspondence with Ellen Terry, a strong objection to Henry Irving, and a considerable dislike of Edward Gordon Craig. So, all those characters were waiting for me when I started *A Strange Eventful History*, which originally I thought would just be about the life of Ellen Terry. I found myself writing a much longer book. Sometimes I have a feeling my subjects chose me. Not I them.

NOTES

1. For Holroyd's discussion about Hugh Kingsmill's influence on him, see his essay "How I Fell Into Biography" (1988).
2. More is known about Ida John's perspective with the publication of *The Good Bohemian: The Letters of Ida John* (2017), edited by Michael Holroyd and the artist Rebecca John.
3. See Michael Benton's discussion about Holroyd's group biography of Ellen Terry and Henry Irving in *Towards a Poetics of Literary Biography* (2015). Benton argues that Holroyd's portrayal of Ellen Terry "allows us to observe a biographer deconstructing a nineteenth century cultural icon

as he simultaneously reconstructs her 'Life' in twenty-first century terms" (2015, 139).

4. *In Tell Me True: Memoir, History, and Writing a Life* (2008), Patricia Hampl and Elaine Tyler May have edited a collection about the connections between historians and creative writers who write memoir on the basis that there is a need to continue the debate about the connections between fact and fiction in this genre. They argue that these are not opposing disciplines but in dialogue with each other (2008, 7).

5. Holroyd, *Basil Street Blues and Mosaic*, 90.

6. Ibid., 315.

7. Ibid., 141.

References

Bostridge, Mark, ed. 2004. Lives for Sale: Biographers' Tales. London: Continuum

Couser, G. Thomas. 2012. *Memoir: An Introduction*. New York: Oxford University Press.

Curtis, Anthony. 1996. Shilling Lives: An Interview. In *The Literary Biography: Problems and Solutions*, ed. Dale Salwak, 121–129. Basingstoke, Hampshire: Macmillan.

Hampl, Patricia, and Elaine Tyler May (eds.). 2008. *Tell Me True: Memoir, History, and Life-Writing*. St Paul, MN: Borealis Books.

Holroyd, Michael. 1964. *Hugh Kingsmill: A Critical Biography*. London: Unicorn Press.

———. 1967. *Lytton Strachey: A Critical Biography. Volume I: The Unknown Years (1880–1910)*. London: Heinemann.

———. 1968. *Lytton Strachey: A Critical Biography. Volume II: The Years of Achievement (1910–1932)*. London: Heinemann.

———. 1973. *Lytton Strachey: A Biography*. London: Heinemann.

———. 1981. Literary and Historical Biography. In *New Directions in Biography*, ed. Anthony Friedson, 14–24. Honolulu: University of Hawaii.

———. 1988. How I Fell into Biography. In *The Troubled Face of Biography*, ed. Eric Homberger and John Charmley, 94–103. Basingstoke, Hampshire: Macmillan.

———. 2003. First published in 2002. *Works on Paper: The Craft of Biography and Autobiography*. London: Abacus.

———. 2010a and 2010b. BSB first published 1999 and Mosaic first published 2004. *Basil Street Blues and Mosaic*. London: Vintage.

———. 2010c. *A Book of Secrets: Illegitimate Daughters, Absent Fathers*. London: Chatto & Windus.

———. 2011. *Augustus John*. London: Pimlico.

————. 2012. *On Wheels: Five Easy Pieces*. London: Chatto & Windus.

————. 2014. *A Dog's Life*. London: MacLehose Press.

MacCarthy, Desmond. 1953. Lytton Strachey and the Art of Biography, Circa 1934. In *Memories*, by Desmond MacCarthy, 31–49. London: MacGibbon & Kee.

Okri, Ben. 2014. The Mental Tyranny Keeping Black Writers from Greatness. *The Guardian*, December 27: 43.

Strachey, Lytton. 1986. First published in 1918. *Eminent Victorians*. London: Penguin.

Wroe, Nicholas. 2008. Life in Writing: Interview with Michael Holroyd. *Guardian Saturday Review*, September 13: 12–13.

Woolf, Virginia. 1967. First published in 1927. The Art of Biography. In *Virginia Woolf Collected Essays*, Vol. 4, 1882–1941, Virginia Woolf, 221–228. London: Hogarth Press.

BIBLIOGRAPHY

Ellmann, Richard. 1985. Freud and Literary Biography. In *Freud and the Humanities*, ed. Peregrine Horden, 58–74. London: Duckworth.

Holroyd, Michael. 1988. *Bernard Shaw: The Search for Love Volume I 1856–1898*. London: Chatto & Windus.

———. 1989. *Bernard Shaw: The Pursuit of Power Volume II 1898–1918*. London: Chatto & Windus.

———. 1991. *Bernard Shaw: The Lure of Fantasy Volume III 1918–1950*. London: Chatto & Windus.

———. 1992. *Bernard Shaw: The Shaw Companion Volumes IV & V*. London: Chatto & Windus.

———. 1994. *Lytton Strachey: The New Biography*. London: Chatto & Windus.

———. 1996. *Augustus John: The New Biography*. London: Chatto & Windus.

———. 1997. *Bernard Shaw: One Volume Revised Edition*. London: Chatto & Windus.

———. 2009. First published 2008. *A Strange Eventful History: The Dramatic Lives of Ellen Terry and Henry Irving and their Remarkable Families*. London: Vintage.

———. 2011. *Augustus John*. London: Pimlico.

Lee, Hermione. 2010. From the Margins. *The Guardian*, 3 April: 2–4.

© The Editor(s) (if applicable) and The Author(s) 2017
J. McVeigh, *In Collaboration with British Literary Biography*,
DOI 10.1007/978-3-319-58383-9

INDEX

© The Editor(s) (if applicable) and The Author(s) 2017   215
J. McVeigh, *In Collaboration with British Literary Biography*,
DOI 10.1007/978-3-319-58383-9

Printed by Printforce, the Netherlands